What People Are Saying About
Nicole Gabriel and
Healing Your Dog Naturally

"*Healing Your Dog Naturally* is a revolutionary look at the kind of care we provide to man's best friend. Nicole Gabriel balances deep affection for her canine kids with practcal questions and research that will make you rethink and make positive changes to your dog's lifestyle so you can hopefully enjoy a longer time together."

— Tyler R. Tichelaar, Ph.D. and Award-Winning author of *Narrow Lives* and *The Best Place*

"Thank you for a book that has been needed for a long time! I just knew there were better options for my dog than were offered by our vet. And WOW, there really are great alternatives that are natural that I would never have thought of. I'm so grateful for this book!"

— Connie Warden, Licensed Accupuncturist, Lifestle Coach, and Author of *Self-Leadershipping*

"If you have ever been in the situation where your dog suddenly doesn't feel well and you imagined the worst or worried about a huge bill that you aren't sure how you'll pay, then this book will ease your mind and your pocketbook as you learn how to resolve many issues at home naturally."

— Patrick Snow, Publishing Coach and International Best-Selling Author of *Creating Your Own Destiny*

"My instincts have been telling me that there is a better solution. I just didn't know what it was until now."

— Sandra Hickson-Mathews, Author of *Kiss Your Food*

“I have known Nicole for a number of years now and followed the stories of her dogs and her struggle to find and share better ways to support our furry friends while they are with us on this earth. I know her to be a compassionate, resourceful, and highly-educated woman who will leave no stone unturned in her life’s work. God bless you, Nicole.”

— Livjot Kaur, Victoria, BC

“I am a friend and neighbor of Nicole’s, and I smell the great meals that come out of her home. Those are blessed pups! I see them heading off and returning from hikes, hear them playing, and can honestly say they are by far the healthiest and happiest dogs I have ever seen. Nicole is authentic and true—you can be assured that all her tips and advice have been thoroughly studied, tested, and proven!”

— Jaimie Brown, Real Estate Agent
in Maui, Hawaii
www.FindMauiProperty.com

“My beautiful golden, Ike, passed onto the Rainbow Bridge in 2012. The vet never quite figured out what was wrong with my sweet pup (he was thirteen and a half). I wish Nicole’s book *Healing Your Dog Naturally* had been around back then. She reveals proactive strategies to help you take control of your dog’s health. Read it now so you can start helping your sweet pup today.”

— Debra Jason, Author of the Award-Winning Book,
Millionaire Marketing on a Shoestring Budget

“I can’t tell you how many times I’ve been guilted into buying all the options for my dog’s care. After reading *Healing Your Dog Naturally*, I understand what is really necessary, what is actually dangerous, and what I can do without.”

— Melissa Woods, Author of
Getting Past Anxiety

"I'm tired of feeling like a hopeless and confused mess about my baby's care! It's time for an alternative way of being and living for you and your best friend. It's here now!"

— Angie Engstrom, Author of *Getting Yourself Unstuck: Transforming Your Mess into Your Mission, Masterpiece, and Money*

"Veterinarians gave my dog, Meg, a week to live eight months ago. She has malignant tumors and the one on her face is inoperable. I remembered my time in Vietnam and a drug the Viet Cong soldiers carried called Yunnan Baiyao. It's used as commonly in China as penicillin is in America, but it's virtually unheard of in this country. The Viet Cong soldiers carried it in war and used it to stop bleeding from wounds. I bought this drug on Amazon, and we give it to Meg every other day in her food. She hasn't had a bloody nose since she started taking Yunnan Baiyou, and her tumors have shrunk. She's regained lost weight and has more energy. It's a miracle drug for us. There is so much more we still need to learn about veterinary care and Nicole teaches many different ideas in this book that go beyond the traditional model. We do have other choices. We just need to become aware of them."

— Terry Gargus, Author of
Witness for the Butterflies

"*Healing Your Dog Naturally* is a fantastic book on how to take care of your dog so it will live longer and happier. Nicole shows you how to think differently about traditional dog injections and unnecessary pharmaceuticals. So often, veterinarians rush to tell pet parents just to pop pills or they over-prescribe medicine, rather than go to the source of the problem or issue with your dog. So many people follow this advice without giving it a second thought, and they wonder why their dog is having liver or kidney problems after their dog is given drugs to fix another issue.

"I'm a huge dog lover. We have five dogs and feed them fresh home-made food and fresh vegetables every day. But what I learned from Nicole took me to another level of understanding. Now I am more confident in knowing the right way to take care of my dogs."

— Renee Gordon, Author of
Finding Your Love at Last

"Nicole has been a long-time lover of the Chinese Shar-Pei breed, both as an owner and as a supporter of Pei People Shar Pei Rescue. The fact that she can take her knowledge and learnings over many years and provide valuable information to Pei owners and prospective owners is wonderful! Information that teaches owners to work with vets and discusses both Western, Eastern, and homeopathic treatment options, in order to keep our four-legged friends optimally healthy, is advice every Shar-Pei owner should heed."

— Sue A.,
Pei People Shar Pei Rescue, Inc,
www.peipeople.com

"Nicole writes from her heart of her experiences supporting her beloved dogs through a lifetime of health and vitality to a peaceful death. What she learned through research, energy study, and her deep intuition can guide us to greater understanding and natural solutions for our animals' needs."

— Wanda Buckner, EdD., Author of *Choosing Energy Therapy: A Practical Guide to Healing Options for People and Animals*

"My son has been labeled many things, Autistic, OCD, ADD, but healing Matthew from the inside out naturally is what made the most difference. Nicole shares through her experience that dogs are no different nor should they be. They can benefit from a holistic living and live their purest lives. This book is a must read to gain an understanding and appreciation that life for this woman's best friend is lived best when done with compassion, love, and Nicole's undeniable knowledge."

— Jennifer Witten,
Author of *Goodbye, Short Bus*

HEALING YOUR DOG NATURALLY

DISCOVERING
THE CONNECTION
BETWEEN YOU AND
YOUR BEST FRIEND

NICOLE GABRIEL

AVIVA PUBLISHING
New York

Healing Your Dog Naturally:
Discovering the Connection Between You and Your Best Friend

Published by:

AVIVA PUBLISHING
New York

Aviva Publishing
Lake Placid, NY
(518) 523-1320
www.AvivaPubs.com

Nicole Gabriel
www.NicoleKristinGabriel.com

ISBN: 978-1-943164-82-0 (hard cover)
ISBN: 978-1-9431649-9-8 (soft cover)
Library of Congress Control Number: 2016954827

Editors: Tyler Tichelaar and Jeannine Mallory
Cover Design: Angel Dog Productions
Interior Book Design: Angel Dog Productions

Every attempt has been made to source properly all quotes.

Printed in the United States of America

First Edition

2 4 6 8 10 12

To all those I have lost,
because you have become my greatest teachers.
Thank you for guiding me from the other side.

To all those who know there is a better way,
because you are the future.

To my Leilani, Bella, and Blue.
Thank you for trusting me, loving me, and humoring me
during our short earth journey together.

To God,
because I'm listening.

Acknowledgments

Thank you to all who gave me the space to research and write this book and didn't question why I was doing it or whether I'd make a profit. Sometimes God just speaks through you and you feel strong enough about the cause to sit down and write, teach, or share… because you know there has to be another way. If you feel that calling, don't let others tell you that you are not good enough to do it. This book is not about making a profit, but sharing what I know for a better planet. What a waste if I didn't! Thank you to those who really get that! I bow my head to others on the journey of enlightenment, whatever the subject.

As always, thank you to my fantastic editors, Tyler Tichelaar and Jeannine Mallory. You make miracles happen!

Thank you to my printing team: Marlana, Todd, and all those who print, pack, and ship.

"Yesterday I was a dog.
Today I'm a dog.
Tomorrow I'll probably still be a dog.
Sigh! There's so little hope for advancement"

— Snoopy

Contents

"Acquiring a dog,
may be the only time a person
gets to choose a relative."

— Unknown

"He is your friend, your partner, your defender, your dog. You are his life, his love, his leader. He will be yours, faithful and true, to the last beat of his heart. You owe it to him to be worthy of such devotion."

— *Unknown*

Preface

Let me make it clear that this is not a book about bashing the veterinary world. Rather, this book is meant to complement veterinary science and support the concept of conscious, healthy mind-body-spirit living, versus reactionary doctoring. This book is about finding solutions that don't mask the problem with short-term fixes. This book is about learning to have a conversation with your dog and finding a natural option before you resort to pharmaceuticals or other costly or temporary solutions. This book will take you beyond the traditional models of care and into the mystical, spiritual, sacred, and natural rhythms of all phases of not just the life of a dog, but also its owner.

It's a comprehensive look at what ultimately makes for happy dogs and happy owners. Most of all, this book is about caring for your best friend (and yourself) in an aware, fluid, and proactive way. Please take a leap with me into an observatory and practical exploration of all things dog!

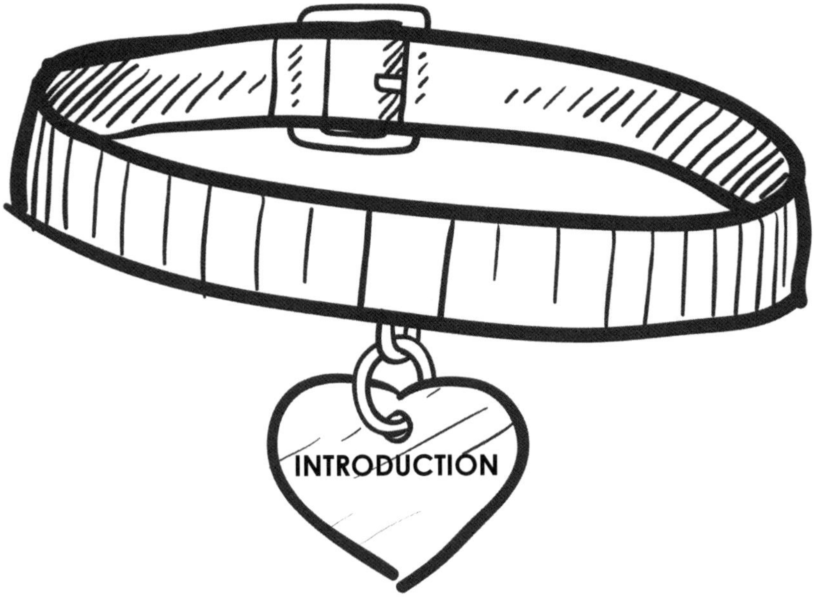

Earth Mission: Tree Hugger

"Outside of a dog, a book is man's best friend.
Inside a dog, it's too dark to read."

— Groucho Marx

There's an inexplicable energy about a dog. You've no doubt experienced it. You know that despite the chaos and care sometimes involved, that special energy always leads you back to your sacred and loyal canine companion. You know a dog's love is nonjudgmental, pure, and true. Yep, you're a dog person!

I've had dogs nearly all my life, but I really wasn't aware of our purposeful union until I separated from my ex-husband. At that time, I realized just how important my dogs were to me. They became my best friends, my confidants, and the most loyal figures, showing me compassion, love, and trust that went beyond anything a human ever offered.

When it feels like the world has abandoned you, remember you can count on the love, companionship, and loyalty of a dog to get you through the tough spots in life. So it goes without saying that in good times, they are right there and ready to celebrate with you. They are happy to be with you no matter what state you're in, no matter your mood, no matter how you look. As a thank you to my best friends, as well as to yours, this book has become a kind of homage to pay my respects to those I have lost and pay it forward to all those here now and yet to come.

Throughout this book, I will share some of the experiences I've had with dogs. Many times, my dogs became my greatest teachers in expanding my consciousness, deepening my soul, and, unfortunately, breaking my heart.

For a living, I help people publish their books. Also, I have published two of my own, prior to this book. Still, there was always a calling for me to write a book about my truest love—dogs! You may wonder why this is my third book—instead of my first. Well, for a subject so close to me, emotionally and professionally, I doubted my ability to write a book that was comprehensive and trustworthy. Why? Simply put, I am not a veterinarian nor a health practitioner.

I've watched many people publish books over the years, and most are not medical doctors. They are people like you and me with a voice and experiences that need to be heard. They have spoken on many topics over the years. But one gal in particular wrote a book that opened my awareness of what gives an author credibility—experience! She wrote a book titled *Goodbye, Short Bus*. It is a moving story about the struggle in her and her family's lives. When he was very young, her son was diagnosed with autism. She and her family went on a personal crusade to find a way to find a cure, or if not, learn how to live with it. She was not a doctor, but the mom of a suffering child. Reading her story made me see that sometimes our personal experiences alone give us the credibility to write a book, to stand up, and to be an experiential expert. We are all humans, doctors or not. We're all here to have the human experience, and my experience has been deeply influenced by my relationship with dogs. Thank you, Jennifer Witten, for giving me the courage to share what I have experienced. It's my hope and dream that this book will start to change how we look at things related to the well-being of man's (or in this case, woman's) best friend.

I take the term dog "owner" lightly because I know I'm truly the one who's owned! You know what I mean if you have a dog in your household. Not only have I had dogs for all my adult life, but I've chosen to have a complicated breed (Shar Pei) that requires more attention than most other breeds. When you set out to "own" a Shar Pei, your dog quickly begins to teach you more than you ever imagined. I've found something rather unique about their owners as well. They are very knowledgeable about how to care for their Pei.[1] In most cases, it's more trial by fire. You see, these dogs are known to have numerous health issues (eye problems, ear problems, skin issues, issues with high fevers, renal failure, and behavior challenges), yet we are somehow lured by their personalities, appearances, and dispositions to take on the task not just once, but over and over again! I sorta think that once we've acquired the knowledge to care for them, we hate to see it wasted by not getting another Shar Pei. Masochists, we are.

I am thankful for all that my dogs have taught me over the years. In fact, I've often forgotten they were even dogs and looked to them as master teachers, gurus, or confidants. Unfortunately, they often end up teaching at their own expense...and challenge our sanity in the process. There's nothing worse than a late night or weekend fever flare-up when all the veterinary clinics are closed. This situation either forces you to find a solution on your own, or pay the outrageous fees of an emergency visit with whatever doctor is on call—experienced with the breed or not. I learned the hard way more than once! Now I always have all the tools on hand in case of an emergency. These experiences, with multiple dogs,

1 To dispel any confusion, please know that Shar Pei is both the singular and plural version of the breed's name.

over many years, have had me not only taking their health, but my own, into my own hands. I've learned about taking responsibility for my dogs and me. I've learned more about the power of prayer.

The American Pet Products Association says that, in the United States, 77.8 million dogs are owned.[2] That's a lot of dogs–and a lot of dog people! If you're a dog person, then you know it's hard to refrain from bragging about your dog, or dogs. Well, I'm going to do just that. I'll start by telling you that my dogs have been my greatest teachers. I would be doing them a disservice not to talk about all they have taught me. They, and the lessons I gained from them, are my reference point. Bear with me; I hope you will find these stories aren't so much about "mine is better than yours," as they are about the valuable lessons I've received from my dogs. The stories are relevant because, to some degree, they are repeated in many homes. I will keep the stories brief when I can, in hopes of getting my point (or theirs) across. I, honestly, owe my life to a few of my dogs. I might not be here today to share if they hadn't been there for me when they were.

In the early 2000s, my life was drastically changing. Even though I've always been a dog person, "all things dog" began to shift for me with the loss of my Tia Maria (a female Shar Pei) in 2005. I made a vow to myself and to her that I would find a cure for the kidney issues/failure known to their breed (and that took her life). Though I still haven't found a cure per se, I have discovered other great ways of being in the process. I now realize it's not so much about the cure, but the concept of living differently (healthily) so you don't unnecessarily invite the problems or place yourself in a reactionary situation. If it's true that the idea of knowledge is only as powerful as what is shared, then I'd like to empower you with everything I've learned over the years.

From my heart to yours, I wish I could snap my fingers and make things easier for you and your best friend when challenges arise. My hope is that you won't have to struggle. May the stories, experiences, and information shared in this book guide you on an easier path to holistic healing for you and your dog. I hope that my perspective and

2 Source: http://www.americanpetproducts.org/press_industrytrends.asp

experiences will outweigh my credentials and that you will see that it is with love I share the words in this book. I understand some of what I share may be controversial, and it may even lack a certain level of proper veterinary terminology, but know you are welcome to disagree.

A brief bit about me before we begin. Not only do I have twenty-five years' personal experience as a dog owner, but I also have a passion and love for all animals and nature. In fact, when I was maybe four years old, my mom decided to wallpaper our dining room walls with a birch tree mural, popular in the '70s, I guess. Anyhow, the next morning she looked for me, and I was plastered up against the wall, hugging the trees! I guess that was the beginning of my love of nature. It wasn't much different as I got older. It was guaranteed that any place we went, I was sure to bring home an animal. We found out that the bunnies at the farmers market were not being sold as pets, so each time our family went, at least one was purchased with my saved allowance and "mysteriously" ended up in a purse or pocket, without my parents' knowledge, finding its way home with us. Thank goddess my parents were good sports! I once had a pet iguana, a pot-bellied pig, as well as an octopus, of all things. The octopus was the final straw with my best friend, though; she threatened never to spend the night at my house again! I've wanted alpacas since I was a young adult, and well…I'm still working on those. Anyway, my point? I've always loved animals!

Although not entirely applicable to this particular book, I have an MBA in Technology Management, a BA in Communications, and an Associate's degree in Graphic Design and Commercial Art. I spent the first part of my adult life bouncing around in marketing and advertising. I have studied Kundalini Yoga since 2005, beginning shortly after I lost my six-year-old Chinese Shar Pei, Tia Maria, to kidney failure. I have since acquired more than 500 hours in training and many more hours in personal practice. My yoga practice allowed me to see past my pain, delve deeper into my psyche, connect with those I've loved and lost, and get answers for those still living. In addition to my more formal training, I've spent many years studying alternative health and healing—shamanic healing in particular.

During the most trying years of my life, I traveled all over Central and South America, looking for help in healing myself and finding alternative solutions or cures for the kidney failure that, at that time, had actually taken the lives of three of my pups (Tia Maria, Mai Tai, and Sangria). In an effort to find a solution for the pups, I found parts of myself I had no idea were even missing. I found alternative ways to care for myself, the dogs of my past, and our futures.

At one point later in my journey, I was intuitively guided to create a dog treat I could use to reward Shiitake (now deceased) as she battled lymphoma. She was diagnosed just prior to our relocation to Maui, Hawaii, and was only given a month or two to live. Through prayer, meditation, healthy eating, and as much love as I could fill my heart with, she lived almost a year beyond her projected lifespan. Later, I will share more about her and what we learned together. She divinely inspired my treat business, Vegan Dog Treats. I am acutely aware that she is smiling beyond her grave with every bag we sell—reminded of all the things we did right, and how we can now help others before it is too late. It also took her death to make me wise up about living and find the courage to write my books.

Today, I live in beautiful Hawaii with my three healthy and active pups—Leilani the English Bulldog, Bella, and Blue the Shar Pei. My undying love for them made me think, "How will I ever leave instructions for their care in case something happens to me?" My list suddenly became a book, this book.

It is winter here now, and the cool flower breezes have been blowing through our open doors and windows as we hear about the cold and snowstorms raging all over on the mainland—making us even more grateful for being here. It hasn't been an easy journey to get here, but I finally see that the past challenging experiences have been purposeful in making life and this book a reality. I also now acknowledge that my views on veterinary care are embraced with a more open mind here on Maui than they probably would be on much of the U.S. mainland. Here on Maui, much is done with appreciation, respect, gratitude, and aloha (love) of the aina (the land) and all that dwells upon it. Whether it be a result of the high cost of living or the connection to the aina, many that live here tend to reject phamaceuticals, alopathic medicine, and rely on alternative medicine for healing as well. On the mainland, my views may tend to be a bit more controversial. I see them as simply more natural.

If you'd like to know more about me, the journey that led me to Maui, my travels across the globe to learn about connecting with spirit, integrating the alternative healing practices I learned along the way, and the love and loss of my canine best friends, I'd be honored to have you read my first two books: *Finding Your Inner Truth* and *Stepping Into Your Becoming*. For me, the book you are about to read is the true purpose for all the challenging experiences in my past.

In this book, you will learn when it's time to make a change in your and your dog's life. We will talk about diet and nutrition, meal planning, what I needed to do for my dog Bella's health concerns and allergies, and how I began to integrate homeopathy into our lives—with suggestions for you as well. I will talk about vaccinations and natural alternatives, the natural energetic system, the connection between you and your dog, and how to use certain essential oils and flower remedies for healing. I hope to give you a better understanding of what to do when there are signs of a problem. Finally, we will discuss death and the transition process. These topics are broad, but the content and discussion is deep. I have spent many nights in front of my computer, researching and reading everything I could absorb for many years, as well as countless hours meditating on every issue I needed help resolving.

Therefore, it is with much emotion and love that I share with you *Healing Your Dog Naturally*. I hope the words on these pages shift you from the chaos and confusion of veterinary care to a proactive and knowledgeable expert. May you happily coexist with your best canine friend, and may your journey be filled with grace, love, peace, and light.

Sat Nam (I acknowledge the truth within me is also within you).

Your Friend,

Nicole Gabriel

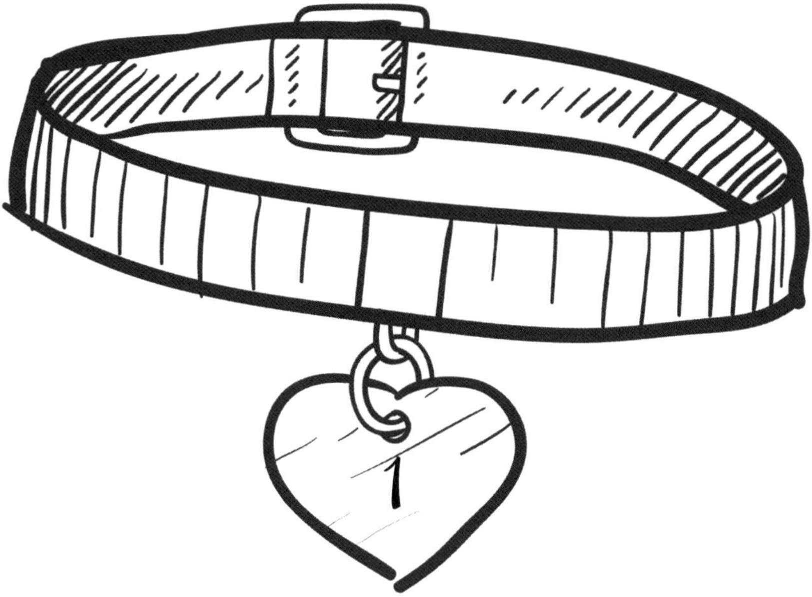

Time for a Change

"If you pick up a starving dog and make him prosperous, he will not bite you. This is the principal difference between a dog and man."

— Mark Twain

Have you ever been in the situation where your dog suddenly doesn't feel well? You dread the thought of taking him or her to the vet, imagining you'll only be given a prescription or two, a huge bill you aren't sure how you'll pay, a directive to schedule a return check-up appointment, and then sent home. But you go anyway, and when you get there, there's the anxiety-ridden wait in the treatment room and apprehension of the door opening only to find out your worst nightmare about your pup. How horrible is it to learn you have to leave your baby overnight? How many times have you been guilted into buying all the options for his or her care? How many times have you blindly gone into a situation where you were left broke and filling your pup with trial medications and/or other quick fixes, only to find even repeat visits and refills were not the solution? How many times were you told your dog had a certain problem, but instinctively, you knew that wasn't it? Are you tired of feeling like a hopeless and confused mess about your baby's care? If so, then I'd like to propose the following pages as an alternative way of being and living for you and your best friend.

Start by looking at a proactive approach—not just for your dog's care, but for your health too! You see, your dog depends on you to change into the solution. Not find the solution, but change into it. In other words, by unknowingly living your life in unhealthy ways, you are affecting your dog. I hate to start our relationship by telling you this. I hope I haven't offended you, and you are not about to set down this book! Please, hang in there with me; I have much more to share. Obviously, you love your dog, or you wouldn't have picked up this book.

YOUR DOG DEPENDS ON YOU TO CHANGE INTO THE SOLUTION. NOT FIND THE SOLUTION, BUT CHANGE INTO IT.

Dogs are pack animals. When they come into your home, a tone is set, a ranking defined, and you are a part of their pack. They feed on the environment you create, your physical and emotional state. If you are not taking responsibility for things in your life, then your dog knows it. I don't want to blame you for whatever is going on with your dog because it's horrible to live with the guilt. I know; I've been there. But understand me; you're taking this journey in tandem with your dog.

You need to look at yourself in order to help your dog live a healthier life. When we live healthier lives, our dogs benefit. Are you a smoker? Guess what? So is your dog! Do you eat unhealthily? How's your dog's diet? I might even guess that your dog even eats better than you do. True?

Before we look at any problem going on with your dog, we need to start designing the solution as a whole. And before we can get there, we are going to go somewhere entirely different. Are you confused yet? Well, let's take this one step at a time. Before we end up on the other end of that huge vet bill, let's take a deeper and more complete look at how dogs coexist within your life. Now congratulate yourself for taking the first steps on a journey into yourself and all things to help your dog not just heal naturally, but to coexist with you peacefully and healthily.

DOG AS A TOTEM ANIMAL

Many cultural traditions believe that a totem is something that is with you for life. It is a sacred emblem, a spirit, or a being that symbolizes a kinship. As dog people, we might say we are all part of the "Dog Tribe." We resonate with our dogs and with each other. How many times have you met people and sized them up based on their interest, or lack of, in all things dog? If you, like me, are part of this tribe, then you understand it's not entirely about judgment, but it's about knowing who and what fits into your tribe, your belief system, your likes, and dislikes. We all have certain categories and ways of being we could classify ourselves into, but that doesn't mean we are locked in them forever, either. My canine buddies create a lifestyle, and I want to know that my human friends can handle that. Otherwise, they might not be close friends—more like acquaintances. I don't mind, on occasion, hanging out with people who aren't dog people, but honestly, there's nothing more painful for me than having people over who require us to relocate the dogs elsewhere in the house. Or worse yet, to relegate them to the garage. And in our home, nonetheless! At times, I even wonder whether my partner is a good fit as my partner when this happens. Nothing in my world would even make me consider removing any member of my human family from a room and placing him or her in the garage.

So why would I do so with my four-legged kids?

I can't even focus on the conversation when I know my best friends are clawing on the other side of the garage door in an unfamiliar and confined space, and not a part of a friendly visit. It pulls too deeply at my heartstrings. And, when this happens, it becomes quickly evident that I don't want to put myself (or my kiddos) in this situation anytime real soon.

Therefore, I'd rather not have people over unless I've already pegged them as part of my tribe. It's just easier to befriend and invite my tribe into my home instead of someone who isn't a "member." I know they will enjoy my canine companions and take the time to know my babies. The worst offense I've ever received from someone outside the tribe was when I was struggling to make ends meet financially. This person told me that perhaps I should leave my dogs behind and move elsewhere because it would be a more sound financial decision for me. If I'd had two-legged human children, I have to think the same advice wouldn't have been given. If you tell me that leaving my dogs is my best solution, then you don't know me at all! I've just become very cautious of you. I would starve myself before I would give up my children...my angels, my spirit guides, my best friends. If you are like me, then you likely have dog as your totem animal, and you already understand.

Many great teachers or shamanic healers have studied and documented the behaviors of various animals. It is believed that, if an animal shows up regularly or consistently in your life, by studying the animal, or specific breed, you will learn more about yourself.

THE DOG TOTEM

Ted Andrews was, of course, a leading author and animal behavior teacher and observer. He wrote the book *Animal Speak* and had this to say about Dog as a totem:

- The Dog totem is about faithfulness and protection.
- People with this totem have great spirit and a great ability to love.
- It takes a lot to break a dog spirit.
- A Dog totem is a great spirit booster.
- People with a Dog totem are usually helping others or serving humanity in some way.
- Dog medicine embodies the loving gentleness of best friend and the fierce energy of protector.
- Most Native American tribes had dogs for protection and warnings.
- In India, the dog is a symbol for all caste systems.
- In Greece, it was a companion to, and guardian of the place of the dead. It has also been a symbol of motherhood because dogs are caring and nurturing parents.

Dogs were revered as very important animals in many traditions. I think this makes great ammunition to share with those who still say, "It's just a dog!" Perhaps one of these statements resonates with you more than another. Perhaps studying a bit more about Dog as totem or even creating a kind of altar to honor your dogs, by placing pictures of them beside symbols of your chosen god or spirit guide, will show them just how much you love and respect them or allow you to connect with them on a deeper level.

OTHER HISTORY AND DOG TOTEM BELIEFS

- Great leaders were buried with their pack of dogs in many traditions. Dogs were considered guides in the afterlife.
- Dogs represent fidelity and devotion and the symbol of a good friend who is always there when needed.

- Dependability, loyalty, and faithfulness are primary virtues of those with whom you associate. Dogs have all these virtues.
- Dogs represent unconditional love from Great Spirit.
- Dogs teach us how to communicate heart-to-heart with others, as many times we must communicate as a dog does—sharing and knowing that you are my reason for being.
- Dogs teach us how to celebrate life.
- Dogs only take abuse for so long before they become aggressors. They will protect all that is held dear.
- Dogs are said to be spirit helpers and dependable guides into explorations of higher consciousness and ones who warn of dark-side entities. They are aware of low vibrational sounds and excel at detecting scents on our shared journey.
- In early Christianity, dogs were a symbol of guardianship. Five Christian saints have dogs as their animal symbol: St. Bernard, St. Dominic, St. Roch, St. Eustace, and St. Hubert.
- Dogs are associated with mother goddess and symbols of healing in Northern Europe.
- In Ireland, wolf and hunting dogs were symbols of young warriors.
- Artemis/Diana was known to be the "Goddess of the Hunt" and "Protector of Animals" and was known to be always surrounded by her pack of dogs.
- Sarama was the Vedic goddess of intuition and mother of all dogs, in particular, the mother of the dogs of the god of Yama. Sarama is also depicted as the dog of the gods and the ancestor of all gods. Indra, Yama, and Rudra were associated with dogs. Sarama uses the "path to truth" (the highest path of existence) and intuitively tracks down and finds Indra's stolen cows.
- In Greek mythology, Kerberos is a three-headed hound that guards

the entrance to Hades and prevents ghosts from joining the living.

- In the Welsh Celtic mythology, Culhwch rode to King Arthur's court with two "otherworld" dogs accompanying him. The Hounds of Annwn were spectral hounds of the otherworld, associated with the wild hunt, presided over by Arawn, King of the Otherworld.
- The Irish Celts believed that true curses could be cast with the aid of a dog.
- The Pan-Celtic Crone or the Triple Goddess represents old age or death, the end of all things, the waning moon, winter, post-menstrual phases of women's lives, and all destruction that precedes rebirth. Crows, black creatures, and dogs are sacred to her. Dogs often accompanied her and guarded the gates of her after-world, helping her receive the dead.
- Norse mythology foretells that the hound Garm will set in motion the events leading to Ragnarok (the end of the world) and the wolf (Fenrir) will break loose at the time of destruction.
- In Irish mythology, the Morrigan is the goddess of war and conflict—a shape-shifter that enjoyed taking the form of a wolf.
- Native American tribes believed the dog was a guard to the Way of the Departed Spirits.
- Anubis, in the ancient Egyptian traditions, was the dog-headed god and a gatekeeper of the Other World, responsible for admitting souls to paradise. Anubis protected the souls en route to the afterlife, and was also the god of mummification and the dead. Set was also an Egyptian canine deity, depicted as a man with an animal's head. Wepwawet is yet another canine creature whose name means "owner of the roads." He has been associated with war and the newly dead and accompanies souls to the underworld.
- Hecate, the Goddess of Death, is always attended by her dogs. Cerberus was a three-headed dog that guarded the gates of the underworld.

- The Angel of Death is said to be seen only by dogs in an old Semitic tradition. It is believed that this is why dogs howl at the moon—to announce death.
- In English folklore, Black Dog appears and guides you to death.
- In the Chinese zodiac, those born in the year of the dog are said to be loyal, generous, and honest.
- Bau, whose name derived from the sound of barking ("bow" from "bow wow"), was the Sumerian goddess of fertility and healing and the patron deity of the ancient city of Lagash in Babylon. She was often depicted with the head of a dog.
- In the Shinto tradition, Kitsune are otherworldly foxes with supernatural powers that are able to grow as many as nine tails and some can take human form.
- Xolotl was an Aztec god of lightning, sunsets, and fire. He was often depicted as a man with the head of a raggedy-eared dog. He was often paired with Quetzalcoatl.

How does any or all of the above relate to you and your dog? The real question is: How does it not? You see, we are mirrors of our surroundings, and our surroundings mirror us. What did you feel drawn to here? Have you ever heard that some people even look like their dogs? Perhaps there is a deeper and richer connection worth pursuing? I have two Shar Pei and a Bulldog, so I guess that means I'm okay with my wrinkles, one of the great treats of the breeds that live in my house. What fits here for you? What do you resonate with? Take time to make a few notes here: ______________________________

____

____

____

____

____

____

____

Our dog-lovers tribe is pretty rich and pretty deep, no? If your aquaintances—or sometimes worse, your partner—don't match up with the qualities of our tribe, then it's not likely you will find them to be loyal or relationship-worthy, no matter how hard you try. If you've ever tried to date someone outside your tribe, someone who either doesn't mesh with your dog or someone your dog doesn't mesh with, then you know you have a better soulmate in your dog than in your partner. The truest test of any relationship is how your dog responds to potential friends or partners. Many times, new relationships in my life have been thwarted by irreconcilable differences between my loyal friend and a new companion.

Because you have picked up this book, it is likely that you are an honorary member of the dog tribe. Welcome! We are pretty loyal here. We are glad to have you!

When God had made the earth and sky,
The flowers and the trees,
He then made all the animals,
The fish, the birds, and bees.

And when at last He'd finished,
Not one was quite the same,
God said, "I'll walk this earth of mine,
And give each one a name."

And so He traveled far and wide,
And everywhere He went,
A little creature followed Him,
Until its strength was spent.

When all were named upon the earth,
And in the sky and sea,
The little creature said, "Dear Lord,
There's not one left for me."

Kindly the Father said to him,
"I've left you to the end.
I've turned my own name back to front,
And call you DOG, my friend."
GOD DOG

— Author Unknown

ANIMAL PRAYERS FOR HEALING

If your dog is in need of healing, there are many gods, goddesses, and angels available to assist. There is Nuada (Nudd or Ludd), the Irish/Celtic chieftain-god of healing who presides over dogs, but also the following: the sun, childbirth, magic, beauty, ocean, poetry, sorcery, writing, weapons, warfare, and youth. Nudons (Nodens, Nodonti, and Nodente) is a similar character in the Welsh traditions, an Anglo-Celtic sea god like Poseidon. He is the god of healing, water, ocean, fishing, the sun, sailing, childbirth, dogs, hunting, youth, beauty, spears and slings, smiths, carpenters, harpers, poets, historians, sorcerers, writing, magic, warfare, and incantations. There is the Buddhist goddess Quan Yin, renowned for her power over the animal kingdom or the forces of nature. Archangel Ariel is associated with lions and animals, protecting and healing nature, and is considered the Patron Angel of Wild Animals. Archangel Raphael is the Patron Angel of all those in the field of Medicine (for both humans and animals). There are many more, so do some research, and then choose one to work with. You can ask any of them for help.

There is also St. Francis of Assisi, the patron saint of animals, who believed that all animals were our brothers and sisters. Francis often prayed that God would work through him to help animals as well as people. He said of animals:

"Not to hurt our humble brethren is our first duty to them,
but to stop there is not enough.
We have a higher mission—
to be of service to them wherever they require it."

Here are a few prayers that are associated with St. Francis that may help you and your animals:

A Prayer for Sick Animals

Heavenly Father,
you created all things for your glory
and made us stewards of this creature
If it is your will, restore it to health and strength.
Blessed are you, Lord God,
and holy is your name for ever and ever.
Amen

Individual Blessing of the Animals

(Name of Animal) may you be blessed in the Name of the Father,
and of the Son and of the Holy Spirit.
May you and (name of pet guardian) enjoy life together and
find joy with the God who created you.
May God, who created the animals of this earth as a help to us,
continue to protect and sustain us with the grace his blessing brings,
now and forever.
Amen

For All Animals

Blessed are you, Lord God, maker of all living creatures.
You called forth fish in the sea, birds in the air, and animals on the land.
You inspired St. Francis to call all of them his brothers and sisters.
We ask you to bless this pet. By the power of your love, enable it to live according to your plan. May we always praise you for all your beauty in creation. Blessed are you, Lord our God, in all your creatures!
Amen.

Here are a few other prayers that may help you in your time of need:

Buddhist Animal Blessing Prayer

May all sentient beings in the animal realm subject to unbearable pain in labs throughout the world be free from suffering. May alternatives to animal experimentation and testing be used immediately. May Bodhicitta fill the hearts of those who imprison them.May all sentient beings from the animal realm who suffer endless days, months, years locked in tiny cages unable to move, be filled with peace and calm. May the many billions waiting in slaughterhouse lines be free of fear. May the hearts of those who work in abattoirs be filled with Bodhicitta so the very thought of harm is purified. May they never kill again and may the slaughterhouse lines become immediately empty. May no animal be afraid or depressed. May their bodies be free of injuries, disease, and illness. May those who need homes, or who have been driven from them find shelter, plentiful food, and water. May there be liberation for those tortured for fur, entertainment, or who are hunted. May those who believe they are superior to our brother and sister animals develop perfect equanimity. And may they realize in their hearts that all sentient beings possess Buddha nature And they are not ours to kill or exploit. May the many billions of land and sea dwelling sentient beings who are abused, exploited, and killed due to greed, hatred, and ignorance be free of suffering. May they experience complete and perfect enlightenment, through the virtue of my efforts and prayers.

Wiccan Pet Blessing

O Gracious Lord and Lady, protectors of all creatures who walk this earth, guard my pet (pet's name) against harm and illness. Watch over (him/her) with every step (he/she) takes. Help me to protect (him/her) and strengthen the connection of love between us. Let this charm be blessed with protection. Blessed be!

DOG SPELLED BACKWARDS

Have you ever encountered a life-changing event that was inspired by a dog? Is it possible that dogs are inspired by God to be a part of our human miracles? To teach us something about humanity? To uplift and inspire us? To help us to know we are loved by the Power that created us? Could dogs be angels? If our creator, or God, is in everything, then why wouldn't he/she be in a dog? And how is it that beyond abuses, neglect, mistreatment, etc., dogs still love us? Doesn't God do the same? Dogs forgive, and so does God. When dogs act as angels of God, perhaps we ought to pay attention to what God may be showing us through them. Dogs love us deeply, no matter how we treat them, and whether we deserve it or not. If you've met a dog, you've likely met an angel. Have you ever met a rescued dog? When it finds a new home, it thanks you for its food, shelter, toys, walks, etc., like no other being on the planet. The loyalty of the rescued dog will never betray you. He or she will spend the rest of his or her life thanking you. And best of all, dogs remind us to be thankful for all that we have, not what we don't have. They do not judge; they just love.

"God couldn't be physically with us, so he gave us dogs...
and notice dog spelled backwards is God.
And they both show unconditional love."

— Author Unknown

I recently met someone who was about to end his life, but just as he lifted the gun to his head, his dog reminded him that he was needed.

When I was sad and depressed going through my divorce and had many drastic changes in my life, my two dogs reminded me that if I left them, there would be no one to care for them as I could. I had given them the best life I could, and I knew no one could do a better job, so I stuck around. One dog was a senior, and one was just a pain in the ass, yet I still loved her. I knew their fate would not be good if I left them, as senior dogs are hard to rehome, and aggressive dogs generally end up being euthanized.

And you know what's funny? I've met many people who treat their dogs better than themselves. I've known many a woman, in particular, who ends up in a relationship where her dog is her world, and her partner is not as fond of her four-legged friend(s). Here's the reality, ladies and gentlemen; if something happens to you, guess who has to take care of the dogs? So perhaps dogs teach us to be in better relationships—relationships that are more loving and divine. Does your partner treat you like he or she treats your dog? I once met a district attorney in Michigan who represented battered and abused women and children. He told me that the way a person treats his or her dog or child is a great indication of how that person will treat his or her spouse and vice versa. What about the dynamics of relationships will divinely inspire you to honor yourself with healthier associations? Sometimes when we can't honor ourselves, we can honor our pets or kids, and make a better choice on their behalf, but not our own. Perhaps, for that moment, when we are weak in self, we are gifted with the care of a dependent innocent being to pull us from our darkness.

The animals of our planet remind us that our purpose is much simpler, joyful, playful, and peaceful than the way we live our lives. When a dog goes for a ride in the car, it doesn't know whether it's going a mile up the street or taking a cross-country trip. Dogs don't have to pack bags or plan. They just get in, smile, hang their heads out the window, and live fully in that very moment. They live in the now. Can you stop thinking about the past or the future and focus entirely on the now? How many days does it take us to plan the trip, pack the right outfit, get the gas, check the tires, etc.? Why don't we live with the faith and trust of a dog? Dogs live in the moment, and as long as we're with them, they are happy. Could the secret of life, or happiness, be shown to us through our dogs?

I've studied yoga for many years. In the yoga community, we understand that Prana is life. Life is breath. If you've ever watched dogs sleep, heard them snore, or watched them as they stretched, you might begin to see the frailty and strength that is life. The magic of life (and simple comforts) can be found in the sleeping dog.

"The human considers himself as 'master' to his dog, but the dog considers his master 'God.'"

— Jack London

Dogs were created by God to be cared for by humans. Have you ever asked why that is? Why are some dogs brutally abused, and others deeply loved? God has a plan, and the dog was designed to turn around humanity. Dogs bring us messages from the divine to let us know we are not alone and that we are loved. We are protected and guided by a more divine and higher power. Have you heard the voice of God whispering through your dog? Dogs have been welcomed into our homes and domesticated in a beautiful way. We can relate to them in such a way that they elicit a human response that mirrors us! When we can't find our own kindness and peace, we can find it in our dogs. For some that is scary, but for others, we see their light. Imagine your dog was sent from another planet, or as an angel from heaven, to study humans and then enlighten and awaken our consciousness. Dogs sleep in our beds and watch us shower naked and go to the bathroom. Who else do you share this kind of close personal space with? If you weren't prepared for that, you might feel threatened. Surprisingly, some of us don't deal well with peace. But if you are curious and choose to follow your heart, you might see that your consciousness will expand because of dogs.

"God sent angels down to earth in the form of dogs with notes saying "Don't judge, just love." They ate the notes, but they keep trying to deliver the message."

— Author Unknown

WHERE IS GOD?

I went through a period of loss where I lost four of my pups within a few short years of each other. I became so angry when all the deaths started occurring. I hated God because I believed God hated me.

But as time went on, I knew God had to love me more than words could express. After the final loss, I thought about it and asked myself again, "How could God take my loves away from me?" Then I paused. I realized God had given them to me to begin with.

If God created them, and I felt so much love from each of them, I could only imagine what love God has for me. God allowed them to show me this love, and I experienced love and devotion from each like I had never experienced with another human. And while God had overseen the experience for us, the connection between us, our mutual love and trust, ultimately showed me the infinite of which they were now a part.

But it was when my almost six-year-old Chinese Shar Pei, Shiitake, died that I was given a big gift. I was shown that my soul's composition is the same as the collective consciousness to which she was to return. If that collective consciousness is some kind of God, then God is within me, around me, and is me! Is it possible that "DOG" really is "GOD"? I think there is no way it can be separate. I have heard yogic chants and speeches over the years claiming that God is not merely outside us, but until Shiitake showed me, I had never confirmed this. Really, our pups are here on loan...a gift from God. We are all here temporarily, and then we go back to the consciousness that knows all and fuses into oneness. I began to wonder how to interact with this consciousness…to connect with her. Would I be able to call on it? Of course—because it is within me! Not only is it within me—it *is* me. I am not just the light of God, but I am the God light. I learned that I connect with Shiitake and the source of her in that same soup of consciousness. Her death showed me how.

Shiitake was gone physically, but present in every other way. I could see the spark of her soul with my psychic awareness. She taught me that spirit energy resides in the pineal gland (the place between the eyes at the root of the nose) here in our earthly body. She showed me this was how I would recognize her when she was without her physical body. It is like a golden ball of light of her essence. It is her recognizing factor when in spirit form. It's a unique calling card we all have. It is how we recognize each other's spirit, with or without the physical body.

I loved her even more for showing me these gifts! I became grateful for what she was teaching me.

Through her love and my trust, I would be the closest to God I had ever been. She was proving that Spirit is active in all sentient beings, and no single one is more or less important than another. Our life, just like our death, is purposeful. No one will ever convince me that she was "just a pet," because that would mean I had ownership over her. Her soul was grand in her physical body, but even more splendid when it was no longer trapped in her physical body. She was teaching me that we might have physical limitations, but our soul can be everything. She taught me never to doubt in God's love. I know God is watching at all phases of our life and in spirit.

My curiosity to know more would be sparked, and that interest proved to be nearly enough to snap me out of the emotional wounds of my past and the emotional loss of her physical presence.

What would snap you out of where you are now and move you into becoming a more intentionally-aware being? What would it take to move you from where you are to where you want to be? Is it one moment or several? Are you aware that these moments transform you? How can you place these transformation nuggets into your everyday awareness? And how did the presence of a dog give you the gift of self-transformation?

"God made the earth, the sky and the water, the moon and the sun.
He made man and bird and beast.
But He didn't make the dog. He already had one."

— Native American saying

DEPROGRAMMING

Why is it that, as human beings, we feel the need to alter the beautiful beings our Creator made? Where do trust, faith, and medicine meet, and which one wins? If, as a human race, we never vaccinated ourselves, would we have become extinct, or at the very least, very sickly as a race? Perhaps illness ultimately teaches us how to gain a well-rounded and natural holistic approach to living? The debate about immunizations may continue indefinitely, and perhaps there is/was a time and place for them. Personally, I think that taking any extreme stance on any subject—strongly swinging toward one side or another—can be dangerous. I originally approached my immunization research believing that there can be a happy medium, and that's the best answer, but I believe that the more I learned, the more my opinion became swayed. I'm open to learning if there are strong facts supporting either side of the argument, but now that I've done my research, I honestly don't understand the need for immunizations in most cases.

I like to consider myself a pretty open person, but when it came to whether or not I was going to choose vaccinations for my current pups, I was a bloody mess! I had been programmed to believe it was best to take them to the vet and then to stay on a regular maintenance program of annual vaccines. I had no idea what the veterinarian was putting into them, and I had no idea there could be side effects. I assumed my dogs would get deathly ill if I chose not to vaccinate them. So for twenty-five years, I stuck with the plan and took them in regularly. I'd pat myself on the back and feel like a responsible, proud momma each time I went. I thought I'd done the right thing as a responsible pet owner. In those days, I was proud to pay that veterinarian bill.

But, as life would have it, things were about to change for me as a dog owner when I decided to move to Hawaii. You see, to get your pets into Hawaii, you must put them through two rounds of rabies shots because Hawaii is a rabies-free state. I took comfort in the fact that someone had done the research, and this was completely safe. I filled out all the paperwork and proceeded as planned. The final tests went in. Sushi, Shiitake, and my cat, Penelope, had the proper levels of antibodies and were cleared, after a three-month period of in-home quarantine, to enter the islands. We purchased the plane tickets, along with their travel crates, cushions, water and food containers, cooling fans, diapers (in case of an accident), and even a baby monitor to check on them during the flight. Their bright-orange agricultural clearance tags and forms arrived and were secured to their crates.

But, just ten days before their travel, Shiitake started acting funny and got a runny nose. Her eyes looked sad and were set deep in her sweet little face. She had been in dog training because her daddy couldn't deal with her sudden onset of aggressiveness, but we had to cancel our last class because she was not feeling well, and the trainer knew she had recently attacked Sushi. He made the decision to quit with her because he didn't think he could help her. He was my last hope for her behavior, and I was beside myself as I worried about the stress and strain it would put on my relationship with my partner because he had threatened it would be me or the dog if I didn't find a way to control her. I was put in a tough place, but it was going to be a cold day in hell before I gave up on her. When backed into a corner, I will always choose a dog over a person. The loyalty is always greater! It was a point in my life that caused significant strain in my relationship, but I knew my girl, and something was wrong. You don't give up on your kids.

Shiitake wasn't herself. Her lymph glands were very swollen, and I knew this was not a good sign. I also knew immediately, and without question, that the vaccinations caused her issues. Then the dreaded call came after our check-up, and it was cancer—lymphoma to be specific. First, I cried and hugged her, but then I was so, so, so mad! I was mad because I'd trusted her doctors, trusted the state of Hawaii, trusted myself, trusted God, and went along blindly believing there were no side effects, and this "system" was tried and trusted. This was the start of another awakening in me. How can we trust a system that fails us? Is it the fault of the system, or a test from the divine?

I believed that through the spiritual awakenings I had experienced for many years prior, traveling the world and working with healers, doing my work and healing, I would be guided into a peaceful life, where these kinds of things didn't exist. I was just mad, mad, mad! What was God doing to me? I thought all the choices I'd made had been at Shiitake's expense. I figured I had made the decision to kill her. Because I wanted to go to Hawaii, she had to die. Because I couldn't see what was in her best interest, I was being punished. My mind raced. I lost sleep. Then I panicked to find a cure.

SHIITAKE'S LYMPHOMA

My heart was in pieces as I prepared to board the plane to Maui, Hawaii. The vet's office had given up on Shiitake, and so had her trainer. The vet told me to put her down and not put her through the travel or even try to save her because she was terminal. That didn't even register. She was my baby, and I wasn't about to give up on her. After all, I believed it was my fault, and I had done this to her. I was barely existing in a fog in a strange new land. Have you ever felt so very alone in your choices and life decisions? I hated Maui and Hawaii for doing this to her. I rejected paradise as soon as I arrived. But I knew that on Maui, there was a doctor who called himself "The Cancer Vet." I figured Shiitake's prescribed prednisone would get her lymph swelling down and get us safely to the vet upon arrival.

I paced the floors awaiting a call back to get an appointment scheduled. I went in thinking we were aggressively going to kick cancer's ass. But what I wasn't prepared for was that I would have to choose between a natural method or treatment with chemotherapy right then and there. I guess I just thought the vet would wave a magic wand and make the cancer all go away. It turned out to be our first visit in a string of many. I made the decision, after many late nights of research, that if I were put in the same situation as Shiitake was, I would not choose chemo. Chemo scared me. I also felt as if I would accept the disease if I chose chemo. I was still in a bit of denial at this point. I just thought she'd snap out of it and get better. I didn't want to see her throwing up and growing weak after a chemo session, and I didn't want to alter her life severely. I wanted to make her comfortable. I have to admit I questioned my choices after many months when she wasn't improving. She was projected to live just thirty days when we left her vet's office on the mainland. However, once we arrived on the island, we had a glorious and emotional additional eight months together. She was able to go for car rides, hikes, see the scenery, taste the rivers, smell the upcountry air, and meet the cows of Maui.

We spent many days in the cool upcountry air above the lavender farms. We danced in the rain, watched cows, smelled eucalyptus, and meditated together. The mediation proved to be valuable in preparing to say our goodbyes. It took us much time to separate and prepare for her eventual passing. It took a lot of forgiveness on my part. I learned to listen to her. She explained to me that Sushi and Penelope (the cat) had also been through their immunizations and were healthy. She explained to me that it was her time to go. But she had some things to teach me before she did.

WE DANCED IN THE RAIN, WATCHED COWS, SMELLED EUCALYPTUS, AND MEDITATED TOGETHER.

By going through this experience, I learned from Shiitake how to make a healthy dog treat to help other dogs that were also sick and on limited diets. Shiitake taught me incredible things about diet so each dog I had in my life in the future would live a better life. She taught me that immunizations are not always best and never to trust an "unconscious system." She taught me to believe in and trust myself, to question things, and to take ownership of every situation, but to balance that ownership with a level of confidence in the creator. She taught me to know that when God calls you back home, it's because your life on Earth is only temporary for a small spectrum of your soul's growth and evolution. She taught me that the soul is endless, and our lost loved ones are never far away. She taught me to open and expand my heart. She taught me that when something doesn't feel right, it isn't. But, most of all, she taught me that you can't mess with God's plan, and no matter how much work you do on healing yourself or your past, planning for your future, or walking through life's lessons—God has a plan. Trust and have faith in the plan and know that, no matter what, you are never in the wrong place, and you will never make a bad decision. To believe that something is wrong just means you do not have faith in the power that created you. You are given choices; how you handle those choices—the power of the mind—is the ultimate place for human growth.

SHIITAKE'S CANCER PROTOCOL

Since Shiitake didn't survive, I leave it up to you whether you choose to believe in the protocol we used. Because she didn't survive, I hemmed and hawed about even writing this book, but I pushed on, knowing I had something I needed to share. I'm doing it for her and for you, too, because she needed you to know! From what I understand, what Shiitake endured is a typical protocol for treating cancer without chemo. I feel it's relevant to share that protocol here because, in all my research, I did not find anything that showed me an entire treatment protocol. I found bits and pieces, but mostly, I would find just one product with instructions for how to use it or an article about the benefits of one particular herb or combination of herbs. I want to document everything I learned here so you'll have a place to start from if you are also opting to try an alternative method for care beyond chemo.

We also opted for home massage care, as well as in-office acupuncture, which was used mostly for body aches and pains, versus treatment per se. However, if you understand both, they are also perfect for releasing energy and circulating herbal supplements. I worked as a massage therapist for several years and am acutely aware that you must be somewhat cautious with massage because it heightens circulation. Just imagine circulating cancer more readily into the lymph system. You have to know how to direct it. I will explain this in a bit.

Here is what she was taking for her cancer care. As far as doses and portions, I am not a doctor. I am not prescribing, so I will ask you to talk to your vet about what would work best. This protocol is something you might consider in the care of your baby. Again, I was never able to find a treatment plan, probably because anyone who could have come up with one feared that it would be followed and was concerned about legal risks if it didn't work. This is why it is great that I'm not a doctor. I have no license to lose. I am not suggesting this is best for you and your baby. I am simply offering the following as an example of what the vet prescribed for Shiitake. She was a fifty-five pound dog if that helps you understand portioning. I left out some information intentionally since it was relevant to her, but may not be to your dog; therefore, simply use this as a guideline in working with your veterinarian on specifics for your dog. Most of the items here can be easily found on Amazon. Neoplasene, however, cannot.

Morning Regime

3 K9 Immunity capsules

½ tab K9 Transfer Factor

2 calcium citrate capsules

1 krill fish oil capsule

3 Wobenzym pills

2 Apocaps pills

2 methylprednisolone (sub-prednisone) pills

1 mirtazapine pill

1 Denamarin pill

1 Proviable pill

1.5 ml Neoplasene (taken orally)

1 taurine capsule

1 acetyl-L-carnitine capsule

Evening Regime

3 K9 Immunity capsules

½ tab K9 Transfer Factor

2 calcium citrate capsules

3 Wobenzym pills

2 Apocaps pills

2 10-20 mg prednisone (sub-methylprednisolone)

1 mirtazapine pill

1 Proviable pill

1.5 ml Neoplasene (taken orally)

1.5 ml melatonin

1 taurine capsule

1 acetyl-L-carnitine capsule

In conjunction with this regime, we also moved her from the diet she was on to an all-natural, home-prepared, starch-free nutraceutical (food sources with extra benefits) diet with lots of dark leafy greens. I began to add Essiac tea toward the end, but I didn't talk to the doctor about that. I found out about it a bit late in the game, or I would have used it from the beginning. About the same time, I heard about the following as alternatives, but it was too late to try any of them:

- Boswellia serrata and frankincense oil
- Cancer nosode (more about nosodes later)
- Cannabis juice/oil
- Chinese herbs of Yunnan Baiyao (equal to penicillin) and Artemisinin (isolated from a sweet wormwood plant)
- Coriolis mushrooms (many other kinds are good too)
- Essiac tea
- Graviola (also called soursop)
- Intravenous Vitamin C and B

Even if you moved away from dry food and just fed your dog chicken and brown rice, you are far better off than with a dry food diet. In my opinion, there isn't much nutrition gained with a dry food diet. In fact, some dry food can even be dangerous.

Since Shiitake's passing, I have found numerous ideas, concepts, herbs, and homeopathic approaches that may have assisted her along the path to good health or prolonged her life even after her cancer diagnosis. For example, homeopathic medicine doesn't fight against the cancer growth or see it as separate.

The attitude of homeopathic care is not one of attacking something separate from the patient. When you are patient-oriented, cancer is just a symptom. Healing starts with the whole patient and the immune system. Instead, nutrition and homeopathy work naturally to rebalance the life energy, so the life energy of the cancer is no longer supported. It's reabsorbed or expelled. In fact, some reports I read stated that if chemotherapy, surgery, or radiation were previously used, fewer would survive with conjunctive homeopathic care, so in the long run, I felt we made the right choice not to do chemotherapy.

If you turned to this book for cancer care in particular, perhaps it will help you understand more about why the cancer happened and give you a few suggestions on how to ease the current situation you are facing. Many things here can be beneficial to know, but they are not pointed out specifically for cancer care. I want to change the way you think about cancer. It's not about bombarding your dog's already-compromised body with chemical poisons, but strengthening it with nutritional tools that take power away from cancer. It is far better to live well (and longer) with cancer present but under control. I think you will understand this concept better as we move along.

In the world of energy, cancer is an entity, meaning another consciousness altogether. When the body grows weak and the spirit waivers in its container, it makes room for other life forms to come in. Celebrating life is cancer's best cure. We will begin with diet and nutrition. Cancer or no cancer, let's start here.

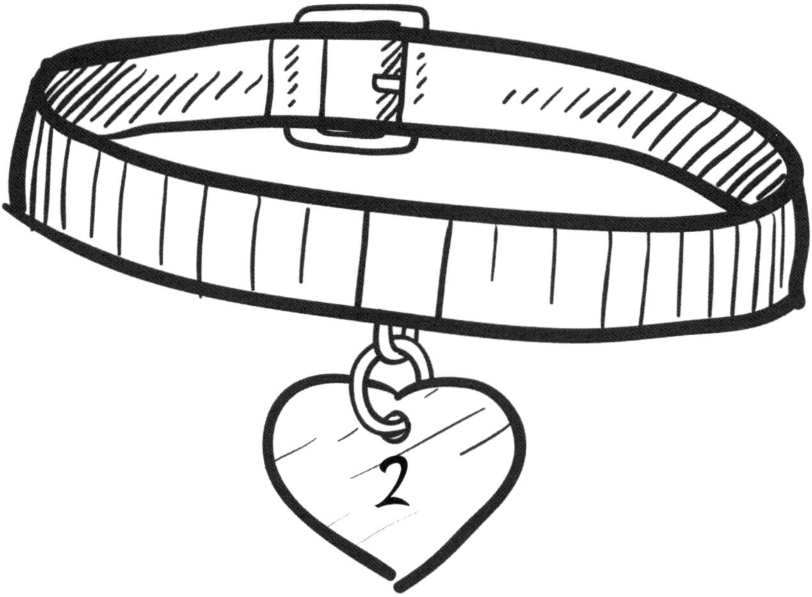

Diet & Nutrition

"In the Book of Life, the answers aren't in the back."

— Charles M. Schulz

Before we begin talking about the subject of diet, I want to walk you through a little exercise. Grab your favorite dog food. List the ingredients here. Circle the ones you recognize.

____

____

____

Now ask yourself the following:

- Where can I find those ingredients?
- Do I know what they are? Plug each item into a search engine and read more. What did you find?
- Now look to see whether you can find specifically which animal any of the listed proteins came from.
- Were those animals healthy when they were slaughtered?
- What state or country did they come from?
- Were they humanely treated before their deaths?
- Take a minute to imagine the whole process from slaughter to your dog's bowl.
- Can you find any dates on the bag?
- How long has your bag of food been in circulation? How long did it take after processing to make it to your home?

Now here's the real test. I want you to eat it! Do you dare? Whether you can or can't stomach it, I want you to imagine your dog eating that food day in and day out for the average age of your dog, say eight to ten years? If your dog eats twice a day for ten years, that's as many as 7,300 bowls of what you just ate. Imagine how your body would feel. Do you know now why your dog always begs to eat what you're eating? Can you blame him or her? Are you ready to make a change? To find a better way? Great! Let's get started here by talking about diet.

Diet is not only the greatest way to ensure a long healthy life for your best friend, but it's also an excellent way to deepen your friendship and begin to discern your dog's needs.

WHY DIET IS SO IMPORTANT

Eating 7,300 bowls of food in the average lifetime (fed twice a day for ten years) means that what you give your dog matters! His or her life depends on it. If you wouldn't choose to live on a diet of potato chips and candy bars, then you need to get your dog off commercial dry food immediately! There is little to no nutritional value to a dry food diet. And canned commercial dog food isn't a whole lot better. Ask yourself, "Where does my dog's food come from?"

EATING 7,300 BOWLS OF FOOD IN THE AVERAGE LIFETIME (FED TWICE A DAY FOR TEN YEARS) MEANS THAT WHAT YOU GIVE YOUR DOG MATTERS!

If you don't know the answer to this question, you have a problem that needs to be addressed. Did you know that more than 95 percent of dogs derive their nutritional needs from a single source—processed pet foods? Just like humans, dogs need a quality source of protein, fats, and vegetables. Not only do good sources of quality food need to be given to them, but because of our modern ways, it needs to be supplemented as well. Fruits and vegetables contain fiber and antioxidants that are no longer available because domesticated dogs no longer hunt for their prey. Fatty acids, minerals, and vitamins must be added because the soil where our food is often grown is lacking in nutrients. Our pups need fresh, whole foods that are moisture-dense. Some say that grains aren't necessary. Many people don't correlate disease to diet. Others realize the correlation. Some just don't care. The attitude you develop for your dog will likely stem from the attitude you keep in your household for your own family's beliefs and standards.

What truly fascinates me is that diet is not studied in much detail in our human educational systems and certainly not in detail in the veterinary community. With the advent of GMO issues, and talk surrounding the subject, this situation is beginning to change. We are starting to question where our food comes from and how it is grown and processed before making it onto our dinner table. I find it alarming that there isn't a store today where you can find out what additives, soil, or chemicals were a part of the growth cycle of our fruits and vegetables. If you can go into any natural foods store, the closest you might find is "organically grown," and we are forced to trust that it was. The only way we'd know any better is if we grew it ourselves.

And what about the pet food recalls that made news a few years ago? I'm sure you've heard of some of these, but did you find out what was going on? Did you know that not only was something found in these foods that was a danger to your pets, but in many cases, something was also discovered that would be a threat to humans? Rat poison, cyanide, molds, fungus or fungal products (aflatoxins), excessive vitamin additives, and enamels from flaking container cans were found in many of them. Some pet foods have even been said to contain euthanized cats and dogs. There have even been tests showing that pentobarbital (the euthanasia drug) has been found in some of the foods tested.

WHAT'S REALLY IN COMMERCIAL PET FOODS?

Processed grains, corn or wheat gluten, starchy vegetables (carrots, peas, potatoes), and other cheap carbohydrate fillers are the least of our worries. What ends up in pet foods is whatever doesn't make it to our grocery stores. It's the ugly stuff that would likely be considered waste to be thrown out. With few regulations, I'd have to bet that the ingredients are mind-boggling. I've even heard that there isn't much concern with public health, and that products made from unhealthy, diseased animals were fed to healthy dogs through these pet foods. I've heard of this referred to as "4D Animals." This stands for Dead, Dying, Diseased, and Disabled. I understand that 4D animal meat was only recently banned for human consumption, but it is still a legitimate ingredient in pet foods.

The World Health Organization publically named common chemical preservatives in pet foods. Here are some they disclosed:

- Propylene glycol (anti-freeze)
- Ethoxyquin (a pesticide and hardening agent often used in rubber manufacturing tested by the FDA as a possible cause of canine liver and kidney cancer)
- BHA (a chemical food additive that helps prevent foods that contain oils from going rancid. Butylated hydroxyl anisol, now being defined in California as a carcinogen)
- BHT (butylated hydroxytoluene) (a preservative)
- TBHQ (a preservative)
- Propyl gallate (an artificial food additive that is also used in cosmetics and pharmaceuticals)

Many additives that are supposed to help are killing or making our pets very sick. DL-Methionine is an amino acid used as a urinary acidifier. The problem is that it was found in excess in many bags of a well-known brand name and recalled. A prescription dog food was found with a serious overdose of Vitamin D, which caused calcium deficiency and kidney disease. One might even ask whether some kind of population control was going on here.

The scariest of all, which I believe personally affected me, was the most lethal pet food recall in our history. In 2007, the FDA received more than 17,000 complaints from consumers. Thousands of pets were sickened, and an estimated 20 percent died from acute renal failure caused by the food. What was the culprit? It was initially believed to be rat poison! Aminopterin was listed as one of the ingredients. Later in 2007, the American Society for the Prevention of Cruelty to Animals reported that symptoms described in affected animals are not "fully consistent with the ingestion of rat poison containing aminopterin." Some time after that, the U.S. Food and Drug Administration (FDA) announced a possible source of the sicknesses, indicated by the presence of melamine, an industrial chemical, in wheat gluten imported from China. The FDA then prohibited the import of wheat gluten from a specific Chinese company, saying that the contamination may be in dry pet foods as well, but it was primarily used as a thickener in gravies and wet food. Apparently, it was also used to feed cows, pigs, and chickens. Thousands of animals were destroyed, but just one month later, the rapid onset of kidney disease appeared in dogs and cats. High levels of melamine and cyanuric acid were found. Much of this information can be found on the FDA website. It's not hidden in most cases, but it's also not openly talked about in the public. Nor is the public being accurately informed and warned. Is it possible that pet food provides a convenient income for slaughterhouses—a way to turn waste into a profit? Isn't that just part of the American way? Smart business? Hmm, I beg to differ. Life is more important than profits. I believe this is a wake-up call to humanity.

Regardless of the exact issues going on here, my point is that I was not feeding any of the foods on the recall lists to my dogs, but whether you were or weren't, you need to be concerned for the safety of your animals if you don't know what you are feeding them.

Again, I question the concept of population control (and I'm not a paranoid person). I lost three dogs in 2007, all to renal failure. It brings tears to my eyes all these years later to think that I was unknowingly poisoning my babies with each bite they took. At more than sixty dollars a bag, I was buying what I thought was the best food on the market. I thought the more I paid, the better the food. Premium food brands may boast of being higher quality, but these meats are still mainly leftover scraps. The chicken is likely backs, bones, feet, and beaks because breast meat is expensive and can be sold to humans. Is there any guarantee that the premium brands kill animals specifically for the pet food market to provide a better quality product? There is no guarantee unless you do it yourself!

A big profit is turned for that which is unfit for human consumption. It's astounding to learn that half of the animals killed are considered unfit for human consumption. And I'm not talking about them as a whole animal. I'm talking about all that isn't appealing in a grocery store. Be prepared...I'm talking heads, feet, intestines, lungs, spleens, livers, ligaments, fat, and unborn babies. Many government bodies claim that what is considered unpalatable to us is desired by our dogs. Possibly so, but is it right for them? What is also found in some cases are all the other waste items you might find on a farm... animal feed, fertilizers, industrial lubricants, soap, rubber, and other "byproducts." More than 50 percent of meats are contaminated. An animal that died on a farm might not even reach a dog food processing plant until several days after its death. And if it died, have we asked why? Surely not all die of natural causes. Do we know what bacteria are present? No law says it must be tested. And we haven't even talked about GMOs yet! Corn and soy are some of the most genetically-modified plants and among the most likely to be found in pet foods.

No wonder 50 percent of dogs develop cancer in their adult years![3] Dogs are twice as likely as humans to develop leukemia, four times as likely to develop breast cancer, eight times as likely to get bone cancer, and a whopping thirty-five times as likely to get skin cancer.[4] And the FDA has no requirement that pet food products have to get pre-market approval by the FDA. However, if you visit the FDA website,[5] you will see that the FDA ensures that the ingredients used in pet food are safe and have an appropriate function in the pet food.

3 *See "The Canine Cancer Crisis" from* The Whole Dog Journal *at http://www.whole-dog-journal.com/issues/1_8/features/5321-1.html.*

4 *Source: VPI (Veterinary Pet Insurance) data*

5 *http://www.fda.gov/AnimalVeterinary/Products/AnimalFoodFeeds/PetFood*

But, if there is no requirement, how can they ensure anything?

Cancer care costs for dogs can vary widely depending on the type and stage of cancer your dog has. According to the National Canine Cancer Foundation, major surgical procedures that require wide and deep tumor removal, or major reconstructive procedures, will likely range from about $1,500 upward, depending on the extent of surgery and the recovery period. Chemotherapy costs vary with the pet's size, but for many treatment regimens, the cost of chemotherapy may range from several hundred dollars for palliative oral treatment to several thousand dollars over a three- to six-month period.

Radiation therapy will range from $2,000 to $6,000, or more, per patient. Does it sound like there's big money in making dogs sick?

THE PET FOOD MARKET

The United States pet food market is a $23-billion industry and is rapidly expanding into other markets. According to Optimum Choice's website,[6] the "With Rule" allows an ingredient name to appear on the label, such as "Made with real Chicken," as long as each such ingredient makes up at least three percent of the food's weight, excluding water processing. The "Flavor Rule" allows for a food designed as a certain flavor, as long as the ingredients are sufficient to "impart a distinctive characteristic" to the food. Thus, a "beef flavor" food may not contain any actual beef at all. Nothing addresses the digestibility or nutrients in the pet food, and there is no way to know whether sufficient nutrients are being satisfied. In fact, what is left of the animal is mostly bones and other byproducts, causing the food to lose all nutritional value.

The process of cooking and forming the food into little round balls of kibble uses heat to such a degree that even more nutritional value is lost. To interest our pets in actually eating this food, many foods are not only fortified, but they are also sprayed with flavors, animal fats, and

6 http://www.optimumchoices.com/whats_in_pet_food.htm

oils that are deemed inedible for humans. Did you know that restaurant grease has been used, as well as more lucrative, biodiesel fuel?

Now, here's what is scary: How many times have you decided to mix your pup's dry food with something wet to make it more flavorful? Well, when the food is cooked, the final product can pick up more bacteria when drying, being coated, and packaged. Some experts have warned that getting the food wet can allow the bacteria on the surface to multiply, which can make pets sick.

So you may argue, "Buy better food!" But what food is "better"? You would think natural food would be, but if the label says "Natural," it's a broad term adopted by AAFCO (Association of American Feed Control Officials). And AAFCO has no regulatory function, as stated at http://www.aafco.org/Consumers/What-is-in-Pet-Food.

"Organic" would likely be the safest bet if you still think buying commercial dry food is right for you and your pet. It has a very strict legal definition under the USDA National Program.

But don't be fooled. Some companies are great at evading the intent of these rules with tricky marketing and labeling. The name of the product or brand can be misleading and use terms such as "Natural" or "Organic" in the brand name. And "Organic" implies nothing about animal welfare in factory farms. Also, be aware of claims of "human grade" ingredients. This term is meaningless, as is "USDA inspected." There are many ways around this. For example, a facility might be USDA-inspected during the day, but the pet food is made at night after the inspector goes home.

Pet food laws are not being regulated as strictly as our human foods, and not much is being done to enforce what little is in place. But many benefit from these unethical practices, including farmers, biodiesel companies, and pet food manufacturers. And, of course, once our dogs are sick, there is a whole new market for veterinary care and health support products. And this is not just happening in the pet food market. It's going on in our lives too.

MAKING PEOPLE AND THEIR PETS SICK IS BIG BUSINESS!

Did you know that pet food manufacturers and pharmaceutical companies award many grants and scholarships? Surgery, neurology, internal medicine, dermatology, etc. are becoming more tantalizing to new vets, and nutrition is rarely even taught. I'm not blaming the veterinarians, necessarily. I believe they are just a part of a broken system that is bigger than they are. In the United States and many other countries, we are taught a way of living that supports the whole of it. It's a system based on commercialism. It's hard enough to get by, let alone stand against it. In fact, many veterinarians are given a commission on vet-only brand foods and special prescription diet foods. How can they recommend a food if they have minimal to no training in nutrition or the ingredients in the products they sell? It truly angers me! But isn't it the same for the human medical community? Doctors almost always will prescribe you a drug before they will talk to you about nutrition. If any of these veterinarians did true research on diet, you would not find one of them selling dry food in their offices. In fact, you might even want to walk away from a veterinarian if you see the bags and bags of dry food in the office's lobby when you walk in. These reasons alone are enough for me to be happy that I didn't choose veterinary medicine as a career path. Did I say how much this situation angers me?

The average annual veterinary pharmaceutical sales representative's salary, according to a national salary trend report from Indeed.com, can be as high as $210K per year. Do you realize this is even higher than for human pharmaceutical sales reps? In that case, the same source lists average incomes as high as $135K for medical equipment sales, but only $30K for pharmaceutical sales.

National spending on pets is even higher than on many other household items for the humans in our homes. The American Pet Products Association says that in 2015, $60.28 billion was spent on our pets in the U.S.

ACTUAL SALES WITHIN THE U.S. MARKET IN 2015:

Food	$23.04 billion
Supplies/OTC Medicine	$14.39 billion
Vet Care	$15.73 billion
Live animal purchases	$2.19 billion
Pet Services: grooming & boarding	$5.24 billion

Source: http://www.americanpetproducts.org/press_industrytrends.asp

If $23 billion is being spent on pet food, and this is happening for all animals, not just dogs, then we have a big problem. According to the same source, 54.4 million households own a dog. How many are feeding their dogs dry dog food? Isn't that generally the norm? Let's start making a change in what we feed our pets. If the amount of money being spent on cancer care was redirected into a proactive healthy diet to begin with, maybe we could create healthier futures for our dogs.

"Change is never painful,
only the resistance to change is painful."

— Buddha

FINDING A NEW WAY TO EAT

The pet food recall scares in 2007 were some time ago now, but we still have dogs dying of cancer at alarming rates. In fact, I was just on social media watching a momma's status updates in the many stages of cancer that were literally eating up a sweet, innocent English bulldog. The latest in procedures was a rear leg amputation that has haunted me ever since I laid eyes on the poor pup. I hate to see cancer winning in a battle.

Many people have begun to wake up to the problems in commercial pet food and have started to prepare their pets' meals at home. One solution to commercial pet food is a raw meat, or B.A.R.F., diet. Since our pups are relatives of wolves, this diet is preferred by many people because it tries to mimic what would happen in nature.

I might argue, however, that we don't have domesticated wolves in our homes. Here on Maui, we have chickens everywhere, and they peacefully co-exist with cats and many dogs too. We also have pigs and cows, and on a few occasions, we have been out hiking and run into them. Even though the dogs are startled at their presence and occasionally want to chase them, I'm not entirely sure they associate them with food. So if they were left to fend for themselves, would the dogs kill these animals to survive? I've noticed that when left alone, dogs tend to be scavengers.

I like to study things…behaviors. They pique my curiosity. I've spent time watching starving dogs throughout my travels. (And feeding them when I could.) If it became an issue of life and death, I would tend to think they might actually starve before they would kill. Perhaps dogs don't go directly to killing when they are hungry. Is it because they are dependent upon humans? Are they not truly connected to their wolf instincts? Are they more omnivores than we think? My curiosity gets the best of me, and sometimes, with no solution, but merely an observation.

Please understand: I am vegan, and much of the subject of diet has been a morally-challenging aspect of daily life with my babies. I tried the raw B.A.R.F. diet on them, and I found it has a few dangers to be cautious of (for example, bacteria). Plus, there is my dislike of the entire process, not to mention the cost. I was broke! And I had blood dripping all over my fridge all the time. I couldn't stand the sight of my vegan kitchen being covered in blood. And I was only able to do it when I got into the mindset of, "I love you enough to kill for you."

A holistic vet once told me (as a vegan) that I needed to buy a meat grinder to prepare their food at home, but before I ground it, I needed to sear both sides to remove bacteria. There are a lot of bacteria in raw meat. These bacteria can be deadly to your dog if not handled appropriately, and they are extremely dangerous if your dog is suffering any immune condition like cancer. Raw meat can also be dangerous if whole bones from it are swallowed or chewed on, causing a potential risk of teeth breaking or internal punctures. The next question might be, "Where does your raw food come from?" You still run the risk of unsafe practices, GMO, and pharmaceuticals showing up. Did you see the animal it came from? Was the animal healthy?

Many have swung to other extremes and tried vegan diets; I have as well, but you have to be very cautious that the diet is balanced with proper amino acids. Too much of one thing or not enough of another can cause issues. Although, just as people have found positive health changes in switching their dogs to a raw food diet, people have found benefits in having their dogs go vegan or vegetarian. Again, watch out for commercially-created foods because they are not much better. Both diets have been shown to balance body weight, give healthier coats, increase health and vitality, and clean eyes and ears. Also, an overall happier disposition has been noticed in dogs. As far as I'm concerned, anything is better than commercial dog food. I think the benefits we are seeing are due to a switch from a toxic, non-nutritionally appropriate commercial diet to something more wholesome. It may just come down to personal preference for you and what works best for your lifestyle.

"Nothing will be attempted if all possible objections must first be overcome."

— Author Unknown

DOGS AS OMNIVORES

I bet you didn't know that dogs are now classified as having evolved biologically into omnivores. Just like humans, dogs can gain nutrients from a wide variety of sources: fruits, vegetables, grains, legumes, as well as animal products. Their systems are capable of digesting various forms of proteins in just the same way a human's system can. As scavengers, they will naturally eat a wide variety of foods.

I wanted to understand more about diet so I started looking deeper into what dogs with long lives ate. I noticed that certain breeds naturally lived longer than others did, probably regardless of their diet. For example, Australian Cattle Dogs (ACD) have the longest expected lifespan of any dog on the planet. Bluey (twenty-nine years) and another ACD in the Outback named Jerry (twenty-seven) lived on a diet of kangaroo and emu, while Bramble (twenty-seven) was vegan. But after doing more research, I noticed that the most common factor was that their diets were almost all holistic. And just in case you are curious, Bluey is in *The Guinness Book of World Records* as the oldest dog alive.

TOP 10 OLDEST VERIFIED DOGS BY AGE

The following canines' ages were authenticated via Guinness World Records. Age of dog was rounded up to nearest year for this book.

Rank	Name	Birth Date	Death Date	Age	Breed	Country of death
1	Bluey	6/7/1910	11/14/39	29 years	Australian Cattle Dog	AU
2	Butch	1975	2003	28 years	Beagle	USA
3	Taffy	-	-	27 years	Welsh Collie	UK
4	Bramble	9/1/75	3/31/03	27 years	Border Collie	UK
5	Adjutant	8/14/36	11/20/63	27 years	Labrador Retriever cross	UK
6	Pusuke	4/1/85	12/5/11	27 years	Shiba Inu mix	Japan
7	Sugar	8/18/52	8/13/77	25 years	unknown	USA
8	Piccolo	10/1/87	12/26/10	23 years	Mutt	Italy
9	Kathy T. Dog	1/8/91	2/6/13	22 years	Mutt	USA
10	Mister	11/28/91	10/26/13	22 years	Shepherd mix	USA

Source: https://en.wikipedia.org/wiki/List_of_oldest_dogs

Dog Breed Life-Expectancy Chart

The following is a dog life-expectancy chart, sorted by the twenty-five most popular registered breeds from the past decade.

2013 Popularity Rank	Dog Breed	Average Lifespan
1	Labrador Retriever	11 Years
2	German Shepherd	11 Years
3	Golden Retriever	11 Years
4	Beagle	12-15 Years
5	Bulldog	8-12 Years
6	Yorkshire Terrier	13 Years (possibly up to 20 years)
7	Boxer	9-10 Years
8	Poodle	12 Years
9	Rottweiler	9 Years
10	Dachshund	13-15 Years
11	French Bulldog	8-10 Years
12	Doberman Pinscher	10-13 Years
13	German Shorthaired Pointer	12-14 Years
14	Siberian Huskie	12-15 Years
15	Shih Tzu	12-16 Years
16	Great Dane	6-8 Years
17	Miniature Schnauzer	12-14 Years
18	Cavalier King Charles Spaniel	9-14 Years
19	Pomeranian	14 Years
20	Australian Shepherd	12-18 Years
21	Shetland Sheepdog	12-13 Years
22	Chihuahua	17 Years
23	Boston Terrier	11-15 Years
24	Pembroke Welsh Corgi	12-15 Years
25	Havanese	14-16 Years

Source: http://www.caninejournal.com

DOGS AS VEGANS

Because I am vegan, I was intrigued by Bramble's diet. I have studied and tested the vegan diet on and off for many years with my pups at the onset of sicknesses, skin issues, or other allergies. When it comes to healing myself or those I care about, I know it to be a tried and true diet for more than twenty-five years as a vegan myself. When I get stuck, it's the only thing I know that will always give me a sure healing or transformation. In fact, I'm rarely ever sick or not feeling well. It's a tool that's always in my back pocket to offer others when they ask me what I do to take care of my health. But I always struggled with knowing what was biologically appropriate for a dog and worried about doing everything right.

When I tried going vegan with my dogs, I worried when they wouldn't eat a meal I had prepared for them. I wondered whether they knew something I didn't. Then, of course, there were the naysayers, the same ones who asked how I did it myself, but even more who stood up for the dogs, harassing and joking, "Don't dogs eat meat?" They would tell me to respect each species for what it was meant to be and to get a rabbit, not a dog.

Bramble was fed a vegan diet of mostly boiled lentils and fresh vegetables. The dog was also kept very active and very toned. I always want to do what is best for my pups, but I do admit that I love animals so much that I'd rather not have to end one life to feed another. I understand that many dogs live quite well on a raw meat diet, but it's just not a diet I enjoy in my home.

As a vegan myself, not only did I worry about ending one life to feed another, but I also knew about the environmental impact of being a meat eater versus not. The book *Time to Eat the Dog?* was written by Brenda and Robert Hale. They calculated that a medium-sized dog has twice the environmental impact of a large SUV when all factors are considered. Many of the same types of reports have been produced in the vegan communities over the years. They are reporting similar findings, based on the idea that a certain amount of land is required to grow enough food to feed either a dog or a human for a lifetime. Factors such as the amount of energy and resources or cultivated land are compared to various running costs.

In the Hales' book, they state an average medium-sized dog will eat 361 pounds of meat and 200 pounds of grain per year. Meat production requires about 15 pounds of grain and about 26,000 gallons of water to produce just 2.2 pounds of beef. They concluded that a medium-sized dog will require 2 acres for food and leave an environmental impact of up to 2.7 acres. They say that to build a 4.6 liter Land Cruiser requires just 1 acre—half as much as for a dog. In comparison, humans require from 4.4 to 14.8 acres. Depending on who you are, perhaps it makes more sense to walk, but for others, eliminating overpopulation seems more reasonable. Still others simply choose to adopt a vegan or vegetarian lifestyle.

A friend of mine, David Robinson Simon, wrote *Meatanomics*, a book about the challenges that meat-producing places on our planet. Many other sources, such as *Scientific American*, *New Scientist*, *Reader's Digest*, and the World Health Organization have made similar conclusions of their own to show the amount of land and water that meat production requires. Many have suggested that the following are the top five violators of our environment, in meat production:

> **Cow Gas:** The methane produced by cattle farts has been joked about, but it is a factor in global warming.
>
> **Plant Displacement:** Specific crops are needed to house and feed cattle. Therefore, plants, trees, grasses, and other year-round plants that absorb CO_2 and capture carbon are displaced.
>
> **Water Pollution:** Animal waste, antibiotics, pesticides, fertilizers, and hormones enter the water cycle along with chemicals from the creation of its byproducts, such as leather production.
>
> **Water Usage:** Raising cattle for food requires 1,500+ gallons of water to produce a single pound of beef.
>
> **Overgrazing:** Overgrazing by cattle makes it challenging to maintain any productive vegetation.

Now we know that dogs are omnivores. We've learned that meat production creates a variety of moral, ethical, and environmental issues.

If a dog (or person) can exist without having to pollute the planet or kill a being to survive, perhaps it's worth looking at a vegan diet for you or your dog. What do you think? Even if you don't agree with the whole vegan thing, you might at least agree that a vegan diet is healthier than commercial dog food (now that we know more about it). I'll let you decide what's right for you and your dog. I'll support you doing just about anything, as long as you never buy another bag of commercial dry pet food again!

On another note, in a fourteen-year study conducted by the University of Pennsylvania and published in the *Journal of the American Veterinary Medical Association* (May 2002), researchers found that a restricted-calorie diet results in dogs living a median 1.8 years longer than the average dog. In addition, these same dogs are slower to develop chronic diseases, such as osteoarthritis, implying that not only the quantity, but also the quality of life is extended. "Dogs in the calorie-restricted group didn't require treatment for osteoarthritis until a mean age of 13.3 years, fully three years later than the dogs in the control group," said Gail K. Smith, Ph.D., V.M.D., professor of orthopedic surgery at Penn. "Because osteoarthritis is painful, this deferral represents a substantial boost in quality of life."

A holistic approach that gives pet owners more power over their pets' diet has been gaining ground since 2007, when contamination of commercial pet foods caused people to take a deeper look into what they were feeding their pets. Even though it was a horrible time for me (losing three of my own), that year was a turning point that led to more home-cooked meals for our pets, whether raw food, vegan, vegetarian, or a combination of all three.

"Never doubt that a small group of thoughtful,
committed people can change the world.
Indeed, it is the only thing that ever has."

— Margaret Mead

DIET AND DISEASE

Whatever is or isn't inherited in the genes can be altered, to some degree, by diet. Food is truly medicine. What many won't do for themselves, they will do for the love of their dogs. Of course, I'm in all kinds of animal groups on social media, and if you are, too, then you see a lot. If you pay attention, then you see all kinds of stories about animals being abused, the dog meat trade in China, people grieving over lost pets, and others using the power of community to find viable solutions for their pets that maybe vets aren't seeking or most people can't afford.

If your pups are like mine, they'd rather not go to the vet's office, and I'd rather not pay for an office visit, just to get another medicine to try out to see whether it might work. Instead, I prefer to go to dog-focused chat groups on Facebook, for example. There, I can see whether other people are having (or have had) the same issues, and what they used for a solution. You can even get comparison pictures, comparative test results, or other information you couldn't get with an office visit. In some way, we are becoming our own doctors with the birth of these communities. At the very least, we're beginning to own our health and the health of our dogs.

But I have to tell you, nothing drives me crazier than when people post pictures of their dogs and the list of problems they have, and then want to know what other dry food to try. Or they wonder why their dog isn't eating it. Or they ask about things that are obvious side-effects of a commercial dry food diet. It really makes me BONKERS! Now, I know this isn't their fault since we are a culture of instant gratification, fast foods, and social programming, but I've been holding out for change for a long time now. I'm always made to feel like an extremist when I suggest to such people making a home-cooked meal for their dogs. Then, when people really consider it, there is the barrage of questions about what to feed or not feed. As with trying anything new, there can be hesitation. We have choices. Yes, it's easier to go through the drive-thru or open a bag of potato chips, but begin asking yourself (for you or your dog), "Is this nutritionally feeding the body?" Your dog doesn't have any other choice but the one you make for him or her.

"Every once in a while
a dog enters your life and changes everything."

— Author Unknown

Sometimes either we, or our dogs, become so ill that we have no choice but to make a change. Switching from one religion to another, moving to a new place, starting a workout regime when you've never been to the gym before…these new things can be hard, but the benefits can be amazing.

Twenty-five years ago, I decided to give up eating all animal products; back then, I was quite the rebel. In fact, I think my dad was embarrassed about it. My mom still isn't quite sure how I exist, or what to prepare for me for family functions. But I got tired of not feeling well. I got tired of stomach pains so severe that I had to be taken into the hospital, only to find out (after all the drugs given) that I was just lactose intolerant.

Unless you have gone through something similar yourself, it may be hard to relate to a change in diet that benefits you or your dog. So maybe for you, it's about just starting slow. When you learn new diet tricks for yourself, then you can begin to try them with your dog. In fact, it can be quite fun to enjoy time in the kitchen together. Isn't that where everyone in the home gathers anyway? If we cut those 7,300 bowls of dog food fed per year in half, maybe we would make a difference.

CLEANSING WITH YOUR DOG

If your dog has been on a diet of commercial dry food for any part of his or her life, then it may a good idea to take a short break and do a cleanse of some kind. There are many techniques and styles of cleansing the body, but basically, it means giving the body a break from ingesting foods that may cause a negative reaction in the body, such as allergies, for example. In some cases, it even means going "cold turkey" and not eating anything at all. Many cleanses will even use various supplements that aid in the digestion and elimination of the limited food selections you do eat. In fact, it might be a great idea for you to join your dog in this journey. Humans and dogs are both bombarded with all kinds of environmental toxins as well as food allergies. This can really tax the liver in particular. Taking away your dog's food for a day doesn't have to be looked at as a punishment, but simply as a break to allow the body to reset itself naturally. If you are curious about this, we can talk a bit more in person to find the right solution for both you and your dog.

I also used to do a lot of fasting when I was teaching more yoga, and my body felt the best it ever has during that time. After 3-4 days without food, the kidneys and gall bladder begin to cleanse themselves. It can be a bit scary if you've never seen anything like it before. Things come out of your body that make your head spin. I used to date a guy who ran a fasting business, and he told me the most gruesome stories of worms and bugs coming out. Yuck! I often feel a sense of guilt that I haven't recently taken the kind of deep dive into cleansing my body that I did just a few short years ago (even though I just completed a twenty-one day light food and herbal supplement cleanse). I've needed to do a lot of emotional healing, and I needed the energy to do it. So I ate a bit more to be stable enough to get through my more challenging days.

I've been a "veg head" for twenty-five years, so my diet is healthier than that of most people, but I still always feel better when I fast or cleanse. I used to do seven-day water fasts, and boy, does the mind play with you a few days in! I noticed my pups and their eating cycles. I watched as I sat nearly lifeless and barely able to move, wondering whether I was slowly killing myself. I noticed that my dogs barely ever ate out of their full bowls. I noticed that if I wasn't eating, they weren't interested in food. It was only the crinkle of a bag or the opening of the fridge door that sparked their interest in food beyond their bowls. I began to see that not only do we overeat as a society, but when we overeat, so do our dogs. And we worry an awful lot when our dogs aren't eating. Maybe we are just feeding them far too much? When we take a time out and allow our bodies to balance out, everything can correct itself naturally. Sometimes, dogs instinctively just know how to do this when they are not feeling well.

I've done many cleanses and have found a few ingredients in most good cleanses that also make sense to give to your dog. You can get all of these items in a dried herb or capsule form on Amazon.Then just add them to your dog's daily food for a period of time in order to complete the cleanse. There is a chart further down (Daily Herbal Intake Based on Dog's Weight) that will help you with portion size. But you might consider a fast (no food at all) if your pup is struggling with a chronic condition that just won't go away. Here are a few things to add to assist the body in cleansing:

- Apple cider vinegar pills/caps (overall parasite cleansing)
- Activated charcoal (will strip out all metals and supplements so use by itself)
- Alpha lipoic acid (increases oxyen)
- Alfalfa (digestion)
- Barley grass powder (digestion)
- Beet root (antioxidant, liver cleanser, and general detox)
- Bentonite clay (pulls out heavy metals)
- Burdock root (liver cleanser)
- Cayenne pepper (be careful, it's hot; don't overdo it!)
- Dandelion leaf (liver cleanser)
- Fennel seed (detox and liver cleanser)
- Fenugreek seed (detox and liver cleanser)
- Garlic pills/caps (detox, build immune system. Note: stronger in capsule form and you avoid the taste)
- Psyllium husks (gut detox and digestion)

- Red clover (lymph cleanse)
- Zeolite clay (gut and heavy metal detox)

Always take it slow with adding new things to your dog's diet, and taste it yourself when you can. If you won't eat it, your dog might not either. When you cleanse your system with your dog, you can both release all that doesn't serve either of you. The cleaner you get together, the more you can harmonize with all good things in your lives and manifest them together. The power of two creating a good healthy life together will create more energy and awareness for far greater results! Many of these things above can be planted in a special dog garden for your pup too.

GROWING A PUPPY GARDEN

Recently, I've been experimenting with a garden for my pups. Because I'm renting a home here in Hawaii, it can be a bit challenging to figure out how to create the space, so I do a bit of container gardening. If you don't have much space, it's a great way to try growing a few things and placing them right on the floor in your apartment or setting them on the ground outside. Place herbs or sprouts in places where your pup can reach them easily and where you don't mind if they make a little bit of a mess. Your pups might pull a bit of dirt out as they attempt to take a few bites. One of the best things you can grow for your dog is wheatgrass. It's very easy to grow. In fact, we had a little place in the yard that was known as "the dig spot" where no matter what we did, there was always a hole. I decided I had nothing to lose so I just planted some wheatgrass there that I had sprouted in the window in my kitchen. I placed it in the yard and it rooted the next day and it is absolutely a new favorite thing for all three of my pups to enjoy. Not only did we stop a digging problem

with it, but we developed a new digestive solution they can access anytime. I've also been playing with a few sprouts. I like to start the sprouting in the kitchen window in a standard sprouting jar you can pick up at most health food stores. Then once it's off and going, it's easy to plant elsewhere. I am always trying new things to allow my pups to choose their own healthy options. It's really a lot of fun to see what they help themselves to. They adore parsley, cilantro, and sometimes basil. It really surprises me on occasion what they will attempt to eat. My boy Blue actually eats all my strawberries. He also loves papaya and banana almost daily. I kinda laugh because he's not such a tough guy like people think. His pallet has actually become quite a bit more sophisticated than those of many dogs I know. He tries just about everything. It really tickles my heart to see what they all will eat.

There aren't too many things to be cautious about when feeding dogs. Chocolate, onions, and grapes are the ones we hear about, but the list of things not to feed is smaller than the list of what you can feed them. Letting them choose can often be an indicator of something lacking in their diet or showcase a potential problem going on that you might have missed. For example, a craving for the dangerous chocolate often means there is a lack of magnesium in the body. Suplement with magnesium and hide the chocolate. Okay, so let's start doing some diet planning for you and yours…this is gonna be fun!

"Thorns may hurt you, men desert you, sunlight turn to fog;
but you're never friendless ever, if you have a dog."

— Douglas Malloch

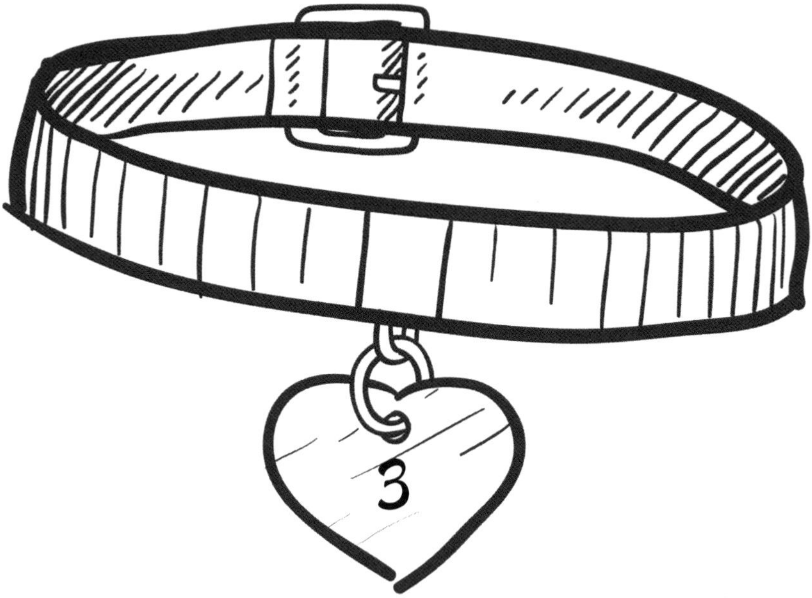

Meal Planning—Before We Begin

"Try not to have a good time…this is supposed to be educational."

— Charles M. Schulz

Dogs need high-quality protein, fats, and veggies, just like we do. Veggies and fruits provide antioxidants and fiber for animals that no longer hunt their prey. Natural sources of vitamins, trace minerals, and healthy fatty acids must be added too. We need to make sure the foods we prepare

are moisture-rich, fresh, whole foods. We want to stay away from foods on the toxic list (http://www.aspca.org/pet-care/animal-poison-control/people-foods-avoid-feeding-your-pets), fillers, artificial preservatives, colors, additives, chemicals, byproducts, and processed foods. If you looked at the ingredients on pet food labels, would you even know where to find some of them if you tried to buy them in a store individually? Isn't it just easier to find whole meats, veggies, fruits, etc.? You can approach this two ways. You can decide to eat healthier with your dog by making a bit extra of what you eat or you can keep eating your way and prepare a special meal for your buddy. My suggestion is that you take this as a healthy eating challenge to do together.

I've noticed over the years that if I only bring things home that I would feed my pups, it keeps me straight on eating just the good stuff. Sometimes, it's harder to honor yourself than to honor another. In my social media dog groups, I often find people circling around in them looking for how to prepare a certain thing for their pets, but if they were eating (and living) healthy, they might already know how to do this. I once ran across a woman who claimed she didn't often leave the house by herself, but she was on her way to the market with a list of what was needed to make turmeric golden paste for her sick dog. We are sometimes forced into making healthier choices for both of us.

When you wake up to nutrition, you begin to question everything. This is not a journey that is just for your dogs. Have you gotten that yet? We are all doing this together. This is a pack effort. What you choose for you, you choose for your dog and vice versa. We've been taught to eat based on what is quick, convenient, and easy. We are also taught to eat to support commercial industry. Don't even get me started on the food pyramid we are programmed to believe as children… the one that supports not just meat and dairy farmers, but eventually ends up also supporting the pharmaceutical industry, as we get sick living by it. What is our government teaching us? Here is a healthier version—the vegan food pyramid. I suggest using it as a foundation for preparing great foods for the whole pack. Yes, that means you too! If you choose not to go totally vegan, just swap out the beans and seeds with animal proteins and pare down on some of the other foods.

THIS IS NOT A JOURNEY THAT IS JUST FOR YOUR DOGS.

THE VEGAN FOOD PYRAMID

The best way I have found to prepare a meal for my dogs is to choose a few ingredients from each category and make something that resembles a thick stew or give it a kind of broth for more dog-friendly palatability. Please note that it's important to watch your pups' stools and digestion when switching to a new diet. Approach this a little at a time. You might start with adding some of the ingredients to your current food, and then remove your old food altogether after about a week or two of transitioning.

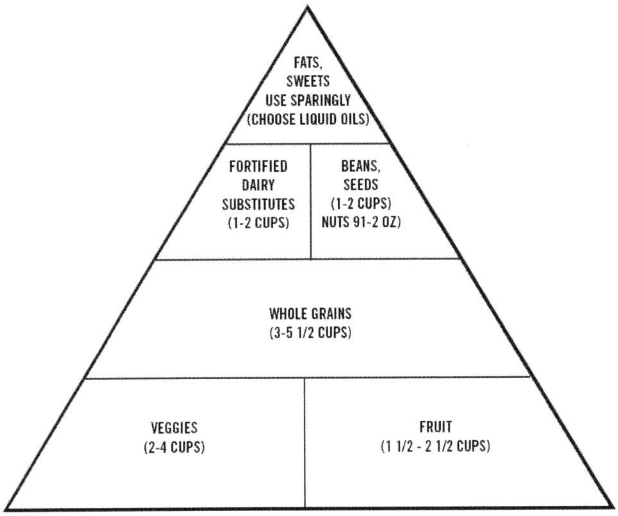

FEEDING YOUR DOG A HEALTHY, BALANCED DIET

Over 2,500 years ago, Hippocrates talked about the many health benefits of food. Food is the fuel that gives the energy needed to perform. Food can be used to prevent disease and enhance health. With increased health care costs, we are starting to understand how diet affects disease. Many are starting to look at the health-promoting properties of food and create what is now being called "nutraceuticals" and separating them out from "functional food." This is creating a birth of all kinds of new products, but I like to stick with just what God gave us—real food!

There is something fun with using real food as medicine too; it often will look much like the body part or organ it helps to heal. For example, many of the roots, such as turmeric or burdock roots, are good for the blood veins. Keep that in mind while you are preparing food for your dog. Also ask yourself this question when you eat or you feed your dog: "Is what I'm about to put into the body going to provide healing and serve a particular need?" For example, what does the glass of wine do for me, or the couple of cookies do for my dog? If you can't find a functional or life-promoting need for eating it, then how does it serve? Remember to eat to live, not live to eat.

When you make a change to any new diet, you might feel overwhelmed and not know where to start. However, if you've welcomed healthier eating habits into your own life, then you've already begun! With every change, you're likely to encounter some opposition. If you are vegan or vegetarian and you talked about changing your diet, or better yet, you did it, some of your friends probably told you that it wasn't ideal for your blood type or teased you about eating like a bunny rabbit as you opted to be a "veg head." Maybe they started questioning where you would find your protein. Or if you stopped eating or drinking certain things, like alcohol, for example, maybe you encountered the same line of questioning. Or how about dieting or cleansing...? Have you tried to do that and maintain the same social life? It really is almost strange how what we put into our body has such a large social effect on our lives. I once tried to join friends out to dinner while I was fasting. It's funny, but they almost didn't even invite me just because I wasn't eating. Do we do social things around food to be together, or do we use it as an excuse to eat or even gorge?

If you've experienced anything like this yourself, then you will possibly hear some of the same opposition when you talk about doing something different for your dogs...maybe even more so. Let's face it; for your dogs, it usually comes down to whatever is easy and convenient as you run out the door. People associate dogs with a bowl of dry dog food. Why would you go against the grain? Well, would you eat a few bowls of dry food per day and be satisfied? Where would all your nutrients come from?

If, as a society, we were feeding our dogs healthier, I could actually almost not write this book. Diet is the key to our dogs' health and longevity (and our own). Fresh live food versus dry commercial food is more easily digestible. It is also full of more natural vitamins, minerals, antioxidants, and probiotics. The less heat-processed, the more likely the nutrients are preserved in their natural state, and the healthier they are for your dog.

We know that when we make healthier living choices for ourselves, we spend less time in the doctor's office. The same goes for your pup. It can be hard to set time aside to prepare meals for your pup at home. Would you rather spend time (and money) with repeated veterinary visits or just take a few extra minutes in the kitchen? The choice is simple—be reactionary or be proactive. What would you rather do? I prefer to hike with my dogs versus sit in a vet's office all day and night. Not only is it good for both of us, but it builds a deeper bond. In fact, my dogs are now over two years old and only two of the three have ever even been to the vet's office. Leilani was spayed and also had the misfortune of spending the night on IVs and getting enemas after innocently swallowing a small rock. Bella had her entropion eye surgery and a few checkups regarding her allergy and skin issues, but to no avail. We spend our lives happily playing together because I've made healthy choices with diet in particular. I'm too busy enjoying life with my pups to go to the vet's office!

WOULD YOU RATHER SPEND TIME (AND MONEY) WITH REPEATED VETERINARY VISITS OR JUST TAKE A FEW EXTRA MINUTES IN THE KITCHEN?

I know it's time-consuming to prepare natural healthy food, but you might find it's easier to prepare a few days to a week's worth of food in advance. It's kinda like grabbing for the bag of potato chips versus the salad. Whatever is prepared in advance will tend to be the go-to food. I like to make a big stew, keep it in a large plastic container in the fridge, and just scoop out of it for each feeding. Or easier yet, placing meals in portioned containers is quick and easy for mealtime food bowl filling. Also, I keep healthy treats I made in large containers ready for rewards.

I bet you like to have a bit of variety in your food, so try to do the same for your kiddos. Variety also provides more complete nutrition. Perhaps you've heard the phrase "eat the rainbow"? When you eat foods in each color group, you are not only getting a variety of nutrition, but you are also eating to balance the chakras. We'll talk a bit more about chakras later on. I have a weird practice that I usually keep to myself, but I like to provide variety (in brands as well as food types) just in case there is an unknown allergy or some weird food recall down the road; then I (or my pups) aren't coexisting on it solely...becoming victims of some science experiment gone bad. In the last two months, I've actually been contacted in regard to recalls on the food items I've purchased. Unfortunately, I was told there was a recall on what we had already eaten. One recall was salmonella and the other listeria. So it's good that we are doing things in our daily diets to boost the immune system to prevent such issues becoming larger problems. I suppose that you live and learn. The dog food scare of 2007 might have changed the way I will eat or feed until the end of my days. I also think that repeated foods over long periods of times might also begin to cause food sensitivities or even allergies.

PROTEIN

Many dry dog foods might only contain about 20 percent protein. AAFCO recommends that adult dogs get around 18 to 22 percent protein at a minimum. But what is the rest of a dog's diet supposed to be made up of? Isn't this a funny fact? We are trained to think of our dogs as wolves or meat eaters, yet only a small portion of protein is actually in their food or recommended. Is AAFCO saying it's okay to feed 20 percent protein and have the rest be corn or a corn byproduct? I've watched trends in dog diets over the years, especially since the scare of 2007. Now that we are forced to become more accountable for our best friends, people are scrambling to figure out what is best to feed their dogs. In many ways, this has been a wakeup call, not just for our dogs, but for humans. We are forced to learn healthier ways of living. God has a funny way of teaching us sometimes.

Many might consider the volunteer-based AAFCO an expert advisory board, but with a focus on pet food labeling versus home cooking, I believe any recommendation to eat commercial dry food showcases a lack of understanding about a nutritious diet. And since the FDA is actually the decision maker, it gets to make the final call anyhow. Where do health, money-making, and politics merge? I certainly question how the relationships work between the FDA, the meat industry, and big pharma. After all, advisors and committee members of the AAFCO include representatives from the major manufacturers, not folks like you and me who love their dogs. Perhaps lowering the protein levels required for our dogs has been a cost-saving method in the production of commercial dog foods. But I'm a skeptic. I've had to be.

Many experts (and when I say "experts," let me point out that there really doesn't seem to be any real official authority on the subject because research done is likely skewed due to budget constraints and political agendas) seem to recommend 30 to 60 percent be comprised of raw meaty bones. Many "dog foodies" suggest including some organ meats like liver and heart as another portion. And the remainder is a mix of muscle meat, eggs, dairy, and any combination of healthy leftovers you don't eat yourself. There doesn't seem to be much in-depth discussion on fruits, veggies, grains, or other supplements. With no real authority figure speaking out (or research being done) about dog diets, that leaves us a bit dark in the kitchen. My take is that we really aren't all that different from dogs. If you wouldn't eat it, why would you assume your dog would?

But we do have some important issues in our past to learn from. Much like the scare of 2007, back in the 1970s, there was a scare with thousands of dogs dying from something called "dilated cardiomyopathy," otherwise known as heart failure, from the dry commercial food they were eating. Cats fed the same dog food reportedly went blind. In the late '80s, the issues (for cats at least) were traced to a deficiency in a basic amino acid called taurine. Taurine is found primarily in muscle meat and is generally absent in commercial dry food. Why is that so?

Earlier in the twentieth century, our cats and dogs were fed wet, meaty commercial pet food from cans, but the metal was needed in World War II, so most foods were converted to a dry food. In the late '50s, a machine called an "extruder" was introduced to make dry food. Later on, in order to get the right texture and save costs on production, more starch was added. As well, meat was getting expensive and less of it was added. The result was a low meat (replaced with animal byproducts), high grain food with higher profit margins than canned food. The same process is actually being used today. All of this has caused taurine levels in pet foods to decrease. So what really is taurine, and why is it needed? And could this be the clue I needed to determine whether dogs can be vegan?

TAURINE—THE FACTOR IN GOING VEGAN?

Many times, I looked into what would be required for my dogs to become vegan. I love animals too much to harm them, and I could skip many of the meat-industry scares and align with my own diet as well. Issues like this low-taurine concern seem to resemble a vegan style diet to some degree—a diet with low animal protein anyhow. I kept seeing that taurine was the magic missing ingredient that vegans said they needed to supplement their dogs with for the vegan diet to work. I never wanted to think my dogs would be harming another animal each time they ate, so I did a bit of research to determine whether taurine was the magical missing piece of the "Can my dog be vegan?" puzzle.

I found that some researchers said dogs, like humans, are able to make their own taurine in their own bodies, but apparently, not on a diet of cereal grains and meat byproducts. It was believed that dogs were dying from a lack of taurine back in the '70s. But I really wondered how necessary taurine was once I started understanding a bit more about it. Was something just mis-understood?

At first, I was led to believe that if the only place dogs can get taurine is from animal protein, then they might not do too well on a vegan diet. My search was starting to lead me to believe it was not a healthy choice to raise my dogs as vegan. But then, as I mentioned earlier, I discovered the dog, Bramble, who lived to be twenty-seven on a vegan diet. Bramble made me realize a vegan diet was possible for my dogs.

I suppose I really wanted to put my dogs on a vegan diet for my own agenda, out of environmental and ethical reasons. Therefore, my eyes were always open to understanding how to make this a possibility. I knew many vegan folks give a taurine supplement so they can keep their dogs healthy on a vegan-based diet. But I began to question whether it was truly natural, ethical, or appropriate to make my dogs live the same way I was. I wanted to know more.

I always want to know something's food source so I can try to get it naturally versus supplementation. I knew taurine to be a kind of amino acid, but could I get it or supply it to my dogs in the food that they ate? It didn't make much sense to me that taurine was so important for dogs because shellfish is one of the highest taurine-rich foods on the planet, followed by other sea animals like squid, clams, octopus, and oysters. But how many dogs eat this kind of diet? Maybe the salty sea dog?

DO DOGS PRODUCE TAURINE IN THEIR BODIES NATURALLY, AND IS THERE A VEGAN SOURCE OF TAURINE?

Most adult human vegans can produce taurine in their bodies. So the question I was trying to answer next was: Do dogs produce taurine in their bodies naturally, and is there a vegan source of taurine? The answer I was getting back was: 1) More research is needed, 2) It appears as if a dog needs to have animal protein to get necessary taurine, 3) Low taurine in the human body can exist if certain conditions are present in the human body. (Would this mean that the same was true for dogs?) and 4) Dogs might be able to make taurine out of vitamin B and the amino acids methionine and cysteine. So what are those? And how does taurine get low or not be produced in the body anyway?

Low taurine levels in the body can exist if any of the following are deficient:

- Amino acids cysteine and methionine (amino acids that make taurine in your body)
- Zinc
- Vitamin A, B6

If you have any of the following present in the body, the level of taurine produced by the body is reduced:

- Candida
- MSG
- Vitamin B5

So is it possible that any of the above conditions were present when the taurine issues were first discovered? I guess you could argue as to whether or not dogs could be suffering from taurine deficiencies from one situation or another. (And many dogs died so it's not likely they all had any of the above going on at the time the deaths occurred.) I wondered whether this was the answer to my lifetime search to determine whether it was healthy to raise a dog as a vegan. (I also learned dogs could possibly go vegan with enough vitamin D supplementation, but I haven't found much to back that up.)

CERTAIN FOODS CAN ASSIST THE BODY IN CREATING THE METHIONINE AMINO ACIDS THAT END UP CREATING TAURINE.

I was beginning to see that dogs can be vegan with supplementation, or if their bodies produce enough taurine on their own. I did find that seaweed is a vegan option that can help the body produce low levels of taurine. But I began to feel hopeless thinking that I would forever have to kill other animals for my dogs to survive. I thought that perhaps the situation was just not something to mess with until further research was done. But who was going to do that research, and how much longer would I have to wait? I charged on. I was finding that there many huge side effects to the taurine levels being low in the body, such as autism, epilepsy, Alzheimer's, etc. But I also found that certain foods can assist the body in creating the methionine amino acids that end up creating taurine. So maybe I was approaching this all wrong?

According to http://www.immunehealthscience.com/cysteine.html:

> *Food sources of methionine are: all meats and poultry, fish, eggs, dairy, quinoa, buckwheat, sesame seeds, Brazil nuts, and to a lesser degree dry spirulina. While methionine can be found in other foods as well, such as beans and legumes, the amount of methionine is too low to be of any benefit for significant cysteine production and ultimately glutathione production for your immune health.*

So maybe I needed to find foods that would assist the body in making taurine? If I fed my dogs foods that increased the methionine, I could go at this a bit differently. Here is a good list of other vegan foods I've been compiling that contain a higher level of methionine:

- Broccoli
- Chickpeas
- Corn
- Lentils
- Medium grained brown rice
- Mushrooms
- Nuts
- Spinach
- Potatoes
- Seeds
- Soybeans
- Seaweeds
- Pinto beans
- White beans

Note: For humans, almonds, Brazil nuts (best source), and peanuts are additional options, but dogs should generally avoid all nuts. (Don't tell my dogs that; they are peanut butter foodies!)

CONVERSION TO TAURINE

Aha! Did we just conclude how Bramble successfully coexisted all those years as a vegan? (See those magic lentils on the list?) So taurine may not be present in many foods, but you can use a few to increase the methionine, thus enhancing the body's ability to create its own taurine. Therefore, *if dogs can create taurine in their own bodies, they really could be vegan.* It's your choice to make on how you feed—vegan or not vegan—but now you have a bit more information to understand how the body works to make your decision.

Since I have a vegan home, it's always been very hard for me to incorporate some of the blood and guts in my pups' meals. I'll generally bend over backwards for them, but there is also only so much I can handle (on various levels). I personally eat almost no protein in my day, and I've been doing my vegan diet for some twenty-five years.

I know dogs are related to the wolf, but I believe all beings are shifting into a lighter way of being on our planet. I know that for me, personally, I have a very hard time eating large meals, and sometimes, I prefer a green smoothie for dinner as opposed to a giant meal. I wonder whether dogs should also begin to go lighter on their diets as all species evolve.

Protein exists in many forms as a meat substitute. Protein can be a subject of great controversy in our human diet, so perhaps it is as well in the canine. So should you go with raw meat, choose certain animals, or do neither, and swing to what some believe to be an extreme—go vegan? Going vegan was toying with me as I was writing this book; I even wondered whether I should write it because I'm still learning even after being vegan for twenty-five years. But I felt I had understood a pretty good base-line to warrant my continuing to write it.

I have spent many years growing frustrated and not wanting to harm another being to feed my dogs. I intend to keep learning and share what I find whenever I learn more. This is a subject that has plagued me daily for years. I love animals and don't want to kill one for mine to survive. I still just can't completely wrap my head around how I'm the central decision maker on who lives and who dies. On top of this dilemma, we may be faced with social pressures to conform, follow trends, or just plain old lack of finances and time. There is also sometimes nothing better than fear-based marketing to persuade you that you are not doing something right in the care of yourself or your dog. If you are making a choice based on fear, you need to step back and stand in love before you make a decision. With love, no harm is done. If you simply do not know better, you are uninformed. If you are informed and you are feeding from a place of love, great things can happen.

"Let food be thy medicine and medicine be thy food."

— Hippocrates

MEAL PREP

In order for your dog to eat a balanced diet, there are five components to preparing a meal. These steps are:

1. 50 percent (or more) quality protein
2. 25 percent (or less) whole grains
3. 25 percent (or less) veggies
4. 25 percent (or less) supplements
5. The Extras: fruits, oils, seeds, herbs and spices

Let's look at each of these steps in detail now.

Step 1: 50 Percent (or More) Quality Protein

I chose 50 percent protein because I want you to think in terms of real food. If you cooked up a chicken breast and fed just that to your dog, then I guess you have 100 percent protein. When I did a bit of research on the controversial subject of the importance of protein levels, especially during chronic renal failure, the concept seemed to have been debunked, and some "experts" believe phosphorus levels to be the real issue. Everything I read seemed to circle back around to the quality of digestible protein as the more important factor in good canine health.

We will talk a bit later about the concept of energy healing too. I do believe the onset to any disease is due to an energetic response and may or may not be entirely related to food choices. So why spend so much time on talking about food? Everything is energy. Good energy foods give more nutrition to your pups. We'll get to that discussion soon.

Meanwhile, it's important to alternate your choice of protein in order to get all the nutrients your canine needs. If you're still hung up on the taurine issue, many types of fish are high in taurine—as are eggs, dairy, krill, brewer's yeast, and a more vegan option: seaweed. Many commonly used meats have lower levels of taurine, such as chicken, lamb, and beef. Maybe even try vegan beans and lentils one day and animal proteins the next. If you've decided to adopt a vegan diet for your dogs, you will need to soak your beans or lentils, cook them, and then run them through your food processor or mash them; otherwise, they won't get digested and will come out just like they went in. No sense going through all the work to prepare them if they don't get digested!

PROTEIN OPTIONS:

Black Beans: High in fiber, folate, protein, and antioxidants, along with numerous other vitamins and minerals. Black beans also contain a variety of both antioxidant and anti-inflammatory properties.

Chickpeas: High in fiber, protein, vitamins A, B, and C, and in omega-3. (Treats made with chickpea flour are a good option for allergy-prone dogs.)

Lentils: Great additions to your dog's diet for omega-3 and 6 fatty acids. They also have high levels of iron, niacin, B vitamins, potassium, folate, and magnesium. These guys lower cholesterol, stabilize blood sugar, and are also great for adding more fiber.

Pinto Beans: Best for pups with allergies. Can be added to sweet potatoes and fed with nothing else to determine food allergies in your pup. Pintos are great for diabetes and hypoglycemia balancing. They are a great source of folate, B1, B6, and minerals such as copper, phosphorus, iron, magnesium, manganese, and potassium.

Other Vegan Protein Options: Black-Eyed Peas, Cannellini Beans, Great Northern Beans, Kidney Beans, Mung Beans, Split Peas

Feed Sparingly: Soybeans-based foods such as tempeh (fermented soybeans), tofu, edamame, or seitan (vegetarian meat that contains gluten flour and usually some onions or onion powder)

Meat: Depending on where you live, you'll have different options available to you and all at varying prices. When you are dealing with allergic dogs, you'll discover that some meats bring on more allergic responses than do others. Chicken, beef, and pork tend to be the largest culprits. As you know, I prefer not to use meat, but my Bella is allergic to most everything. I have found only one fish, Ono (also known as Wahoo), that is mild enough to keep her allergies managed. I have to admit, it's taken a long time to find a food to re-grow her hair and tame her itch, so from fear of reoccurrence, I stick with it. She doesn't respond well to salmon, and I've heard salmon tends not to work well for other dogs with allergies either. It can also be high in mercury.

It's up to you whether you choose to cook or serve meats raw to your dog. Cooking the meat will eliminate bacteria, but raw has been known to be an option recently adopted by many dog owners, and coincidentally, I have found research indicating that raw meat is richer in taurine than cooked. In my opinion, raw would mimic the hunt in nature, but I believe most domesticated dogs are no longer natural hunters, and I suspect that raw meat could even trigger more aggression in your pup. I understand what people are trying to do by feeding their dogs this way, but it's not a lifestyle I adopt in my home. Although, raw meat is a better choice than dry commercial food. I personally just don't have the stomach for it after trying it on many occasions. My dogs are extremely fussy about eating it too. Not to mention, meat is very expensive here on Maui. If you are looking for support on your raw meat or B.A.R.F. diet, I'm afraid you have come to the wrong place.

I have adopted the same beliefs for my animals as I have for myself, and many spiritually-connected folks tend to believe that, beyond the fact of ending a life, by digesting meat, the karma and possible cruelty of the dead animal can infuse into your pup's sweet little body. When feeding sick dogs, this diet can also be very dangerous because it brings in much more live bacteria into an already weakened immune system.

NOTE ON FEEDING MEATS:

Whether you are vegan or not, please consider that an animal has died in order for your or your pup to survive. I feel it is truly important to honor that life by offering some kind of prayer. By showing reverence, you may find a greater awareness of the entire process opens up for you. I personally tear up each time I prepare a meal where another sentient being has lost its life in order for my babies to survive. I have shed so many tears and prayed so hard to understand why this must be the way in which we live. I am happy to be a vegan to spare many lives, but I have been unsuccessful in finding just the right vegan diet for Bella. My other two dogs could not care less, so long as it's food. Of course, Bella will eat just about anything as well, but then I have to deal with the hair loss, itching and scratching, ear discharge, and infections as a result. I will talk a bit more about allergies later on.

Step 2:
25 Percent Whole Grains

Grains are a healthy source of protein and complex carbohydrates. Many people debate the importance of grains in a canine diet, but they're a great source of B Vitamins. I've heard it argued that grains should be avoided because they aren't found naturally in a dog's diet. But I haven't had an issue with grains in my home.

Sure, the wolf never caught a rabbit boiling a pot of quinoa, but if your dogs are going vegan, it's important to choose something from this group. Otherwise, you may find your pup ends up a bit gassy or with the runs. If your pup isn't feeling well, then a simple grain like brown rice served with chicken breast can help soothe stomach acids. Grains really serve a purpose. I believe that just about anything in moderation is fine. I like to add grains when the stool gets a bit soft. Pumpkin and slippery elm can also be great for this condition.

Twenty-five percent (or less) of your dog's meal should consist of high-quality whole grains. Be sure to alternate between different grains to ensure your dog eats a varied diet. Be sure to cook the whole grains and run them through a blender or food processor to make sure they get properly digested. Following are the advantages of different whole grains for your dog.

Brown Rice: High in fiber, protein, manganese, magnesium, selenium, rich in antioxidants, might promote weight loss or stabilize blood sugar levels. Brown rice and chicken breast can be great if your pup is not feeling well or needs assistance with diarrhea.

Quinoa: One of the highest quality proteins on the planet because it contains all the amino acids and is a complete protein. Technically a seed, it contains all nine essential amino acids. Quinoa is gluten-free; high in iron, antioxidants, potassium, calcium, manganese, magnesium, folate, zinc, and copper; and higher in fiber than most grains. Quinoa is generally my first choice, but it can get quite expensive if purchased in flour form. Quercetin can be found in quinoa; if you don't know much about quercetin, it is often called "Nature's Benadryl" and is a great natural source to assist with allergies. (On a side note, cranberries also have a high level of quercetin.)

Oats: Contain a special type of soluble fiber that boosts the immune system, helps fight bacterial infections, and helps keep cholesterol levels low. The high fiber in oats may also help with constipation. Oats also contain a special antioxidant that protects the heart from free radicals, helps reduce the risk of Type-2 diabetes, and helps control blood sugar levels. Oats prevent the absorption of bile acids. In addition to the benefits of a whole lot of fiber, oats also have high protein levels that may be equal to some soy products as well as meat, milk, and egg protein. They are also a good sources of magnesium, iron, zinc, selenium, and several B Vitamins. Maybe you've heard the term "wild oats"? They have been found to calm the nerves and to aid the intestinal tract in digestion. You can also use the flower essences to calm your pup. (We'll talk about this later on.) As an herbal, they can also be good for the skin, healing as an anti-inflammatory, so they are often used as shampoos, poultices, or soaks for itchy, irritated skin. You can even easily grow your own and let your pup harvest the crop with you…or just graze a bit in the yard.

Other Grain Options: Barley, buckwheat, kamet, millet, rye, berries/flakes, sorghum, wild rice.

Feed sparingly: Cornmeal/polenta, wheat berries, whole grain pasta, and white rice. Some people freak out about a corn diet because we hear it's what most commercial dry foods use as a base. It's fine on occasion, though. Just don't go overboard. Note: High levels of any of these are not good for pups with cancer. Anything that turns to sugar or glucose is not something I generally eat or feed my dogs if I can avoid it.

Step 3:
25 Percent Veggies

Not only do vegetables add healthy antioxidants to your dog's diet, but they are also a significant source of soluble fiber and roughage, which can promote good intestinal health in your dog. Dark, leafy, green vegetables are the preferred choice, but almost all vegetables are super-healthy for your dog (except onions). Twenty-five percent of your dog's meal should consist of finely chopped, shredded, or (ideally) blended vegetables that are part green vegetables and part red or yellow vegetables (listed below). You can even allow them to ferment to mimic the stomach of the prey they might have caught in nature.

Ideally, veggies should be blended or run through a food processor. If you don't "Vitamix" them raw, then cook them to break down the plant matter and "pre-digest" them so they can be absorbed. Sauté at lower heat to avoid carcinogens. (Note: cooking all foods at low heat and avoiding grilled food will keep cancer-causing chemicals called HCAs from intruding on all your good feeding efforts.)

Each vegetable contains a unique combination of special vitamins and minerals, so be sure to alternate between different vegetables. Try adding these to your buddy's bowl:

Asparagus: High in potassium, which helps detoxify the body. Also high in folate, which helps fight against cancer and helps reduce pain and inflammation. Asparagus is also high in Vitamin K, which aids in bone formation and repair.

Broccoli: One cup of broccoli contains the recommended daily value of Vitamin C, an antioxidant necessary for fighting against free radicals. Like other leafy green vegetables, broccoli is high in calcium and Vitamin K, which is important for bone health. Some dog foodies say that too much broccoli can cause gastrointestinal irritation. There is also talk that too much can cause a build-up of toxins in the body. So go easy here.

Cauliflower: Contains a good amount of omega-3 essential fatty acids (great for heart health). Contains other heart-friendly nutrients, including potassium, magnesium, and niacin.

Green Beans: Although technically a legume, green beans are high in protein and fiber, and they aid in digestion. They also contain considerable amounts of folate, iron, magnesium, and potassium. Green beans are also known for helping overweight dogs shed some pounds. If your dog needs to lose a little bit of weight and you are still opting to feed kibble, try replacing some of it with green beans to help him feel fuller while giving him less of the high-calorie foods.

Kale: Its antioxidant and anti-inflammatory qualities work together to prevent and even combat cancer. With more than 192 percent of the recommended daily value of Vitamin A, one cup of kale is an effective antioxidant, boosts immunity, maintains healthy bones and teeth, and prevents urinary stones. Try adding it chopped and steamed to your dog's dinner! Kale is high in calcium. It is the number one choice for me personally, so it stands to reason it would be the number one choice for my pups.

Mushrooms: Are capable of preventing and reversing cancerous cellular changes. Below are the special benefits of various mushroom types.

Special Note: Be sure to cook your dog's mushrooms; avoid serving them raw. Scientists at the University of Nebraska Medical School found that mice who ate unlimited amounts of raw mushrooms developed, over the course of their lifetimes, significantly more malignant tumors than a control group.

> **Chaga** (Inonotus obliquus) is a hard fungi found on birch trees. Russian herbalists favor it as an immune nourisher, cancer preventive, and an aid to those dealing with melanomas.
>
> **Coriolus** (Coriolus versicolor) is used to maintain, protect, or restore immune health. Known as Krestin or PSK in Japan, and as PSP or Yun zhi in China, the hot water extract of this medicinal mushroom is the world's most thoroughly-researched supplement for immune health.

Maitake (Grifolia frondosa) has been shown to be more effective than any other fungi ever tested at inhibiting tumor growth. It is very effective when dealing with cancer.

Reishii (Ganoderma lucidum) is an immune tonic and is a premiere herb in Traditional Chinese Medicine (TCM). It has been shown to increase T-cell and alpha interferon production, shrink and eliminate tumors, and improve the quality of life for terminal patients. A product called Reishii Gano 161 is a powerful preventative, liver tonic, and immune tonic. Even occasional use builds powerful immunity and reduces the risk of cancer.

Shiitake (Lentinus edodes) is highly medicinal. Those who make shiitake a regular part of their diets increase their production of cancer-fighting alpha interferon, reduce inflammation throughout their bodies, improve their ability to produce and utilize Vitamin D, and prolong their lives.

Other options: Beets, bok choy, Brussels sprouts (high in omega-3), cauliflower, celery, chard, cucumber, lettuce, parsnips, rutabaga, spinach, celery, turnips, and zucchini.

Orange or red colored fruits and veggies are excellent sources of vitamins and minerals such as beta carotene. Beta carotene, a vitamin the body converts into Vitamin A, is a powerful antioxidant that has been celebrated for its possible ability to fight cancer. Beta carotene is also thought to play a role in protecting cells and boosting the immune system.

Twenty-five percent of your dog's meal should be from vegetables. Half of that should be from an orange or red veggie! Here are the best choices:

Canned or Fresh Pumpkin: The oils in pumpkin's flesh and seeds are believed to support urinary health. They are also an excellent source of Vitamin A, beta-carotene, potassium, and iron, and they may even reduce the likelihood that your pet will develop cancer. Not only is pumpkin full of vitamins and minerals, but it can also help your furry friend with constipation, diarrhea, indigestion, and an upset stomach. Sometimes pumpkin can be hard to find off season, but I tend to find it stocked in cans near the pet food sections at many natural grocery stores these days.

Carrots: The richest source of beta-carotene, a precursor to Vitamin A, which is essential for good vision, especially night vision, and helps prevent macular degeneration. They're also an excellent source of antioxidants and phytonutrients that help protect the heart and prevent cancer.

Sweet Potatoes: One of nature's most perfect foods. Sweet potatoes are high in Vitamins A, C, and B6. They also contain a potent antioxidant that helps prevent degenerative diseases like cancer (they are not always good once cancer happens, though), and the effects of aging.

Note: If you have a cancer pup, then carrots, peas, corn, and sweet potatoes are not optimal, but they may be a choice otherwise. They break down quickly into simple sugars in the body and may end up feeding cancers. You may decide they are just never the right choice for your pup. I don't mind an occasional sweet potato (and I mean occasional—like, just once or twice a year), but I generally don't use them myself. With carrots, I'm a bit more lenient.

Other Options: Red/orange/yellow bell peppers, squash (acorn, butternut, spaghetti, etc.), yams, and yellow summer squash.

Step 4: Supplements

Taurine and L-carnitine: These two amino acids are naturally found in animal flesh, but they do not naturally occur in plants. Deficiencies can be potentially serious, so a supplement is an important preventative measure, whether you are feeding vegan or not. Deficiency in cats causes blindness. (See the discussion above for more on taurine.)

Nutritional Yeast: Rich in B Vitamins and fortified with Vitamin B12. Whether or not you include nutritional yeast in your dog's food, you should make sure your dog receives an adequate source of B12. If your dog is prone to yeast infections, however, you may want to eliminate it from his or her diet. VegeYeast is a great brand we use on occasion in our home. It is 100 times more acid than other yeasts such as brewer's or nutritional, and it is 35 percent lower in magnesium. The extra acidity is valuable for both dogs and cats, and the lower magnesium content helps prevent urinary problems in cats.

Probiotic & Digestive Enzymes: Help improve immune function and aid in the secretion of nutrients in foods. They're great for when the body is challenged from cancer. In the wild, dogs get their food "predigested" by their prey, so we are mimicking that.

Calcium: Dogs cannot produce this in their bodies and must get it from their diets.

If you do not want to use supplements or add them with food, here are some great vegan sources of calcium that you might play with. They can be served slightly warmed over low heat and pureed:

- Adzuki Beans (1 cup contains 65 mg)
- Almond butter (2 tablespoons contain 85 mg)
- Artichoke (1 medium artichoke contains 55 mg)
- Black Currants (1 cup contains 62 mg)

- Blackberries (1 cup contains 40 mg)
- Blackstrap Molasses (2 tablespoons contain 400 mg, but watch the sugar)
- Broccoli (1 cup contains 95 mg)
- Collard Greens (1 cup contains more than 350 mg)
- Dates (1/2 cup contains 35 mg)
- Figs (1/2 cup contains 120 mg)
- Fortified non-dairy milk (1 cup contains 200-300 mg)
- Fortified orange juice (1 cup contains 300 mg)
- Great northern beans (1 cup contains 120 mg)
- Hemp milk (1 cup contains 460 mg)
- Kale (1 cup contains 180 mg)
- Navy beans (1 cup contains 125 mg)
- Oranges (1 orange contains between 50 and 60 mg)
- Raw fennel (1 medium bulb contains 115 mg)
- Roasted sesame seeds (1 oz. contains 35 mg)
- Soybeans (1 cup contains 175 mg)
- Tahini (2 tablespoons contain 130 mg)
- Tempeh (1 cup contains 215 mg) (use sparingly because it contains wheat gluten)
- Turnip Greens (1 cup contains 250 mg)

Vitamin C: The benefits of Vitamin C are multiple. It helps detox from mercury in vaccines, benefits sick and stressed dogs, treats for viral diseases, increases anti-viral and anti-cancer compounds (interferon), and increases antibodies. Vitamin C is good daily, as well as before and after vaccines to reduce exposure to harmful side effects. It can be a treatment for kennel cough, distemper parvo, abscesses, and other bacterial infections, and for puppy stress.

Some holistic vets recommend Vitamin C for dealing with stress, pollution, pesticides, chemicals, and poor diets. Some vets recommend

100-500 mg daily; other vets recommend up to 750 mg twice daily for acute issues.

Liquid Trace Ionic Minerals: We are no longer able to get all 92 known elements in our foods, but they can be found in dead sea minerals. Add a small amount of liquid minerals to food daily to avoid mineral deficiencies.

Omega-3 Fatty Acids: These are said to shrink tumors, and they protect against weight loss. Decrease Omega-6, especially in cancer pups. Here are some great vegan sources of Omega-3:

- Chia Seeds
- Fish Oil
- Flaxseed Oil
- Hemp Seed or Hemp Seed Oil

Flaxseed Oil vs. Fish Oil: There is always a lot of talk about the difference between fish oil and flaxseed. Some believe the information that claims flax oil isn't as beneficial comes from research funded by fish oil companies. Fish oil is big business with big profits.

I have been curious about this topic and reading about it for a while. What I found is that there seems to be a debate about the chemical conversion process of ALA (alpha-linolenic acid) in the body and which one does the conversion better.

In the case of flaxseeds, virtually all the Omega-3 fat is found in the form of ALA. This specific kind of Omega-3 fat makes up about half the oil in flaxseeds. The debate is over two closely-related fats found in fatty fish—EPA (eicosapentaenoic acid) and DHA (docosahexaenoic acid). It's quite a scientific debate to determine whether the body will convert enough ALA in flax to EPA and DHA and how much is needed.

It's also debated whether the body can make the conversion in just the right proportions. Then there are those who caution about the danger of being "artificially" overloaded. Concerns also exist about the processing of fish oil in high temperatures versus cold-pressed vegan oils.

After some investigation, I determined that not enough research has been conducted to determine how much EPA and DHA are needed in the human body, let alone the canine. I believe flax is great for healthy people and pets!

The only time there is evidence of ALA having difficulty converting to DHA and EPA is when a person or pet has chronic illnesses, is elderly, and/or is very sick. This situation usually occurs because other minerals are needed in the conversion process, and they are very low in an unhealthy person. What I find the most interesting in the whole debate is that Omega-3s are known to help with heart-related issues. Aren't vegans statistically less likely to have heart-related issues?

Note: There are way more books than I can cite here that will explain how a vegan diet can prevent heart disease. One you might look up is *Prevent and Reverse Heart Disease: The Revolutionary, Scientifically Proven, Nutrition-Based Cure* by Dr. Caldwell Esselstyn. I have not read it, but have heard it's very informative. Furthermore, I'm already vegan myself, have done my homework, and determined my belief system. I have not written this book to convert you, but simply to make you aware of alternatives. It's up to you which pieces work for you and which don't. But if you or your pet are struggling with heart issues, you might consider adding hawthorn berry to the diet. I personally put it in my smoothie daily as a preventative.

The real evidence of the benefit of any supplement is when it's consumed and there are health improvements and changes that correlate to adding it to the diet. If coats are shinier, thicker, and healthier-looking after eating flax, isn't it working? In some cases, it's been reported that flaxseed can help dogs with arthritis move better and have less pain. These results would not be possible if the body could not convert AHA to DHA and EPA. Also, flaxseed has more benefits than just Omega-3 oil. Ground flaxseed has fiber, protein, flax hull lignans (the shell of the flaxseed is said to be more potent than the darkest leafy green and helps boost the immune system), as well as Omega-3.

In a final note, in order to get the flax oil, the flax has to be squeezed and the oil separated. This oil is very fragile, and if it is heated at all in this process or during storage, it can become rancid. Then your dog is eating rotting flax that will not have health benefits. Always make sure your flax oil tastes good, smells good, and doesn't have a bitter aftertaste.

Step 5:
The Extras: Fruits, Oils, Seeds, Herbs and Spices

The items listed here would be added for flavor more than as a main ingredient in the meal.

FRUIT

Dogs can enjoy fruit in small, snack-sized, amounts. Be careful that you don't feed your dog fruit too soon before or after a high-protein meal. The enzymes are different, and can cause digestive upset. Be careful when feeding your dogs fruit to make sure they do not eat any seeds. Many fruit seeds contain cyanide, and when fed over a long period, will have harmful side effects. Keep experimenting to find what your dogs like.

Apples: Contain phytonutrients that help boost the immune system and aid in preventing certain forms of cancer.

Bananas: Are high in potassium. Ripened bananas, meaning bananas that have brown spots on the skin and are softer, do, in fact, help prevent and treat cancer. As a banana ripens, it produces a chemical known as "TNF," or Tumor Necrosis Factor. This combats irregular cells, such as cancer cells, and helps aid white blood cells. The riper the banana, the more cancer-fighting power it has.

Blueberries: Are high in antioxidants and fight the effects of aging on the brain, slow the aging process, and protect against cancer, cardiovascular disease, chronic degenerative conditions, and aid in combating skin allergies.

Cranberries: Are rich in cancer-fighting antioxidants, and help promote urinary tract health. They help maintain a healthy urinary pH. Cranberries may also help by removing harmful bacteria from the teeth, slowing the formation of plaque, and reducing the incidence of gum disease.

Watermelon: Watermelon is filled with Vitamin A, Vitamin C, Vitamin B-1 and B-6, potassium, and magnesium, and it is a source of the potent carotenoid antioxidant, lycopene.

Other Options: Blackberries, cantaloupe, honeydew melon, mangoes, papayas, peaches, pears, raspberries, and strawberries.

OILS

We already talked a bit about the more technical side of flaxseed and fish oil, but let's talk about this in a bit more detail. Adding healthy oils to a dog's diet will ensure he gets all the required fats in his daily meals. Include one tablespoon of oil with each meal. For smaller dogs, try giving them one teaspoon to one tablespoon at every meal. Without healthy fats, your dog's skin, nose, and coat will become dry and flaky.

Some oils also contain high levels of healthy Omega-6 and Omega-3 fatty acids that aid in heart and joint health. Omega-6 is not needed as much for dogs, but it is often added to many dry dog foods. On the other hand, most dogs suffer from Omega-3 deficiency. Omega-3 fatty acids reduce inflammation and may lower the risk of chronic diseases such as cancer, arthritis, and heart disease. They are good for cognitive and behavior functions. Deficiency shows up in dry skin, heart problems, depression, and poor circulation.

My personal favorites are first Udo's Oil 3-6-9 with DHA, then others such as Chia Oil from the Chia Company, Biotivia's Green Omega 3, and Algae Omega from Nordic Naturals. Also, soaked chia seeds contain both Omega-3 and Omega-6 fatty acids. They also have significant amounts of fiber and protein. Just keep them in a jar in the fridge and scoop out a gooey spoonful or more on each meal.

Fish Oil: Improves the coat and skin. It reduces inflammation due to conditions such as arthritis, allergies, and inflammatory bowel disease. It regulates the immune system, calms overactive immune systems for dogs with allergies or autoimmune diseases, aids in mental development of fetuses and puppies, and improves cognitive function in older dogs. It lowers blood pressure and triglycerides, and it provides support for dogs with kidney disease, heart disease, and cancer. Fish oil also promotes weight loss in overweight dogs.

Be aware that many fish oils come from mass fish kill operations and are the byproduct of a massive moneymaking and often toxic industry.

Flaxseed Oil: Low levels of Omega-3s can lead to skin and coat problems related to allergies, which are common in many dog breeds. Flaxseed Omega-3s not only improve skin health in dogs, they also help promote a shiny, soft coat. Flaxseed oil—a more concentrated form of flaxseed without the fiber—is especially recommended for dogs' skin and coat health. It also aids in improved immunity, increased bone strength, and joint health. The amount of EPA in flaxseed oil is very low.

Hemp Seed Oil: Hemp seed oil is a balanced source of Essential Fatty Acids that are required for optimum health. Omega-6, Omega-3, and Gamma Linolenic Acid are often lacking in animal diets, resulting in a deficiency of these important nutrients. Hemp seed oil helps reduce inflammation and promotes joint function, cardiovascular health, digestive health, and will give your dog a healthy coat.

Extra Virgin Olive Oil: One of the more affordable options for your dog, olive oil is just as healthy for dogs as it is for humans. Not only will it give your dog a healthy skin and coat, but it also supports a healthy heart.

Virgin Coconut Oil: I could write a whole book on coconut oil alone. The benefits are worth researching. It has antibacterial, antiviral, and antifungal properties. Coconut oil aids digestion by helping the body digest and absorb nutrients. It also helps heal digestive problems (e.g., inflammation of the bowels). It reduces, and may completely eliminate, bad breath, and it helps eliminate hairballs and related coughing. It also aids the bones, immune system, and metabolism. Coconut oil is also great for skin and fur conditions, such as helping to clear-up eczema, flea allergies, dermatitis, and itchy skin. It improves the health and appearance of skin and fur, and it deodorizes, prevents, and treats topical yeast and fungal infections, as well as disinfects cuts and supports healing of wounds. It also aids in the healing of cuts, dry skin, hot spots, insect bites/stings, and wounds.

I leave a plate of coconut oil on the floor all day and night so my pups can access it at any point in the day. I've noticed they take turns lapping it up after each meal. Of course, here in Hawaii, it is always liquid due to the heat. I also play with adding things to it. I find it intriguing what my pups will eat if it's left alongside their plate of oil. I leave many dried greens, and chia or hemp seeds there, and they love them!

Other Options: Pumpkin seed oil, safflower oil, sunflower oil, sesame oil

SEEDS

Seeds are a great source of healthy fats for dogs. They're a good substitute for oils, and they're a great addition to any meal. Too much fat in the diet will cause your dogs to gain weight and may cause an upset stomach, so don't give them too much oil and seeds together. Some seeds have better or different nutritional values than others, so make sure you rotate seeds in their diet for optimum nutrition. Also, they will come out like they went in, so they will need some kind of processing to help them get digested.

Chia Seeds: Chia seeds are a true super food. Not only do they contain Omega-3 and Omega-6 fatty acids, but they're also high in protein, calcium, and boron, which aids in calcium absorption. Soak them overnight, and then put a scoop in their food bowl daily.

Pumpkin Seeds: Pumpkin seeds are a natural source of unsaturated fatty acids, antioxidants, carbohydrates, amino acids, and Vitamins C, D, E, K, and most B Vitamins. They also contain calcium, phosphorous, and potassium.

Unhulled Sesame Seeds: Always buy unhulled sesame seeds. They are a great source of calcium, and they provide manganese, copper, magnesium, iron, phosphorus, Vitamin B1, zinc, and dietary fiber.

Other Options: Flaxseed meal, hemp seeds, peanut butter, sunflower seeds, sunflower butter, tahini.

HERBS AND SPICES

People choose to consume different herbs and spices for taste or for medicinal purposes, and dogs are no different. When creating recipes for your canine friend, try adding small amounts of herbs and spices to enhance flavor or to add special nutrients. There is a chart below for suggested amounts.

Daily intake varies, depending on whether you are using a dry powder, a tea infusion, a capsule or pill, or a tincture.

Basil: Is rich in essential vitamins, minerals, phytonutrients, electrolytes, and oils that are essential for optimal health. Basil is an anti-inflammatory, antibacterial, and antioxidant. Basil is known for its disease-preventing and health-promoting properties. You can use fresh or dry basil. I grow mine in the garden and just clip off a few leaves, mince them, and add them to the food as I prepare it.

Caraway Seeds: Are rich in dietary fiber, vitamins, minerals, and antioxidants. Caraway seeds are considered a warming herb, meaning they help the body stay warm. Caraway seeds are also good for muscle health.

Cinnamon (Ceylon is best): Not only does cinnamon smell and taste great, but it has many health benefits as well. It's an antioxidant, anti-inflammatory, anti-diabetic, and antiseptic. It is warming and soothing, calming, and carminative (anti-flatulent). Cinnamon is great for senior dogs struggling with arthritis. Don't feed your dog too much, though. (Generally, keep it under a tablespoon; if you have a tiny dog, use less.) Excess consumption of cinnamon can cause liver damage in both dogs and humans. Cinnamon is said to have one of the highest anti-oxidant levels of all food sources. Cinnamon can help remove the alfatoxins present in foods (these are cancer-causing elements found in mold, usually in decaying vegetation). Cinnamon is also good for keeping teeth clean, skin issues, and fighting bad breath.

Fennel Seeds: Are rich in dietary fiber, antioxidants, vitamins, and minerals. They have anti-inflammatory properties and help protect the body from infection, disease, and cancer. Fennel seeds are good for the urinary tract. They also help in the absorption of food and help to keep your dog's teeth clean.

Flax Seeds: Are rich in Omega-3 and fatty acids, antioxidants, nutrients, minerals, and vitamins that are essential for optimal health. Flax seeds also help remove toxins from the body. There are two types of flax seeds: brown and yellow (golden). Both are similar in nutritional value. You can use one tablespoon for each 10 lb. to 25 lb. of your dog's weight.

Garlic: You may have heard that garlic is bad for dogs, but holistic veterinarians have used it for years. The debate about garlic seems to have arisen from confusion with its close cousin, the onion. Both garlic and onion contain thiosulphate, the substance responsible for causing Heinz body anemia in dogs. However, the amount of thiosulphate in garlic is much lower than it is in onions. In fact, the amount of thiosulphate in garlic is barely traceable. This fear of feeding garlic to dogs is new, and not proven by any facts or study.

Garlic is a powerful antibiotic. Garlic is also an antioxidant, anti-allergen, antibacterial, antifungal, anti-protozoan, antiviral, and anti-carcinogen. Garlic helps regulate blood pressure and blood sugar levels. It is high in vitamins, minerals, and nutrients. It contains calcium, potassium, zinc, protein, and Vitamins A, B, B2, and C. It is an aid to fighting and treating diabetes, liver, heart, and kidney disease. Garlic contains germanium, an anti-cancer and anti-protozoan agent. It can also be used topically to treat specific ailments, such as ear mite infestation and ear infections. Garlic also contains sulfur, a natural insect repellent. It is a natural de-wormer and a flea, tick, and mosquito repellent.

Garlic is safe for pregnant dogs, so long as it's not ingested in large quantities; it can flavor the milk of lactating females (human and canine). Don't give garlic to puppies six months of age or younger.

Ginger: An anti-coagulant, anti-inflammatory, and antibacterial carminative. Ginger also helps in the absorption of food, keeping your dog's teeth clean and helping with digestion. Ginger helps in treating nausea and motion sickness. It helps boost healthy blood circulation, so it is helpful for a dog that is prone to vascular damage of the extremities. You can also use dry, ground ginger.

Green Tea: Is rich in antioxidants and is helpful in fighting some cancers. It is also calming. Make sure you use de-caffeinated green tea. It can also be applied topically for skin-related issues.

Mint: Mint is effective for indigestion, "doggy breath," flatulence, and motion sickness. Never use extracts, though. Only use the fresh herb.

Parsley: Freshens dog's breath in addition to providing some great phytochemicals. It also contains Vitamin C, Vitamin K, B Vitamins, iron, and limonene (kills bad mouth bacteria). It is high in fiber and rich in anti-oxidants, vitamins, and minerals that help fight cancer and enhance the function of all organs. It also helps the body pass toxins. Fresh parsley is best.

Rooibos Tea (Red Bush Tea): Is naturally antiviral, anti-allergenic, and a mild anti-anxiety mediator. Rooibos tea is also high in Vitamin C and rich in antioxidants, several minerals, and alpha-hydroxy-acid. You can even add it to your dog's drinking water. Rooibos is naturally caffeine-free. The USDA has confirmed that rooibos tea is capable of reducing cancer, heart disease, and other illnesses. It is excellent for dogs with chronic skin allergies. If your dog suffers from anxiety, rooibos can help to relax and de-stress your dog. Caution: It might slow down the absorption of iron.

Rosemary: Is high in fiber and rich in vitamins. Other properties include antioxidant, anti-inflammatory, anti-allergic, antifungal, antiseptic, disease prevention, and health promotion. You can use fresh or dry rosemary.

Turmeric: Is high in fiber. It is anti-inflammatory, antibacterial, antioxidant, antiseptic, anti-carcinogen, and anti-microbial. It is rich in vitamins and minerals and offers protection against anemia, arthritis, cancer, stroke (cardiovascular health), neuritis, and memory disorders. You can use powder (most commonly available), crushed, or fresh root.

Curcumin is the most active "curcuminoid" found in turmeric, and provides turmeric with its bright yellow color. Curcumin is known for its anti-inflammatory properties, but it is also beneficial for accidents and trauma, as it helps lower serum levels that would otherwise cause massive inflammation leading to organ shutdown. It is beneficial in the fight against rheumatoid arthritis and has cancer-fighting properties.

Turmeric is even more powerful as a cancer inhibitor when teamed with cauliflower, of particular importance in preventing prostate cancer.

Many pet food manufacturers are beginning to add turmeric to foods because of growing interest, but don't be fooled since you have no idea where it was grown (possibly with pesticides) and whether it contains curcumin. Remember, many manufacturers rely on consumer ignorance and want to make a profit before they care much about ethics. Your best bet is to add turmeric directly.

Turmeric paste is one of the latest popular fads in animal health. It is known to have many benefits. It contains turmeric, coconut oil, crushed black pepper, and a bit of water. I'll give the details later in the recipes.

Caution: Stop turmeric if using prescription drugs. It will generally reverse the effects of the drug. Also, stop using turmeric if going through any kind surgery because it will keep blood from clotting and may cause death.

Special Note: It used to be thought that inflammation was the body's way of fighting disease. In reality, inflammation prevents the body from recognizing a foreign substance; therefore, it creates a hiding place for invaders. All successful cancers are surrounded by inflammation. Inflammation means the virus is winning. Vaccines cause inflammation. Turmeric is known to be one of the best anti-inflammatory agents. Therefore, it must be an extreme cancer fighter.

What to Reduce or Eliminate:

Chives, cocoa, mace, nutmeg, onions/onion powder, paprika, added salt (can substitute with a small amount of Bragg's Liquid Amino), sugar (for cancer pups in particular because cancer feeds on sugars), and wheat. Also, veggies like potatoes, carrots, peas, and corn can break down quickly into simple sugars in the body and may end up feeding cancers.

Go to ASPCA for a comprehensive list of plants that are toxic to dogs: http://www.aspca.org/pet-care/animal-poison-control/toxic-and-non-toxic-plants?field_toxicity_value percent5B percent5D=01

Daily Herbal Intake Based on Dog's Weight

The table below provides a general guideline for herbs/spices based on your dog's weight. The information provided in the table is an extract from Dr. Kidd's *Guide to Herbal Dog Care*.

Dog's Weight	Sprinkles (on dog's food once/day)	Teas	Capsules/Tablets	Tinctures *
1-10 lbs.	a small pinch	less than 1/4 cup, 1-3 times/day	1/2 capsule, 1-3 times/day	1-3 drops, 2-3 times/day
10-20 lbs.	a bigger pinch	1/4 cup, 1-3 times/day	1/2-1 capsule/tablet, 1-3 times/day	3-5 drops, 2-3 times/day
20-50 lbs.	2 pinches-1 teaspoon	1/4-1/2 cup, 1-3 times/day	1-2 capsules/tablets, 2-3 times/day	5-10 drops, 2-3 times/day
50-100 lbs.	2 pinches-2 teaspoons	1/2-1 cup, 1-3 times/day	1-2 capsules/tablets, 3-4 times/day	20 drops, 2-3 times/day
Over 100 lbs.	up to 1 tablespoon	up to 1 cup, 3 times/day	adult human dose	adult human dose

* This is a safe dose, but to be honest, I generally add quite a bit more. Try muscle testing with the instructions provided later in Chapter 15 to see how many you or your pup need. Talk to your vet about use for puppies, but generally puppies are still using their mothers' antibodies up to as many as twenty-two weeks and may not need too many herbs unless they have a health issue going on. Seek additional care and support if that is the case.

DIET OVERVIEW

We've talked about many things here, but please don't feel overwhelmed. I wanted to spend some time here stressing the importance of diet in both your life and your dog's. I hope I have given you, literally, some food for thought. Many health issues can be eliminated or radically reduced with a healthy diet. I can nearly guarantee that you'll see some improvement in your dog's health if you remove commercial dry food from her diet, and then invest a bit of extra time and money to begin having some food fun in the kitchen with your pup. For me, being a responsible and conscious pet parent means stepping up first in the kitchen.

If you don't choose to put your dog on a vegan diet all the time, maybe just try it some of the time. Alternate when you can. If you put yourself on a healthy and balanced diet, you can always make something extra for your dog. I've found it's best not to go above and beyond—making something you won't eat but your dog will—at least at first. Just make extra, and it will force you to watch what you eat too!

If I'd prepared meals for the pups of my past, I probably wouldn't have written this book, and maybe they'd still be with me today. While I'm grateful for their teachings, I would much rather not have learned and lost them the hard way. When Shiitake was sick, I looked high and low for more information on diet, and I wished I could have taken back time for the others before her. My girl is watching over us. Just call…she'll come guide you on your (and your dog's) path to good health. Perhaps our separation will inform and inspire others. I've included some recipes later, but before we get there, we have more to talk about!

Really, dogs are pretty easy and will eat just about anything, but they prefer certain flavors and foods. Even if you aren't the best cook or aren't very intuitive, as you spend more time in the kitchen with your pups, you will begin to learn what they like and what they don't. My two Shar Pei like fruit, but my Bulldog doesn't care for it. Every morning as I make my smoothie, my Bella and Blue are right there asking for a banana. They just adore them and hardly go a day without one; sometimes, they even have two! After reading the previous chapter, you should be able to use the following table to help you in daily meal planning. Don't stress yourself out about likes and dislikes. It will come naturally over time.

MEAL PLANNING CHART

	AM	PM
PROTEIN (choose one)		
GRAINS (optional with meat, more necessary with vegan meals)		
VEGGIES (choose a few)		
SUPPLEMENTS		
OILS		
SEEDS		
HERBS/SPICES		

SAMPLE MEAL PLANNING CHART DOG #1

	AM	PM
PROTEIN (choose one)	Chicken	Chicken
GRAINS (optional with meat, more necessary with vegan meals)	None	None
VEGGIES (choose a few)	Carrots, green beans, kale, cabbage	Carrots, green beans, kale, cabbage
SUPPLEMENTS	MSM, colloidal silver, taurine	MSM, colloidal silver, taurine
OILS	Turmeric paste	Turmeric paste
SEEDS	Cranberries, hemp seed	Cranberries, hemp seed
HERBS/SPICES	Mullein, milk thistle, nettle, dandelion	Mullein, milk thistle, nettle, dandelion

I usually don't follow any particular recipes and work organically in the kitchen. This drives people crazy when they ask me for a recipe, since most of the time I flow in an intuitive state and pull from a variety of things in my cabinets, cupboards, and fridge. I guess, like all cooks, we develop a few favorites that tend to go into our meals. And, with one of my babies being very allergy-prone, I've had to limit her diet and mentally note what works and what doesn't. So don't worry; you'll get it.

"You can trust your dog to guard your house but never trust your dog to guard your sandwich."

— Author Unknown

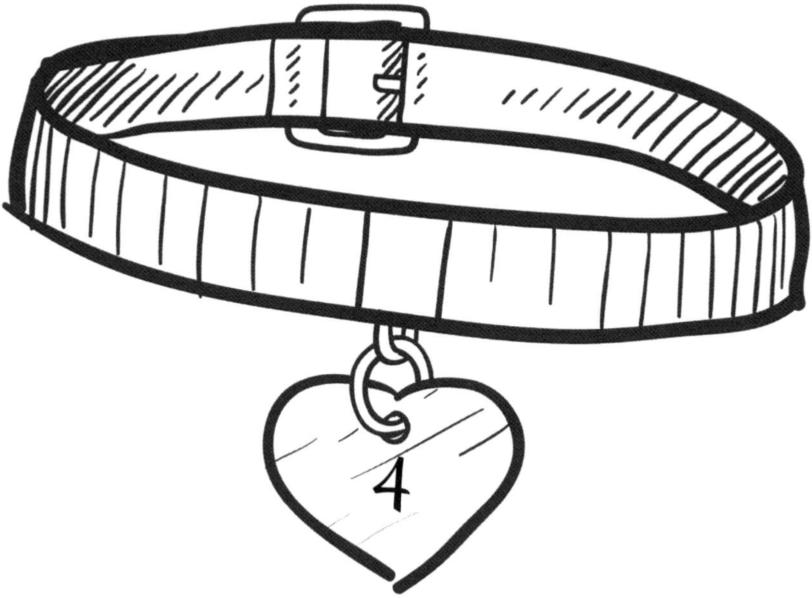

Bella's Allergies

"The difference between an itch and an allergy is about one hundred bucks."

— Anonymous

Many people ask me what I feed Bella for her allergies. Other people are curious about making the Vegan Dog Treats. I don't want to get crazy here with recipes since the previous chapter gave you many guidelines to follow. I just want to give you a few you've asked for. Keep in mind that when I prepare my meals and treats, I prepare them for three dogs or more and in large batches so I have more than one meal or bag of treats. I keep several packaged containers of portioned meals in the fridge for Blue and Leilani's food since their diet is less finicky, and they can be fed for a week on what I make. I just throw chicken and veggies with mixed herbs in a pot of water and boil it up for a stew that lasts all week for my easy two.

First thing in the morning, I prepare breakfast and dinner for Bella. Large batches give you a bit of freedom so you don't feel like a dog slave in the kitchen. I frequently call myself Bella's personal chef and lovingly refer to her as "Dog Princess." I like to think she has some good *dogma*. (But she also might have some bad karma due to her constant allergies.)

I've learned that food has become her medicine, and it can help with one of the most common health issues—allergies. I learned that there is one factor in allergies: atopy. It's a predisposition to produce high quantities of something called Immunoglobulin E (IgE). Atopy is a response to environmental allergens, such as pollens, dust mites, molds, or certain foods, for example. It is generally regarded as genetic. But because food is medicine, we (Bella and I) found a few ways to deal with it. The other, more troubling, thing we found was that Bella had a few vaccines before she came to me at eight weeks old, and they were likely the culprits behind her allergies.

Linking Vaccines to Skin Allergies

After some worry, I researched a few things and found what I believed to be negative information about the possible link between the early vaccines Bella received from her breeder and the allergies she developed. Being an energy healer, I wanted to learn more, and I also trust that it can be reversed. I'll offer my thoughts on that as we proceed.

It's sad that, as a society, we know so little about the long-term dangers of vaccines. They are much broader than just what Bella is going through. Let me explain what I found as it relates, in particular, to food and her skin.

Catherine O'Driscoll (author of *What Vets Don't Tell You About Vaccines*) wrote an article titled "Vaccines and Skin Problems," in the

July/August 2012 issue of *Dogs Naturally Magazine*, in which she discussed atopic dermatitis and how it relates to vaccines. This article really helped me understand what was going on with my Bella, so let me summarize a few key points of this rather technical article for you.

Atopic dermatitis is a hereditary condition that causes an inflammatory skin condition as a reaction to allergens. O'Driscoll states, "There are many accounts from holistic practitioners who say that skin conditions in dogs flare up shortly after a vaccine event…."

Here are a few key points I learned from the article:

- 46.2 percent of dogs with skin problems first started to have problems within three months of vaccination. Latent genetic traits may remain dormant until something (like a vaccine) triggers the predisposition.
- Antibodies (IgM, IgA, and IgE) are proteins that are used by the immune system to identify and neutralize foreign objects such as bacteria and viruses.
- With atopy, the issue is that the immune system recognizes normally harmless proteins as harmful. The body may mistakenly make antibodies against itself (autoantibodies), treating healthy organs and tissues like foreign invaders. This is called autoimmune disease.
- Putting vaccines in the foods dogs later eat might explain why dogs are becoming allergic to their appropriate diets. The vaccines enter the bloodstream and are viewed as invaders by the immune system (a kind of anaphylaxis).
- After vaccination, dogs mistake their own biochemical makeup for the invading cow serum in the vaccine and develop allergic responses. *Science has known about these reactions since 1839, but the practice continues.*
- Aluminum in vaccines is linked to causing atopy and other allergic diseases (increasing IgE response).

- Vaccinated children are more prone to cancer and leukemia than children who have suffered childhood infectious diseases.
- The use of broad-spectrum antibiotics appears to increase the risk of atopy.
- Imbalanced gut bacteria play a role in atopy.
- Being exposed to some disease allows one to develop a strong immune response to survive infection.

I was beginning to understand from this article, and my continued research, that dogs have a few different kinds of allergies, and it seems as if there is a vicious circle that continues to worsen it. The first general response a vet has to a problem is often an antibiotic, when, in fact, that can increase atopy. And the life of a pup is begun with vaccinations, so we can't identify it as a problem when we've never known the pup any other way.

EXERCISE

Go through this list and check each box that is troublesome for your dog(s).

Inhalant Allergies: (related to IgM and IgA antibodies) are characterized by:

- ❑ Biting and scratching
- ❑ Feet chewing and licking
- ❑ Itching worse on feet, hind legs, groin, and armpits
- ❑ Recurrent ear infections

Food Sensitivities (or Intolerance): (related to the IgE antibodies) are characterized by:

- ❑ Aggression and other unpredictable behaviors

- ❑ Coughing (in rare cases vomiting)
- ❑ Diarrhea
- ❑ Ear scratching
- ❑ Head shaking
- ❑ Hot spots
- ❑ Inflammation in ears
- ❑ Itchy skin
- ❑ Licking and biting of the back legs
- ❑ Rubbing face on the carpet
- ❑ Sneezing

Slower acting and chronic symptoms, such as digestive and skin-related conditions, are more commonly associated with IgA and IgM responses.

A Food Allergy: Is a severe, immediate, and acute (IgE) response to eating a particular food. A food allergy is an adverse response to a food protein where proteins become resistant to digestion, so they are not broken down during the digestive process (IgE antibodies). Therefore, the body thinks the protein is harmful.

Finding out what foods cause issues can be quite a challenge—possibly a lifelong one. Dr. Jean Dodds has developed a saliva-based testing tool called "NutriScan" to diagnose food sensitivities and intolerance. (See www.hemopet.org for more information.) Later, in Chapter 15, I will show you how to muscle test and save yourself $300.

Bella's Health Explained

When Bella first came to me as an eight-week-old pup, she was losing large amounts of hair and itching and scratching like she had a bad case of fleas or mange. Her breeder explained she had none of those problems before she came to me. She is a knowledgeable and experienced breeder and I knew she was ethical as well. I then tried to figure out what food Bella was eating—thinking it was possibly a food allergy on my end (or hers). It took me a long time before I started to figure out that she was possibly having an issue with the vaccination just days prior to coming to me, and maybe not actually her food. I looked back at her records. She'd had a large combination vaccine (Nobivac 1-DAPPv—containing distemper, adenovirus, Type 2 parainfluenza and parvo) just three days before I picked her up. I was convinced that her immune system had been compromised, and she now began to attract fleas and ticks that I needed to pick off daily. I learned that when any animal attracts other living entities into its shared physical and energetic field such as viruses, bacteria, or insects, it's usually because the immune system is compromised. From an energy healer's perspective, I knew that Bella's constitution was not strong enough to exist in its own space, and I knew I needed to do something to strengthen her immune system. Meanwhile, her skin grew more red, puffy, and swollen. She and I were both miserable!

After many baths, visits to the vet for skin scrapes for bacterial, fungal, and whatever other bugs, nothing was found to improve her condition. I had never seen a small pup with such issues, and I often found myself in tears. I meditated and prayed every minute of the day. She was nearly bald at one point. I was finally convinced by many Shar Pei friends that the issue might be her thyroid. When I had her tested, the tests came back inconclusive. My "Pei people" told me that means she had a problem and needed meds. The doc gave me thyroid meds. I, however, knew instinctively that this was not her problem. I was just at a loss for what else to do. She didn't need the meds. I went through and ruled out various shampoos. Then it dawned on me that it wasn't something topical—she might just have food allergies. I still wasn't quite sure I could convince myself it was vaccine-related. I trusted the breeder since she had been breeding for over twenty years. I knew she wouldn't knowingly harm Bella.

I'd never had a dog whose diet I had to monitor so strictly. I was even more deeply saddened when I realized this meant it was not likely I would be breeding her. I was heartbroken on many levels, and I even wondered whether I might have to consider something more extreme to end her struggle and put her out of her misery, but I proceeded to monitor things in the kitchen, with lost sleep and tears in my eyes. I realized that nothing I was doing was working, so I just completely stopped everything and went in a different direction.

The vet wanted to put Bella on an allergy medicine, but that would be a lifelong prescription, and the vet said that if Bella stopped taking it, she would return to her reactions with more aggressive problems. All the vet knew to do was give her the typical antihistamines and corticosteroids, and these would simply paralyze her immune system. Everyone in the Shar Pei groups kept telling me to put her on a raw meat diet, which would heal everything. After I spent more than $500 to get the raw, frozen meats shipped and delivered, that diet made things worse. She was severely allergic to chicken—she nearly lost all her hair just looking at it! She was allergic to lamb, beef, turkey, pork, duck, and venison. She loved the meats, but they didn't love her.

THE VET WANTED TO PUT BELLA ON AN ALLERGY MEDICINE, BUT THAT WOULD BE A LIFELONG PRESCRIPTION, AND THE VET SAID THAT IF BELLA STOPPED TAKING IT, SHE WOULD RETURN TO HER REACTIONS WITH MORE AGGRESSIVE PROBLEMS.

I tried every kind of meat for the first eighteen months of her life. The last attempt I made was fish. Salmon cleared up her itching over a period of time, but then the store had a sale on Ono. It seemed to be the best-priced fish, so I chose it only by default. The salmon was bankrupting me. Ono wasn't much cheaper, but her hair started growing in and her itching ceased. The longer I had her on the fish, the better she did.

When I finally had Bella stable, I tried a few more things. She seemed to have an animal protein intolerance, so I knew that going vegan might be an option for her. But, so far, we haven't had much luck there either. I had intended to raise her as a vegan dog, but she required so much care early on that I was nervous to alter her diet once I realized the fish was working.

I started doing more research. I found that the most common animal food allergens in many dogs are fish and seafood, although, for some reason, not for Bella. Several studies I found showed that some ingredients are more likely to cause food allergies than others. The most common offenders for dogs, in order of severity, are beef, dairy products, chicken, lamb, fish, chicken eggs, corn, wheat, and soy. As you may have noticed, the most common offenders are the most common ingredients in most commercial dog foods.

In everything I read, I found that food sensitivity symptoms are similar to those of other allergies seen in dogs and cats. The primary symptom is itchy skin affecting primarily the face, feet, ears, forelegs, armpits, and the area around the anus. Symptoms may also include chronic and recurrent ear infections, hair loss, excessive scratching, hot spots, and skin infections that respond to antibiotics but recur after antibiotics are discontinued. Evidence exists that dogs with food allergies may also sometimes have an increased incidence of bowel movements. One study showed that non-allergic dogs have around 1.5 bowel movements per day, while some dogs with food allergies may have three or more per day. Bella had every one of these symptoms.

Other studies suggested that switching food would not show immediate results. Twelve weeks was considered the normal amount of time required to gauge a new food's success or failure and its effect on food allergies. Think about how few choices we actually have over a dog's lifespan, if that is the case. With Bella, I have spent two years on personal studies of trial and error. If I switched food every twelve weeks over two years (104 weeks), I could only test out roughly nine meal choices for her.

Although it seems like it's taken forever, I've actually had good success fairly quickly. Bella and I found a solution that works for now, as long as we stick to it religiously! And that's hard to do, when you really want to give treats and rewards. However, consistency is the largest key to success with allergies. Once you get things managed, you can experiment a bit and add in a bit more variety. Bella can have my homemade Vegan Dog Treats occasionally, but we even try to keep those limited.

So, without further explanation, here is what Bella ate daily to get her allergies managed. I have since made some changes in her diet now that her condition is more manageable. Perhaps this is a good solution for you to try as well. Just find something and stick with it for twelve weeks before you go back to the drawing board. Allergies take a long time to pinpoint, so be patient. This recipe makes two meals—breakfast and dinner. Note: Bella is a fifty-pound dog.

Bella's Allergy Relief Broth with Ono Fish

In a deep saucepan, combine the following and bring to a boil. (Note: You can find any of these ingredients on Amazon.com.)

- 1/8 cup dry mullein leaves
- 1/8 cup dry stinging nettle leaves
- 2 tablespoons dry roobios tea leaves
- 2 tablespoons turmeric Golden Paste (see recipe below)
- 1 tablespoon Manuka honey
- 1 tablespoon apple cider vinegar
- 1 teaspoon (up to a tablespoon) liquid silica
- 1 teaspoon MSM powder
- 1 garlic clove
- 1/2 teaspoon Ceylon cinnamon
- 24 oz. water
- 1 tablespoon Vitamin C (ascorbic acid)
- 1 tablespoon taurine powder

Once the broth is boiling, you can place three to four small pieces of Ono fish in the pan, lower the heat, and cover until the fish turns white. Do not overcook or it will get dry.

Once it is done, separate the fish flakes and add a daily probiotic. I just drop her cap on top. Cool completely and serve with the broth.

I also include the following as a part of Bella's diet: a good pre and probiotic (I will explain the advantages of each in a bit), and either a plate of coconut oil or Udo's Oil that is available at all times.

Notes: Milk Thistle is also great to detox the liver if you believe the skin conditions or allergies are a result of some kind of toxin being introduced (long-term prescriptions, vaccinations, mushroom poisoning, etc.).

I have a list of a few other things commonly used for allergies later on as well. I rotate a few of these daily/weekly.

Key to Allergies: The key, I've found, in healing allergies is releasing the toxins stored in the liver, in particular. I've found the liver and the gut to be two areas of focus for allergy relief. I also rotate a few other liver cleansers such as dandelion, milk thistle, horsetail, bladderwrack, ashwaganda, echinacea, spirulina, and Essiac Tonic. I also use a good probiotic for gut health and occasionally (if I intuitively sense a need for a cleanse), I give an activated charcoal capsule with bentonite clay. I use Uncle Harry's Natural Products brand. Note that if you give this, it will strip all other supplements out of the body, so hold off a day on those. You can also use zeolite clay to assist in the detox process too.

BELLA'S ALLERGY MEAL EXPLAINED

Let me take a moment to explain why I used the ingredients I did. You can also make any of these herbs (mullein, nettle, rooibos) into a tea or infusion and add it to your dog's water bowl daily, or preferably, leave a separate bowl next to the water bowl. You can use the following amounts 1-3 times per day (or just leave a bowl of fresh tea or herbs out for them all day):

- Small dog 1/8 cup
- Medium dog 1/4 cup
- Large dog 1/2 cup

Mullein: Inhibits some specific body processes that cause inflammation and can sooth inflamed mucous membranes, thereby helping provide relief from respiratory discomfort associated with environmental allergies—runny nose and eyes, difficulty breathing, etc. Since we have sugarcane burning and VOG (volcanic smog) in Hawaii, I like to use mullein in Bella's meals on days of heavier pollution. It is useful for reducing allergy symptoms due to its anti-inflammatory qualities. It also can soothe inflamed skin or mucous membranes.

Caution: If you harvest your own mullein seeds, be careful because they are toxic (the seeds contain rotenone, a natural pesticide). Do not allow any of the seeds to be mixed in with the leaves you harvest.

Nettle (Stinging Nettle): Is nutrient-dense and a great immune system booster. Nettle is also a powerful anti-inflammatory. It is commonly used as relief for pollen-related allergies. It is known to inhibit the release of histamines, increase the production of T cells—vital to controlling allergic reactions. It mimics the action of antihistamine allergy medications (such as Benadryl) and provides respiratory relief without the side effects of conventional chemical-based antihistamines. It can treat skin conditions, such as eczema and hives, be used to relieve the inflammation of arthritis, and aid in digestion.

Nettle is also high in calcium, chlorophyll, iron, and Vitamin C, which increase the body's red blood cell count. The anti-allergy impact of nettle may be due to its quercetin content—having the ability to inhibit IgE-induced histamine release. I was using quercetin more often, but learned long-term use may cause issues with the liver, so I stuck with nettle.

Caution: Bacteria needs iron to spread. Nettle is high in iron, so do not give your dog nettle when your dog has a bacterial infection. Nettle may also interfere with prescription medications for diabetes, high-blood pressure, and NSAIDs (aspirin).

Rooibos Tea: Contains anti-allergy properties and can aid in treating allergies and related skin problems, asthma, etc. It is high in alpha hydroxyl acids (AHA), which help facilitate healthy growth and maintenance of the skin. It can be applied as a soothing rinse or foot soak too.

Ceylon Cinnamon: Is an insect repellent, skin odor neutralizer, antibacterial, and antimicrobial to stop the growth of bad bacteria, fungi, and yeast. It's also good for dental care.

Caution: Ceylon cinnamon is safe, but avoid Cassia cinnamon. It may pose a health risk since it contains measurable amounts of coumarin.

MSM: Relieves skin problems, leathery cracked skin, wrinkles, and itchy skin. MSM reduces scar tissue, moles, brown spots, black spots, skin tumors, cuts, and burns.

Garlic: Repels internal and external parasites, and it acts as a digestive and circulatory tonic. It is a great prebiotic. As we discussed earlier, garlic has gotten a bad rap as of late because it is a bit misunderstood. Much of the bad press comes from a study done at Hokkaido University where four forty-pound dogs were given twenty cloves of garlic for seven straight days. It was deemed toxic and caused damage to the red blood cells. Too much of anything is bad, so just be cautious not to give too much and you should be fine. I like to rotate one week on and one week off to manage better the risks and benefits. I personally believe that no medicinal herb should be used for an extended period. According to Dr. Pitcairn (*The Complete Guide to Natural Health for Dogs and Cats*) here is the appropriate dosage:

- 10 to 15 pounds: 0.5 clove
- 20 to 40 pounds: 1 clove
- 45 to 70 pounds: 2 cloves
- 75 to 90 pounds: 2.5 cloves
- 100 pounds +: 3 cloves

Honey: If your dog suffers from allergies caused by pollen in the environment, you can use a wildflower blend of locally-produced (within a fifty-mile/eighty-kilometer radius of where you live) honey. Use local, unpasteurized natural honey to inoculate your dog against locally-occurring pollen.

Honey is really fascinating. It contains minute amounts of pollen, negligible enough that, when consumed in a proper dosage, won't cause an allergic reaction. It actually acts as an antibody or vaccine, inoculating the system against pollens that cause allergies. When your dog ingests a small amount of the honey over a period of time, say a month prior to allergy season, your dog's system builds up a tolerance, or develops a natural immunity, for the pollens that arrive in allergy season. About ¼ tsp for every twenty pounds of bodyweight should be sufficient.

Caution: Processed, pasteurized, mass-produced commercial honey does not have the health benefits of locally-produced natural honey.

Manuka Honey: Manuka honey comes from New Zealand. It is rich in antioxidants, vitamins, and minerals. It is known to be an antibacterial, among other things. Topically, it heals wounds. Internally, it provides numerous sources of nutrients, such as Vitamins A, B complex, C, D, E, and K, plus minerals such as calcium, magnesium, and more. It helps dogs with allergies, fights infections, and helps with digestive problems.

CAUTION: When buying Manuka honey, remember to consider the UMF (Unique Manuka Factor) rating. UMF is a phytochemically-derived antibacterial property found in certain strains of Manuka honey. If you want to benefit from the healing qualities of Manuka, you need to get one with a UMF rating of 10 or above.

Apple Cider Vinegar (ACV): Is a general detoxifier, high in potassium, and beneficial for dogs with heart problems. It is also good for stomach upset, poisoning, intestinal gas, and constipation. It helps with nutrient digestion and assimilation, prevention of bladder stones, kidney infections, and urinary tract infections. It has antibacterial, antifungal, and antiseptic properties, and it helps prevent growth of harmful bacteria in the digestive tract. It can be spritzed on decaying or splitting toenails (caused by a lack of potassium in the diet). Instill a few drops (you can also add garlic, mullein, and lavender oil) in each ear, massage, and swipe with a cotton swab for a natural ear cleaner. It can also be used to make your own herbal tinctures. Mix with fresh or dried herbs, strain, and store in a cool dark place or amber bottle.

Apple cider vinegar is a great foot soak and skin and coat rinse when used topically. Dogs with itchy skin caused by allergies (seasonal or fleas) can get almost instant relief if it is used as an after-shampoo rinse. If used long-term, it can make your dog more resistant to infections, as well as flea or worm infestations. It can even help with tear stains by being used both internally (add a teaspoon to food) and externally (as a wipe); just don't get it in the eyes because it will burn. Using full strength ACV topically can burn the skin, so use caution. Always test on yourself first before applying to your pup.

Silica: Can benefit dogs with delicate skin or skin troubles. Silica improves skin texture and thickness of the skin, and plays a major role in collagen formation. It's found naturally in skin, hair, and nails. As a supplement, it helps the body naturally heal itself. It helps the body balance pH levels and helps relieve skin rashes and hives. In fact, without silica, calcium cannot be digested and assimilated properly. It can be found in romaine lettuce, cucumber (with skin), hemp leaves, marjoram, burdock root, some spinach, bell pepper, and tomato.

Vitamin C: Bella recently started on a light dose of Vitamin C (calcium ascorbate in a powder form), and we are seeing great improvement in her demeanor. She is much happier and full of energy. Studies are beginning to show more resistance to disease with supplementation of Vitamin C. 100-500 mg per day is generally fine (based on weight of dog). There is a test ("bowel tolerance") where you keep increasing the dose until your dog develops diarrhea. You decrease from there as the stress of the issue releases. Work with a homeopathic vet for issues such as respiratory conditions, arthritis, infected ears, and skin allergies and appropriate dosages of Vitamin C. It's also now being more regularly given (via injection) for cancer care as well.

Bella's allergy diet has shifted since I've learned additional information about possible links to her vaccinations. I've begun to realize that strengthening her body is more important after the possible suppression of her immune system from vaccines. She is still a work in progress, and I study her life and my own daily for clues. She and I have been finding new ways through her issues, and information is coming to me quicker than I can write this book. Today, I'm proud to report, she is free from her skin and hair loss issues and has a full beautiful coat. She is basically a normal dog on a super-charged diet. Hallelujah! I hope to continue to relay new information on her improvements after this publication.

COMMON ALLERGY FOODS

Many of the following can cause allergies, and they should be avoided if you suspect allergies in your dog. If your dog has red itchy skin, bites at its feet, loses fur on the back of its legs and underbelly, is lethargic, or loses energy, make sure none of these are in her diet.

- Beef
- Broccoli (too much can cause seizures)
- Carrots
- Corn
- Cow's milk
- Chicken
- Peas
- Pineapple
- Pork
- Spicy foods, sugars, or salts
- Tomatoes
- Tuna
- Turkey
- Wheat pasta
- Yeast

BOOSTING YOUR DOG'S IMMUNE SYSTEM IN TANDEM WITH DO-IT-YOURSELF ALLERGY TREATMENTS

Your dog's allergies will be more acute if his or her immune system is compromised because of poor diet (commercial dog food); over-inoculation; or chemical-based parasite preventatives, such as heartworm preventatives, flea and tick preventatives, chemicals in household cleaners, over-exposure to antibiotics, and toxins and carcinogens in dog toothpaste, dental chews, and shampoos. Think about what you would do, or not do, for yourself. Why would you do something else for your dog?

Now that we've talked about diet, let's consider adding immune system boosting and allergy fighting items to your dog's daily diet. We've already talked about a few of them as a general addition, but let's just touch briefly on them for allergy relief (e.g., garlic, which is also a de-wormer). Here are a few others to consider:

Bioflavonoids: Also referred to as Vitamin P, bioflavonoids contain compounds, such as quercetin, biotin, folic acid, zinc, and Vitamins E and C that help control histamines. They are found most in many high Vitamin C foods and are full of antioxidants that are believed to deliver an anti-carcinogenic effect. Top choices are: red bell peppers, strawberries, Brussels sprouts, tropical fruits like mangos and papayas, garlic, kale, spinach, dark beans, and many teas such as green tea.

Bladderwrack: A concentrated source of minerals, bladderwrack aids in the production of thyroid hormones, which helps maintain healthy metabolism in all body cells. One of its major benefits is it improves overall skin and coat health.

Burdock: Is best for psoriasis, eczema, and flaky, oily, or inflamed skin that may be related to liver issues. It is a blood purifier.

Coconut Oil: Improves overall skin health, has antibacterial and antifungal properties, prevents yeast infections, is antiviral.

Dandelion: Benefits the liver and digestive system and helps maintain normal blood pressure. Dandelion helps the liver in the detoxification process. When impurities and toxins are released, the liver receives the nutrients it needs to function well, but when the liver is impaired, health suffers. Dandelion helps to keep bacteria and spillover of waste products from the liver so it has less work to do. Many herbs that will cleanse the liver and kidneys will assist the body in the allergy-fighting process. Use it as a dry herb or a tincture.

Horsetail: Is known for its high silica content, which is the main component in all connective body tissues. It has antiseptic and anti-inflammatory properties. It's said to cure baldness and be a natural conditioner when used topically. Great for body tissue and urinary tract health. Best for dry skin, eczema, cuts, and wounds. It will encourage healthy skin and a glossy coat while supporting the immune system—

liver, kidneys (aids in the removal of kidney stones and bladder incontinence), and thyroid—when taken internally.

Kali Sulph (Kalium sulphate): Is a cell or tissue salt known for distributing oxygen throughout the body and keeping cell membranes in peak health. It's also great for reducing inflammation. It treats ringworm, fungal infections of the skin, and promotes growth of new cells.

Lemon: Is a natural de-wormer, antibacterial, detoxifier, antioxidant, and insect repellant (mix with apple cider vinegar as a topical cleanser). I actually prefer to use Young Living's essential oil as my primary choice for lemon, but using it fresh or using the juice is fine as well. The essential oil requires just one drop in most cases.

Licorice: Blended 50:50 with nettle, licorice can sometimes be found in a tincture. Together, they are said to increase palatability. It has been used for allergy patients for thousands of years. It is said to have an antitussive effect similar to codeine. It can relieve inflammation in the digestive tract and eliminate mucus from the respiratory tract.

Omega-3 fatty acids with a balance of ALA, EPA, and DHA acids: Insufficient daily amounts may contribute to or cause behavior problems such as stress, anxiety, depression, or aggression. Insufficient amounts can trigger chronic inflammation such as allergies, arthritis, as well as other conditions such as cancer, diabetes, etc. I use Flora brand (Udo's Oil 3-6-9 Blend).

Prebiotics: Non-digestible food ingredients that promote growth and activity of bacteria in the colon. They feed the good bacteria already present. Studies show that they work to increase acid, making the environment less hospitable to harmful strains of yeast and disease-causing bacteria. They aren't degraded by stomach acids, enzymes, or water, and can be fermented by gut bacteria. In fact, they stimulate the growth of good bacteria and may inhibit the growth of disease-causing bacteria.

Whole food sources of prebiotics include whole grains, bananas, garlic, leeks, artichokes, dandelion root, burdock root, chicory root, legumes, garlic, and some fruits. Chicory, burdock, and dandelion are known by herbalists for their antioxidant properties, and their abilities to strengthen various functions of the liver and gall bladder. This, in turn, improves digestion and aids in removal of systemic waste.

Probiotics: Live microorganisms, usually in the form of good bacteria (lactobacillus acidophilus, Bifidobacterium bifidum, lactobacillus bulgaricus) that help maintain a healthy balance of intestinal flora. They can ease digestion and support the immune system by protecting the gastrointestinal wall. Fermented foods such as kefir and yogurt contain natural probiotics. You can also use fermented vegetables like sauerkraut.

Making Your Own Probiotics

One probiotic you can make yourself is sauerkraut. Shred a head of fresh cabbage, add 3 tablespoons of sea salt, and place it in an airtight glass canning jar or container to ferment for three days in the sun.

This sauerkraut actually contains thirteen strains of bacteria and about 100 times more probiotics than most supplements (not to mention it's a lot less expensive). Feed one-half teaspoon, up to three tablespoons per day.

One of my favorite blog sites is Ottawa Valley Dog Whisperer. You can read more about the benefits of cabbage as a probiotic at http://ottawavalleydogwhisperer.blogspot.com/2012/05/foods-rich-in-probiotics-beneficial-for.html

Note: If you don't mind the smell and aren't doing a vegan diet, green tripe is an excellent digestive enzyme as well. Green tripe is generally considered a form of probiotic.

Spirulina: Contains protein, vitamins, and carotenoids. It supports energy, the immune system, and liver functioning.

Sprouted Seeds: Can help with leaky gut syndrome. Keeping the gut healthy helps protect against allergens. Sprouted seeds are high in vitamins, minerals, enzymes, and probiotics to support healthy gut flora.

Turmeric Golden Paste: Let's talk briefly about turmeric golden paste and how to make it. I already talked earlier about the benefits of turmeric, so go back to reference that if needed. But let me explain why golden paste…turmeric doesn't always get digested. In other words, it isn't always bioavailable. Most of the curcumin in turmeric that is ingested gets metabolized before it can get absorbed. Black pepper contains a chemical called piperine, which increases the bioavailability of turmeric to help the body absorb it. When eaten with fat (virgin olive oil, coconut oil, or meat drippings), as done in India, curcumin can be directly absorbed into the bloodstream through the lymphatic system, partially bypassing the liver.

Turmeric Golden Paste Recipe

- ½ cup turmeric powder with curcumin
- 1 cup water
- 1/3 cup unrefined coconut oil
- 1 ½ teaspoons of freshly cracked black peppercorns

Mix turmeric powder with water until a paste forms. Once you have a thick paste, add the coconut oil and, lastly, the pepper.

You can cool and place the paste in a jar or form small nuggets by placing cooled paste into a baggie, cutting off an edge, and squirting a few dots on wax paper. Then refrigerate until solid.

I find it easier just to keep it on the counter in a jar since I use it in meals. Here in Hawaii, with our warm weather, it rarely gets solid.

You can add the golden paste directly to your dog's meals by mixing it with some water or kefir. Most dogs don't mind the taste at all. Start with about ¼ to ½ tsp, depending on the size of your dog. You can increase the amount from there, up to about a tablespoon for larger dogs.

With all herbs, try a few days on and a few days off to test their efficacy. With allergies, look to see whether your dog itches and scratches more or less on those days to determine the best protocol for home care.

There are many ways to boost the immune system that aren't just for allergy support. A few ways to do so might be with any of the following, some of which we have discussed already or will shortly:

- Boost the adrenals
- Cleanse the gut
- Clear the lungs and lymphatic system (sage, ginger, eucalyptus)
- Detox the liver
- Eat healthily
- Supplement the body (echinacea, mushrooms, turmeric, etc.)

VEGAN DOG TREATS

When Shiitake was sick, I knew of the benefits of creating an alkaline body to help healing because I've been vegan for twenty-five years. It was my first thought when the cancer hit. My second thought was, *Why haven't we always done a vegan diet? Then, maybe she wouldn't have gotten cancer in the first place.* Not only did she have a typical dog diet, but she also had her vaccinations to travel to Hawaii. We're gonna talk about vaccines in more detail in a bit.

But first, I've always wanted to find healthy treats that weren't casually given as a reward when I knew that a life was lost to make them. I couldn't just flip her a treat into her mouth and not think of both the life lost and the fact that I was introducing the karma and possible sickness of that animal into an already sick body.

I was just an absolute mess when Shiitake was sick. I could barely function. All I did was lie in bed with her and cry. It was as if the world ceased to exist, and we were the only two left on it. I barely remember what happened in any other facet of my life at that point. I do recall that a voice came into my head that said, "You must prepare a healthy treat to help her, and help others." I was given all the ingredients without any thought. I just started mixing things up in a bowl, and I knew to dehydrate them as opposed to using high heat to bake them. Both her food and her treats began to look very much the same at one point, except one was wet and one was dry.

Many people have since asked for the recipes. Quite honestly, they are rather expensive to make, and there has never really been much profit for me in selling them, so I'd rather teach you how to make them than spend my whole day in the kitchen and have to charge you for shipping too. I think that once you make them, you will appreciate them even more. Making them takes time, but they have a long shelf-life, and they are full of good stuff.

First, you'll need a dehydrator. I have a nine-tray Excalibur, and I think it's the best on the market. I make the recipes in bulk, and I never measure anything. So please feel free to change the ingredients to suit your needs. I make four flavors, but once you get the hang of it, I think you will see just how easy this is, and you can make your own recipes. More about the specific ingredients can be found at www.Vegan-DogTreats.com.

COCONUT BANANA

Ingredients:

- Coconut oil
- Coconut flakes
- Coconut flour
- Peanut butter
- Bananas
- Nettles (Dry herbs need to be measured for dog and batch size, infused into a tea, and leaves disposed.)
- Quercetin (Open a few caps based on batch and dog size, and mix with water.)

Mix all ingredients with just enough water to make a thick batter. I like to mix the wet ingredients—bananas, peanut butter, some water, and oil—in my Vitamix to make a wet thick additive to the dry coconut flour.

Spread on a series of sheets in the dehydrator to the desired thickness. Once the dough is just about to crack, you will need to cut it quickly by pressing into it with a long knife, making several squares. Continue dehydrating until completely dry and hard. Place in large plastic baggies for indefinite storage (as long as they are kept dry).

PEANUT BUTTER AND JELLY

Ingredients:

- Kidney beans
- Oats
- Flaxseed
- Pumpkin
- Peanut butter
- Turmeric
- Apple cider vinegar
- Dates
- Liquid trace minerals (buy at a health food store)
- Strawberries

Soak the beans overnight. Then cook them and let them cool. Once they are cooled, you can blend them with some water in a food processor until they are a nice thick soup. Place them in a bowl with the oats, dry turmeric, and flaxseed. I like to mix wet ingredients—the pumpkin, peanut butter, some water, apple cider vinegar, dates, and trace minerals—in my Vitamix to make a wet thick additive to the dry.

Mix all ingredients with just enough water to make a thick batter. Once you have a batter, you can thinly slice the strawberries and add them by lightly pressing them onto the top of the batter on the sheet.

Spread on a series of sheets in the dehydrator to the desired thickness. Once the dough is just about to crack, you will need to cut it quickly by pressing into it with a long knife, making several squares.

Continue dehydrating until completely dry and hard. Place in large plastic baggies for indefinite storage (as long as they are kept dry).

CHEEZY VEGGIE

Ingredients:

- Chickpea flour
- Oats
- Nutritional yeast
- Red bell pepper
- Fresh parsley
- Fresh basil
- Liquid trace minerals (buy at a health food store)

Place all dry ingredients in a bowl—chickpea flour, oats, and nutritional yeast. Lightly chop peppers, parsley, and basil in a food processor. Mix all ingredients with just enough water to make a thick batter.

Spread on a series of sheets in the dehydrator to the desired thickness. Once the dough is just about to crack, you will need to cut it quickly by pressing into it with a long knife, making several squares. Continue dehydrating until completely dry and hard. Place in large plastic baggies for indefinite storage (as long as they are kept dry).

PUMPKIN

Ingredients:

- Flaxseed
- Yellow and orange lentils
- Oats
- Pumpkin
- Banana

- Turmeric
- Ceylon cinnamon
- Liquid trace minerals (buy at a health food store)

You will need to soak the lentils overnight. Then cook them and let them cool. Once they are cooled, you can mix them with some water in a food processor until they are a nice thick soup. Place all dry ingredients in a bowl—flaxseed, oats, turmeric, and cinnamon. Vitamix, or blend, the wet ingredients: pumpkin, banana, and trace minerals with a bit of water. Mix all ingredients with just enough water to make a thick batter as you combine the wet ingredients with the dry.

Spread on a series of sheets in the dehydrator to the desired thickness. Once the dough is just about to crack, you will need to cut it quickly by pressing into it with a long knife, making several squares. Continue dehydrating until completely dry and hard. Place in large plastic baggies for indefinite storage (as long as they are kept dry).

Note: If you add a bit of taurine to the pumpkin or peanut butter treats, you really have a whole vegan meal packed into these little snacks. Once you perfect this recipe, you might even consider making treats that more medicinal, such as to keep away fleas and ticks, to detox the body, or maybe make your own heartworm treat.

I watch so many people suffer with the health of their dogs; I know diet is the answer to many things. With a good diet, many problems can be avoided. I hope to introduce a few more recipes on social media or on my website after the launch of this book, so stay tuned. This book would be far too large if I included them all, but a great reference for a few meals might be Dr. Ihor John Basko's book *Fresh Food & Ancient Wisdom: Preparing Healthy and Balanced Meals for Your Dog*. He goes into far more detail than I have in this particular book. We've barely scratched the surface here with the amazing things I want to share with you, so let's move on to our next subject: herbal medicine.

"Folks will know how large your soul is,
by the way you treat a dog!"

— Charles F. Doran

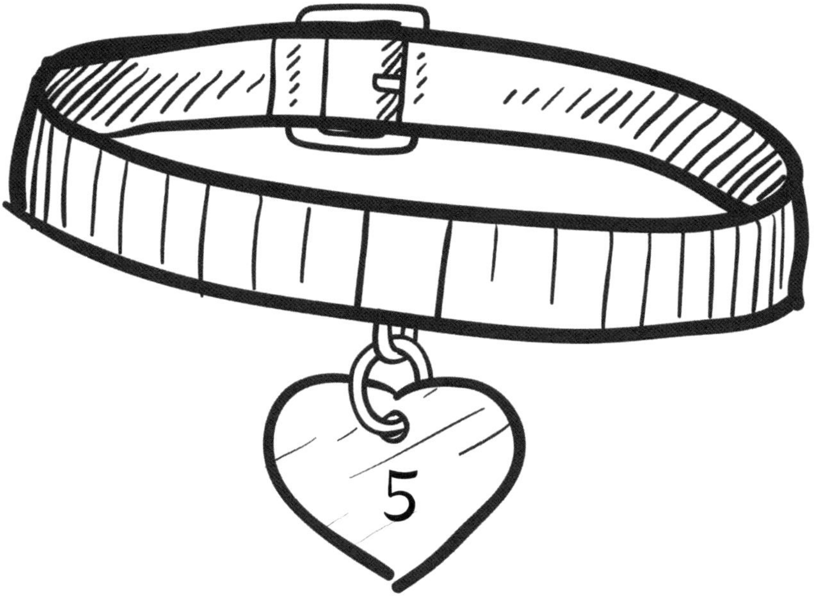

Discovering Herbal Medicine

"A dog lives in the moment and always hopes for the best."

— Author Unknown

Many medicines originally came from plants. For example, morphine is from poppies, and aspirin is from willow bark. Herbal medicine has been used for centuries, but it is often classified as "complementary" medicine. Herbal medicines come in many forms—tinctures, liquid extracts, tablets, capsules, powders, dry herbal tea, or dry medicinal herbs. They have a strong smell compared to homeopathic options.

Liquid herbal tinctures and dried loose tea-like herbs are my choice when it comes to my dogs. Tinctures go through the bloodstream faster. It's very easy to mix the liquids in with their daily food as well. With some herbs, it's a good idea to mix them in with a favorite treat if your pup is sensitive to smell and taste. Sardines or peanut butter are great secret "weapons" for hiding smells and flavors in my home. The more herbs you use, the stronger the dosage (and the stronger the smell). Remember, many herbs are used to create pharmaceutical drugs, so use caution; do not use too much. Do your research.

LYMPH GLANDS

When Shiitake was sick with lymphoma, I found many herbs that would help create a healthy lymphatic system. Cleavers and calendula will aid circulation in the tissues around the lymph glands. They help in removing waste and toxins from the body. Red clover will also help with swollen lymph glands. Astralagus is also good for protecting the immune system against stresses. It has antiviral properties and is an antibacterial and anti-inflammatory. I used it when Shiitake was sick.

I also found a few odd herbs that I can't find much research on in terms of how they relate to dogs, but maybe someone will begin doing more research on them and their safety and efficacy for lymph issues in dogs. There are a few things that need to happen with regard to treating the lymph glands: bringing down the swelling, detoxingifying the body, and boosting the immune system. Many herbs can help with all of this. When Shiitake got lymphoma, I just couldn't do the research quickly enough when I needed help the most. Since her death, I have found references to many things that might have helped. Perhaps you can ask your homeopathic vet about any of the following for lymph health:

- Astralagus
- Calendula
- Cleavers

- Echinacea
- Ocotillio bark
- Red root
- Stillingia root

PARASITES

More and more research is being done on herbs, but as quickly as it's done, more forests are also coming down. We still have so much more to learn. I won't spend too much time here talking about the advantages of using herbs in your dog's diet because I'd need to write another book on the subject. But let me give you a few suggestions that might work well for both allergies and parasites—the two topics that I find people ask about the most.

I've had dogs in my life for two-and-a-half decades, and I have never had a dog get worms. A good probiotic or a dash of garlic given with regular consistency is generally the best cure for parasites, but if that doesn't work, here are a few other herbs to talk to your vet about trying:

Berberine: A compound available in a variety of herbs. Used for intestinal parasites, it can be extracted from barberry and is also found in goldenseal. I like to add goldenseal to my dogs' meals because it can also boost the immune system.

Black Walnut: You can find it in liquid form and place a few drops in your dogs' meals for tapeworms. It is said to oxygenate the blood, which helps remove parasites.

Cayenne Pepper: A dash in their meals to protect against tapeworms. Be careful; it's spicy!

Cinnamon (Ceylon): A dash in their meals to protect against worms.

Clove: Add to meals to detox the body. It also repels fleas and worms.

Dirt: Yep, regular old dirt eaten from your yard is also great for worm treatment, so go ahead and let them eat it. (Of course, you never want to use chemicals in the yard where your dog(s) frequent.)

Fennel: Give internally or externally for tapeworm parasites in the intestines.

Garlic: A dash in their meals is great for cleansing after they have drunk bad water. It also repels mosquitos, fleas, and ticks.

Ginger: A dash in their meal helps protect against tapeworms.

Green Papaya: For roundworms and as a digestive enzyme. You can also purchase it in powder form. My dogs love to eat it here in Hawaii.

Neem: Applied topically for worm and mosquito repellent.

Parsley: A dash in their meals to protect against worms.

Peppermint: A dash in their meals to protect against worms.

Pumpkin Seed: Raw, organic seeds can be added to their meals for hook and tapeworms.

Turmeric: A dash in their meals reduces inflammation caused by worm infestations. Be cautious if your dogs are on medication because turmeric is a blood thinner.

Wormwood: Add to meals to cleanse the blood and digestive tract. Caution: Some have found wormwood to cause seizures in their dogs. Pure oil is considered toxic.

Look for the following symptoms if you think your dog has worms: bloating, gas, diarrhea, fatigue, nausea, worm in stool, stomach pain, vomiting, and weight loss.

Adding things to your dog's diet is one thing, but also avoid refined grains and sugary handouts. Keeping the gut clean and functioning well with a good probiotic is generally the best proactive habit to avoid so many issues and maintain good health.

If you live in an area where you have mosquitos, you don't really need to get crazy with over-the-counter chemical treatments and topicals for your dog. More and more research is beginning to show all kinds of health problems with these products, and companies and the FDA are both issuing alerts regularly now for so many products that used to be applied at the scruff of the neck that unknowingly were harmful. The best way to combat heartworm is to repel mosquitos. Protect your dog from any parasite by boosting its immune system by keeping the gut clean (or adding a dash of garlic in your pup's meal).

ALLERGIES

We've already talked about allergies, so I will make this brief. Allergies occur when an invader enters the body. Allergies are a symptom of an immune system disorder. Many allergies can be linked back to diet…or to vaccines. The trick is not just finding out what caused the disturbance, but also why the immune system is or isn't responding. The next step is figuring out what to do about it. Helping the organs, in particular the liver, release the disturbances, or toxins, can often treat allergies. Some herbs can help do this. We talked about a few, but here are a few more that are less commonly used (generally added to the diet):

- Alfalfa
- Black current seed powder
- Borage seed powder
- Burdock
- Cholagogue
- Dandelion leaf and root
- Evening primrose seed powder
- Flaxseed powder
- Red clover

Again, work with a homeopathic veterinarian to determine what is right for your kiddo.

I recently purchased a book that covers herbs in detail: *Herbs for Pets* by Gregory L. Tilford and Mary Wulff. I highly recommend it. No sense repeating a good thing. We have so much more to talk about, so we will move on.

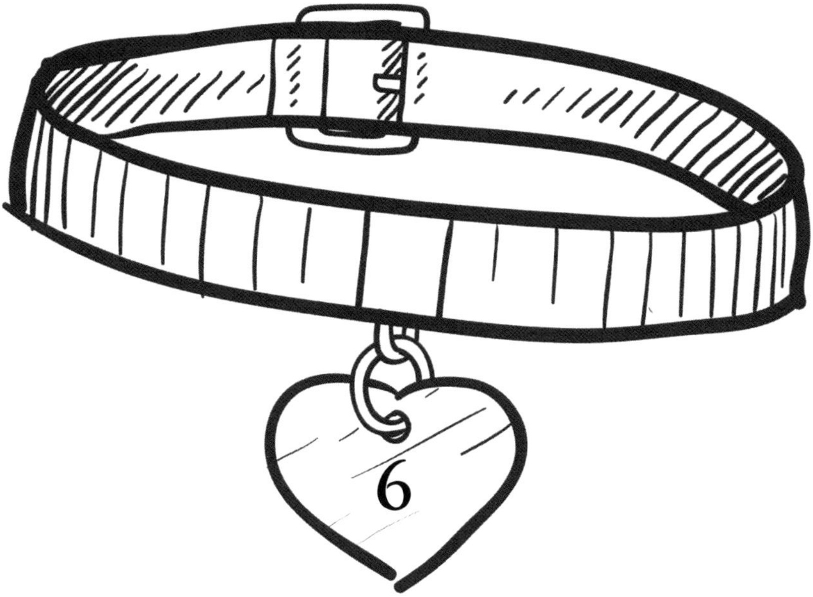

Homeopathy

"The introduction of Homeopathy forced the old school doctor to stir around and learn something of a rational nature about his business. You may honestly feel grateful that Homeopathy survived the attempts of the orthodox physicians to destroy it."

— Mark Twain

Homeopathy has been an option for health care since the seventeenth century, yet little is known about it in the United States. Homeopathy, or homeopathic medicine, is based on the idea that the body has the ability to heal itself. The word homeopathy is from the Greek: homoios (similar) and pathos (suffering). Homeopathic medicine views symptoms of illness as normal responses of the body's attempt to heal itself. The homeopathic belief is that whatever causes the illness can also cure the patient with similar symptoms. Screech, what? Hold on! It's truly taken me some time to grasp this concept. The things that cause the problem can cure it?

Homeopathic medicines are drawn from plant, mineral, animal, and other biological matter and put into a tincture or small white pill form. They are taken from a "mother tincture" and diluted to such a degree that the original substance can no longer even be detected. They work by gently boosting the body's natural energy. Homeopathic remedies are quite safe; there is no danger of addiction or toxic buildup.

They have no smell or taste. The number of drops or pills administered is not as important as the frequency. The drops can be applied to the scruff of the dog's neck and the pills placed in the mouth near the gums, with no need to open the mouth and traumatize your dog. Pills can even be added to water to make a liquid that can be drawn into a syringe and easily placed in the dog's mouth.

Homeopathy treats the whole dog, not just his or her symptoms—it is holistic. Repetition and frequency is the most important factor with homeopathies. If your dog shows signs of stress, is withdrawn, hides, is lethargic, or demonstrates other unusual behaviors, it's an indication that some kind of remedy should be given. After the second or third dose, you should notice a positive change. If there's no response, then it's time to try a different remedy. The great thing is there's no danger in trying a few to get the appropriate remedy. Just because the approach is subtle doesn't mean the results are. I've personally had great results by adding homeopathic remedies to my daily routine…as well as that of my dogs.

Homeopathy is based on the idea that like cures like. If something causes a symptom in a healthy dog, then giving that dog the same substance may cure the illness. The symptoms are not always easy to identify, but when we begin to notice odd behaviors in our dogs, it can be a great indication of a problem. When Shiitake was sick with lymphoma, I read many case histories of sick dogs sloughing off their cancerous external tumors and then being given them to eat. Yuck! But the theory is that by eating them, the body would respond by knowing how to heal from the illness that caused that tumor. This seems crazy, but I'll agree to go along with it. If the "medicine" isn't needed, it isn't used by the body and is simply just absorbed. Homeopathy does great work even if you don't entirely understand all the symptoms.

If you've ever done a water fast, then you understand that when the body goes without food for a period of time, it naturally cleanses the kidney, liver, and other organs. Once, I experienced a lot of pain when my kidneys and gallbladder flushed out toxins during a cleanse, but afterwards, I felt great. Some people freak out when their dogs don't eat (they're fasting!). I believe that dogs naturally understand that going without helps remove toxins. All within reason, of course. In theory, a dose of homeopathic pills or tinctures works much the same way by enhancing the body's normal healing process. Usually these remedies are made from plants. There are others, called cell salts and nosodes, which we will cover shortly.

In the U.S., homeopathic medicine is used to maintain health and treat a variety of illnesses such as allergies, rheumatoid arthritis, irritable bowel syndrome, and minor injuries such as cuts, strains, and sprains. However, homeopathy (especially nosodes) has been more popular outside the country, mainly, I think, due to the expectation of quick fix solutions in our country, thus resorting to pharmaceuticals being used far too often.

HANDY HOMEOPATHIC REMEDIES FOR DOGS

You may want to go out and purchase the most commonly used remedies to have on hand in case the need arises, you are unable to get to a vet, you are unsure whether it necessary to go immediately, or you believe the issue is treatable at home. Homeopathic remedies are small, so you can easily make up a small kit for home or travel.

Homeopathy generally treats a condition, but it can also be used as a proactive measure in some cases. What I have learned about homeopathy is that consistency is the key. Let's take us ladies for example; we have a monthly cycle we have to deal with. We can take an aspirin, and within a few minutes, have immediate results and no more cramping and pain. But if we opt to take something like Magnesia Phos, we might need to take a single dose every 20-30 minutes if we have bad cramps. It's not often you can take one and have immediate all day results. It may take several during a severe condition. Therefore, if your dog has something like foot or pad pain, you can't give one and walk away. It will likely take a bit more management… but it is a natural approach that doesn't have the same kind of side effects. You can train and teach the body not to rely on certain medicines after a few doses of a homeopathic remedy. In essence, your body learns to heal itself. It's like teaching a toddler to ride a bike. Once the body learns, it can't unlearn. Sometimes, a true cure takes time. With homeopathy, it takes time to learn and observe changes, however subtle they are. It might require keeping a journal to document progress, remedies used, and times and amounts taken. It can take up to a month for a remedy to work. And sometimes things may appear to get worse before they get better. Over time, the symptoms will lessen if you have found the correct remedy. Homeopathy can be used in first-aid situations, for acute injuries, or illness. I've highlighted a few of my favorites to have on hand below. I've used the "key words" to indicate what the remedy is best known for (for quick reference). If you do not see the key words, it generally means I didn't find more applicable situations to common dog issues.

TOP HOMEOPATHIC REMEDIES FOR YOUR DOG

Aconite (Aconitum Napellus): Used for fear, joint pain, emotional trauma, pacing frantically/anxiously/restlessly, mental anxiety, early fever states and into fever, and shock. Best used at sudden onset behavior change or start of fear, or in early stages of acute conditions like infection or inflammation, like an abscess or apprehension. Key words: sudden change or disturbance, colds and fevers.

Apis: Use for bee and other insect bites, swollen eyes, or skin eruptions. Look for hot, red, puffy, itchy, or burning skin or eyes. Generally the symptoms come on very suddenly. Key words: allergic reactions, bites, stings, swelling.

Argentum: Fear of performing or being in public places. Great for show dogs or service dogs. Also use if you have to fly your dogs. Key words: fear in public places.

Arnica: Good for general pain, soreness, trauma, stiffness due to overexertion, bruising, and musculoskeletal injuries. If your dog is in great pain and doesn't want to be touched or is restless and having a hard time getting comfortable and lying down, you'll want arnica as your go to. Use after extreme physical activity, like a run or hike. Also try Bryonia with arthritis, rheumatism, and chest pain. Key words: all physical pain/trauma, bruising/muscle soreness.

Arsenicum: Great for GI upsets or acute digestive upset. This could happen from eating spoiled food (getting into the trash perhaps). Symptoms are simultaneous vomiting and diarrhea (foul smell and watery). Symptoms are worse from midnight to 2 a.m. When your pup doesn't want to be alone, won't eat, or drinks very little water, these are also symptoms. Fidgeting when lying down. If the kidneys and liver aren't filtering toxic waste, this might also be an option. Also helps with fear caused by insecurity and restlessness. Key words: poisoning, diarrhea, parvovirus.

Belladonna: For acute or sudden onset of violent fever, redness, inflammation, anxiety or fear, or throbbing pain. Can be useful for epilepsy. Good for extremely moody or angry dogs with sudden outbursts, upset with a variety of different stimuli, or even sudden attacking or lashing out or biting. Special note: One of the first and most important discoveries in homeopathic remedies. Key words: fevers, inflammation.

Borax (the remedy, not the powder): For sensitivity to sudden noises, for example, fear of thunderstorms and fireworks. For in-growth of eyelashes (and eye sensitivities); therefore, a great remedy for entropian issues in dogs with wrinkles such as Shar Pei and Bulldogs. Key words: fear of noise, entropian.

Calcarea: There are three to mention: Calc Flour, Calc Phos, and Calc Sulph. Flour is good for pregnancy when there are mammary gland issues. Use phos for the runt of the litter and for skeletal growth problems. Use sulph for anal gland issues or other abscesses that have burst and become septic—this remedy might replace antibiotics. Key words: vessels, bone health, blood cleanser.

Calendula: Use as an oral remedy for candida and yeast overgrowth in the digestive tract and to stimulate the immune system or as an external ointment for skin infections, wounds, cuts, scrapes, rashes, insect bites, eczema, and to relieve pain and inflammation. It stimulates the growth of healthy scar tissue for open wounds. Key words: Antiseptic, tissue healing.

Cantharis: For burning urination.

Carbo Veg: For sudden collapse where pulse becomes weak or lacks oxygen. Known as the "homeopathic corpse reviver." Great for dogs that can't keep their breath during exercise (like my English Bulldog.) Also use for bloat, gas, heartburn, nausea. Key words: loss of breath, gassy dog.

Chamomilla: Remedy known to assist with teething. Also good to calm heat associated with ear infections, stings, an abscess, or sometimes even a rash or bad itch. My Shar Pei often get warm ears due to build up in the tight ear canals, so this is a good remedy. One of the safest and most versatile remedies. Good for irritation and works much like a sedative and calms nerves. Chamomile tea can also soothe upset bellies. Try a tablespoon every few hours. Also use tea for a calming topical skin cooler for allergies, bacterial, or fungal infections. Key words: teething, cools heat (on skin and in bellies).

China (Cinchona): For loss of body fluid, such as blood loss, dehydration, or diarrhea. For counter-acting dehydration, used with parvo.

Cocculus: For motion sickness or exhaustion after running away.

Colocynthis: For bloating. (Also use ornithogalum.)

Crataegus: For a cardiomyopathy or to strengthen the heart muscle. (Also use digitalis.)

Drosera: For kennel cough.

Echinacea: Use for snakebites or other poisoning of the blood or swelling of the lymphatic system. (Generally available in liquid or caps.)

Gelsemium: For emotional excitement or fear of a person (the vet) or events (dog shows). These events may cause diarrhea. Fear of thunder that may cause your dog to tremble. Key words: fear of someone or something.

Glonoinum: For heat stroke.

Graphites: Used mostly for skin issues such as oozing eruptions, eczema, hair loss, cysts, skin issues of genitals. Key words: skin eruptions.

Euphrasia: For eye injuries and issues such as infections, colds, watery discharge, abrasions, and scratches. (Can also be used as a wash.) Key words: eye problems.

Hepar Sulphur: Used to treat painful abscesses (for example, teeth) or inflammation anywhere on the body. Also useful for painful or infected anal glands. It helps bring pus and mucus to the surface, drain it, and get it resolved. Use if your dog is scratched or bit by another dog. Key words: abscess, cough, runny nose.

Hypericum (also known as St. John's Wort): For any pain due to nerve damage, injuries, or trauma. Great for when you cut your dog's toenails too short or there is damage to fingers or toes or the tail, tongue, or sex organs. Start with arnica for an injury and then go to hypericum in the next day or two to reduce pain. If it's worse when touched, exposed to air, or cold, this is your remedy. Use Bryonia when symptoms worsen with movement. Key words: nervous system.

Combine 30c with Ledum 30c every ten minutes after a snake bite. Alternate Cedron 6x between. Taking echinacea herb every 20-30 minutes is said to "denature" the venom, fight infection, and bring the swelling down. Apply MSM topically for swelling. Lachesis Mutus 30c and Crotalus Horridus 30c are made from snake venom and may also work. Keywords: nerve damage, snake bite.

Ignatia: for loss or grief.

Ipecac: For persistent vomiting and nausea, violent cough, chest full of mucus, blood in the milk, bloody diarrhea, or blood in the stool. Key words: queasiness and vomiting

Ledum: Use for any type of puncture or stab wound that doesn't bleed (thorns, nails, teeth, claws, barbed wire, etc.), stings, animal bites. Use for pressure sores like bedsores. New research is finding it to be a treatment for Lyme disease (also try borrelia). Insect bites that are hot and red may be better served with apis. Said to work like tetanus. Combine with hypericum for snake bites. Key words: bites, stings, puncture wounds.

Mercurius: For abscesses, ulcers, swollen glands, and bodily discharges that are foul-smelling, thick, and greenish-yellow. Key words: ooey gooey.

Myristica: Remedy for abscesses, anal sac infections, and chronic anal sac problems. It is also good for ear infections. It's said to do the work of a knife and help drain the abscess. Key word: infections.

Nux Vomica: For sensitive bellies after a food change or a toxic food like chocolate or onions are eaten. If your pup is irritable, has diarrhea, small hard stools covered with mucus, colic, has over-eaten, is unable to pass a stool, or has belly-gurgling, nux vomica may help. Do not use if you already used arsenicum. Key word: indigestion.

Phosporus: For vomiting, bleeding, couching, anemia, bronchitis, pneumonia, and other bronchial and lung conditions. If your dog is scared by loud noises like thunderstorms and fireworks, this is a good remedy to try. Use at the first sign of blood in the stool or vomiting if you suspect parvo. Key word: oversensitive.

Psorinum: For skin problems such as intolerable itching and eczema behind ears. Ear discharge (bloody or smelly). Also for relapsing or sudden onset fever. Key words: skin issues.

Pulsatilla: For separation anxiety. If your pup is very attached to you and suffers from separation anxiety (throws a doggy tantrum) or likes to be the center of attention, this is your remedy. Also for yellow, pussy, or creamy discharge (also try scutellaria). Key words: timid, emotional.

Rhus tox (also known as poison ivy or the 'Rusty Gate Remedy'): For joint inflammation, joint pain, arthritis that's better after moving around, general musculoskeletal injuries, red swollen eyes, skin infections, and skin itching. Dogs needing this remedy have a hard time getting up after lying down and have a hard time getting comfortable when lying down. Also, dogs seem to be immune to poison ivy, but skin conditions that look like it could be poison ivy (swelling or blisters) can also be treated with this remedy. Key word: arthritis.

Ruta: For any sudden onset injury to tendons, bones, or ligaments with indication of pain. Use it immediately after any injury. Ruta is much like arnica, but your pup won't be as sensitive to touch. Sometimes a loud pop or snap can be heard prior to injury. Ruta is the go to for arthritic conditions, broken bones, sprains and strains, injuries to the brain and spinal cord, and also for post-partum pains. It is said to be a good follow-up after arnica. Combine with rhus tox and arnica for extra pain relief. Key words: sprains, strains.

Silicea/Silica: For skin problems and wounds that are slow to heal. This remedy is known to push foreign bodies like splinters, thorns, grass seeds, or foxtails out of the skin. It can also be great for tooth abscesses. Silica is a good remedy for many things, such as for illnesses that linger, help healing corneal ulcers, possibly helping to fend off cataracts, treating constipation, helping impacted anal glands, and diminishing negative effects of vaccinations. Called the "homeopathic surgical knife." Not to be given alongside of mercurius. Key word: skin disorders.

Staphisagria: All post-surgical problems regardless of how long ago they were. Also use on female if male is attracted post-spay. Give for any problem related to resentment or grief, such as when introducing a new pup into the home, being kenneled too long, and separation anxiety. Key word: resentment.

Sulphur: For skin issues that don't heal or for dogs that aren't good at grooming (the lazy dog). The skin is usually dry, flaky, covered in eruptions, and the dog has a dull, dry rough coat. Bathing generally makes the skin worse. The eyes and gums tend to be red and your pup may scoot on the floor or lick at his or her rear end for relief from itch. Do not use if previously used calcaria. Key word: skin disorders.

Thuja: For ill effects of vaccination.

I have purchased a few remedy cases to keep my top remedies on hand for particular activities. One of my favorite places to order books and catalogs to learn more is from a company out of Germany http://www.narayana-verlag.com. I have a few cases and have organized my remedies for common issues I have with my pups, such as foot pad injuries from all the hiking we do, for Shar Pei fever, and for dehydration or lack of oxygen for my Bulldog when she runs out of steam during exercise, etc. Take some time and answer a few questions about the common activities you and your pups participate in and use the list above as a starting point to create your remedy pack to keep on hand or take with you if you are active with your pup.

BUILDING YOUR PUPS REMEDY PACK(S)

Activity	Remedy
Do you do heavy exercise with your pup where your pup might run out of oxygen?	Carbo veg
Do you live in a warm climate where your pup might become dehydrated?	Cinchona or Glonoinum
Do you travel with your pup?	Cocculus
Do you do shows with your pup?	Argentum
Is your dog prone to other dog bites?	Hepar sulph
Are there many bees in your area?	Apis

Do you live in a high risk snake bite area?	Hypericum, Ledum, Cedron
Does your dog exercise more than usual and may have sore muscles?	Arnica
Come up with your own questions and answers based on where you live and your dogs lifestyle....	

*"Through the like, disease is produced,
and through the like it is cured."*

— Hippocrates

BASICS OF HOMEOPATHY

The Law of Similars

Allopathic drugs are great at suppressing symptoms, but they do not necessarily cure the disease or issue presenting itself. Homeopathy talks about something called The Law of Similars. This means that the remedy that causes certain symptoms in a healthy person will cure the same symptoms in a sick person. The law originated in Greece with Hippocrates.

Vital Force

The idea of homeopathy is to address the "living presence," so the physical, emotional, and mental aspects of a person's well-being would be addressed. Vital force is the level of inner strength and vitality a patient has. Homeopathy looks at what disturbs the life force and uses a remedy that is harmony to restore balance. It is believed that in the case of great shock, the nervous system would be overwhelmed and the vital force would be withheld from vital organs. There are certain remedies that can restore the system after shock and others that can restore the circulation of the vital force in the body. There is a fine balance in the dosages required to shock or stimulate the body so that the body is not weakened or does not become dependent upon it.

Minimum Dose

Another main principle in homeopathic medicine is the Minimum Dose principle. This means taking the original remedy (the mother tincture) and diluting it down so much that the original substances' individual molecules are extremely difficult to detect in samples. The less substance the remedy contains, the more powerful it becomes, or the higher the potency it is.

Not all homeopaths agree on dosage and potency, or techniques of measurement, but some say that chronic illnesses that have been around a long time need lower dosages (6x or 6c), while acute conditions that are relatively new are treated with higher dosages (30x-200c). In general, sensitive patients should be given lower potencies. If you are not sure about potency, I might suggest 6x before a higher potency. This is the one you'll generally find in your local health stores anyhow. If symptoms improve, but not completely, perhaps try a 30c potency.

For a homeopath, a dose is the number of times a remedy is taken, not the number of pellets or squirts. The higher the number, the higher the strength. Again, it's best to start low until you understand your dog's response.

So, what are the xs and cs on the labels? They basically mean dilution ratios of the mother tincture...and the different techniques used. Hang in there; this gets a little confusing! Again, if you are confused, just stick with buying the 6x or 6c for now.

XX = The substance is diluted in a ratio of 1:10. The potency is one part mother tincture to ten parts dilutant (water or alcohol, for example).

K = Refers to a method known as Korsakovian. It means that the substance is diluted in a ratio of 1:99. The potency is one part mother tincture to ten parts dilutant.

C = The substance is diluted in a ratio of 1:1000. (Generally used for seasonal and chronic issues.)

CK = A reproducible processes of using 1 percent of one Korsakovian dilution successed[7] with 99 percent ultra-purified water as a solvent. (200CK means that the substance has been diluted 200 times at the rate of 1:100.)

M = M is the Roman numeral for 1,000; therefore, it means the cycle of dilution and sucussion has occurred 1,000 times.

= The number preceding the letter indicates the number of times the substance has been both diluted and successed.

Note: What can be very confusing about this process is that the more the substance is diluted, the stronger, or more potent it becomes. I've understood this process should be compared to an informational field rather than a chemical or material factor for better comprehension. My head still spins in circles thinking about it, though, so I just know that the higher the number, the higher the potency, and I just generally stick to basic "XX" or "C" labels. It's probably best to work with a homeopath if you want to use higher concentrations.

Once tinctures are prepared, the remedy can stay liquid or be placed into little white pellets that are generally made of milk sugar. I'm not a real fan of the milk because I'm vegan, but there are vegan substitutes for the pellets; they are just harder to find. The pellets seem to be the easiest to find in most natural health food stores.

7 Successed is the homeopathic word for agitated.

I prefer to use pellets for dogs because they are far less invasive. Just slip a little pellet in an open mouth and *voila!* Your dogs aren't too bothered; in fact, they actually seem to like them. Many times, you will find that two or three pellets taken at one time is a standard dose, but how many times that dose is given is based on the condition. For general dosing, you might give them to your pups once or twice per day. For chronic issues, three pellets might be given three times per day. For severe or sudden symptoms, you might give as many as three pellets every fifteen minutes until three or four doses are taken, and then three pellets, three times a day until the symptoms lessen, and you gradually decrease until your dog can go off the pellets entirely.

Most homeopathic practitioners will use one remedy at a time, so as not to confuse the body or produce unpredictable results.

OUTCOMES OF TREATMENT

There are three outcomes of any homeopathic treatment: suppression, palliation, and cure.

Suppression: Rids the body of specific symptoms, but the disease might still exist somewhere else. This is comparable to plugging a dam with something not strong enough to hold the water back. Eventually, the water will creep in or the dam will explode.

Palliation: Repeated dosing so the symptoms don't come back. The pup is not getting healthier or might be getting sicker, so something else needs to be tried.

Cure: The ultimate goal of homeopathy is to eliminate disease, not just symptoms, in order to reach optimal health. The goal is to make symptoms go away and stay away. A true cure.

DISEASE PATTERNS

Energetic Imbalance: When you know something is wrong but you may not be entirely sure what it is. When my Shiitake contracted cancer, her eyes became deeply set, her nose was runny, and her muzzle girth shrank in size.

Functional Changes: There is a behavioral change that isn't entirely a problem yet, but your dog started doing something differently than normal. A vet will not likely pick something up yet at this stage, but you notice a difference. My Shiitake started acting up more aggressively. Aggressiveness is a tell-tale sign that something is wrong. So is sleeping too much.

Inflammation: The body is trying to rebalance itself, and fever or other issues may present themselves. Your pup is sick and it can be seen or diagnosed. My Shiitake started presenting a runny nose, but no other issues. Shortly, thereafter, her lymph glands became swollen.

Pathology: The body is trying to work with the problem. Once this stage is reached, a cure is harder to find. Healing must work backwards through each of the previous stages. Finding the right remedy is critical.

A FEW EXAMPLES OF HOMEOPATHIC TREATMENT

Smelly Skin and Ears

One of the best homeopathic solutions I have found for ears is colloidal silver drops applied daily, or several times daily, until the problem discontinues. It is a natural antifungal, anti-virus, and antibacterial solution.

For the skin, many of the following homeopathic remedies may be right for you and your dog: antimonium (skin lesions), arsen alb (dry skin), cacillinum (nosode for lesions), hepar sulp (lesion with pus), mezereum (rash or eczema), psorinum (nosode for eczema), rhus tox (red rash), sulphur (red itchy skin), tellurium (circular red marks on skin).

Treating a Foot Injury

A common problem with many dogs is foot, toe, or pad injuries. I recently was dealing with an injury with my dog Blue. He is an avid hiker, a real athlete, yet he was grounded in a time out for several days after an unknown foot injury. After our hike, he was limping, but I didn't know what he had done to cause it. I immediately wrapped his foot in cotton batting and covered the pad in arnica gel. After some time, he seemed to get better, but after a short amount of exercise, he got worse. I soaked his foot in a rubber balloon footie filled with warm water and Epsom salt. Again, he appeared to get better, but then when he exercised again, he refused to put too much weight on it. I thought I might have to take him to the vet, but then I realized that I just needed to keep him off of it. The vet was likely only going to shoot him full of x-rays and prescribe prescription pain meds and a foot wrap...then give me a giant bill. There really wasn't much that could be done for a broken or sprained toe if I took him in. Even in humans, there really isn't much that can be done. Therefore, I ordered him a splint called "Walkin' Pet Splint" off Amazon and decided to treat him with arnica for pain, silica in case something was lodged in there, ruta for the tendons and ligaments, hypericum for possible nerve damage, hepar sulphur, and intermittent belladonna in the beginning when there was more pain. I never did get the splint on him, and I ended up returning it, but it sure was a nice one, so I thought I'd mention it. He is doing much better with just a bit of relaxation and a bunch of homeopathic remedies, and I just saved myself hundreds of dollars. The key with a pad injury is to keep your dog off the pad and keep him or her still. The key to treating with homeopathic remedies is consistency. For an injury, it's necessary to dose remedies three times a day or more. Oh, and by the way, it turned out it was a toenail issue, and when treating for possible nerve damage, I was likely addressing the pain. The toenail fell off and I treated with colloidal silver, apple cider vinegar, and potassium—a great combination for strengthening and repairing toenails.

SHAR PEI FEVER[8]

Thanks to the work and research done by Jeanette Ward-Taber, I have found the following to be lifesavers when it comes to a Shar Pei fever outbreak:

- Aconite 30c: for fever

8 Shar Pei fever is a condition found only in Shar Pei dogs. It is unique to the breed. Although, any dog struggling with a fever could benefit from your learning how to manage it.

- Arnica gel or oil: for swollen hocks
- Arnica Montana 30c: for inflammation
- Belladonna 30c: for fever
- Rhus Tox 30c: for pain

Once a fever is gone, continue to treat for two or three days to avoid a rebound of a fever episode.

With belladonna and aconite, one might work better than the other for your particular dog, so it's good to keep both in a Fever Kit.

Other items for your Fever Kit include:

- Baby aspirin
- Pedialyte or coconut water for dehydration
- Rectal thermometer
- Vaseline (for easy insertion of thermometer)

You can find Jeanette Ward-Taber's Facebook group at www.facebook.com/groups/SharPeiHealthEducation. I honor her and all the administrators for the amazing work they do for so many people who are dealing with Shar Pei-specific issues.

TO IMMUNIZE OR NOT TO IMMUNIZE

Homeopathy and other natural options have shown up in my life as a result of the trauma I experienced with Shiitake's death and the introduction of my three new pups. I knew that Shiitake became ill from the two rounds of rabies shots she had to come to Hawaii, so I knew things were going to change if I ever got another dog. I knew those changes would include diet, the addition of herbs and homeopathy, and my newly-acquired belief and practices regarding immunizations.

I can't tell you how many nights' sleep I lost in the beginning when I got my three new pups after Shiitake's death. I was like a mother with a new baby. I prayed and cried myself to sleep for months. I was so worried about what other options and methods of care were available instead of choosing immunizations. I didn't want to be a victim of "I told you so," and I didn't want to poison my sweet babies. I did lots of research, and I relied a lot on my faith in the beginning of the learning process. I just kept talking to God, saying, "Keep these babies safe. I know you created perfect angels, and I don't want to alter that perfection. Teach me how to release my anxiety and care for them naturally." The funny thing was that God just kept saying back to me, "This is not about them; this is really about you. Animals are innately designed to survive." I just needed to learn to come to peace with my beliefs and God's wisdom.

I LEARNED THAT ANYTHING THAT IS PUSHED WITH FEAR TACTICS IS NOT TRULY ALIGNED WITH OUR BEST INTERESTS. NO ONE SHOULD MAKE DECISIONS FOR YOU AND YOUR PUP.

I was frantically looking for answers on the immunization debate when Leilani, our English Bulldog, came into our home. By then, Shiitake had passed and Sushi was elderly and preparing to pass any day. I was worried about Leilani living healthily and Sushi dying comfortably. Also, I was still mourning Shiitake's loss. You didn't want to know me during that time in my life. Family and friends had to deal with a lot. I was so exhausted that I could barely stand. I cried about everything without many triggers.

Learn the basics of homeopathy, and don't let vets scare you about illness. I learned that anything that is pushed with fear tactics is not truly aligned with our best interests. Ask yourself: "Is this fear or is this love?" Then do your homework and listen to your intuition. No one should make decisions for you and your pup. Homeopathy is based on the vital force. As you begin to understand it, it will have you asking, "How can I build health further? Does doing this build the vital force?" Once you come into alignment with these practices, you will begin to see that by asking about the vital force, you will inherently begin to ask, "Does this make my pup more toxic?" and choose differently.

NOSODES

I'm not sure how I came across the subject of nosodes, but before I knew it, I was researching everything about the concept, and quickly, because it was almost time for Leilani to go to the vet's office for her next round of immunizations (after the initial ones given by her breeder), and Bella was moving in.

I had phone consultations with every natural veterinarian I could find (they were not plentiful or easy to find), and was amazed by their answers. Surprisingly, many suggested I not go the route of no immunizations at all, which is what I was leaning toward. Many told me that since we live in Hawaii, I'd be subjecting the pups to higher amounts of leptospirosis and parvovirus than found on the mainland. I'll talk about what both of those viruses are later on, but I was told they were very prevalent in Hawaii and possibly even deadly. At the very least, they said, I should consider inoculation against those two diseases. And, distemper...who doesn't do distemper vaccines?

I was confused when the natural and homeopathic doctors I talked to didn't have a different suggestion or protocol for me to follow. I realized that my idea of going completely natural and not doing immunizations was rather "New Age" thinking, but was it dangerous?

I asked about nosodes, but the concept seemed a bit foreign—even to the natural docs. And, of course, local clinics had never heard of nosodes. I felt as though I was making a poor decision to try something different. Then I realized that the power that created these beautiful little souls created them perfectly just as they were. If I chose to alter them in any way, then I was denying that perfection. I took a deep breath and decided to move forward, with extreme faith. I was going to try the nosodes and research any and everything about parvo and lepto on the islands to learn why they were more dangerous. I found some amazing information. Before I get too far ahead of myself, let me explain what nosodes are.

Nosodes Explained

Nosodes are relatively unknown in today's modern veterinary practice, yet they've actually been used in homeopathic medicine since the mid-1800s. Many growing case studies show their efficacy too, yet they are considered rather controversial solutions as a replacement for traditional pharmaceutical vaccinations. One of the main reasons they've not been accepted in the medical community is because they don't produce specific, measurable antibodies that show up in titer testing. Titer testing is a test to measure your dog's antibody levels to determine whether he or she is immune to a particular disease. It is believed that a homeopathic remedy acts on a deeper level than that of antibodies, so the only way to measure the effectiveness is with clinical results…or to wait for a good health report, I suppose.

Nosodes are prepared remedies that use actual diseased matter (a pathological specimen) from a sick animal. The material is diluted by using traditional homeopathic protocols and methods until virtually no molecules of the original substance remains—rendering it safe for use and creating something called a "mother tincture." This process is called potentization. The specimen could be blood, pus, any other body secretion like saliva, or even a diseased fragment of tissue, such as a growth or tumor. The rabies nosode, for example, starts with the saliva of a rabid dog. It is then "potentized." The final product, or nosode, becomes a remedy that is an energetic blueprint of the actual disease.

Nosodes are safe and can be given to pregnant females. What's amazing about nosodes is that they can provide immunity to momma's litter before the puppies are even born. Otherwise, you'd have to wait several weeks after their birth and use vaccines with their numerous side-effects and dangers. By contrast, a homeopathic nosode contains no dangerous chemicals or additives.

A nosode's purpose is to "immunize" the body against a specific disease at the point the body shows signs of weakness. The major difference between a nosode and an "orthodox" vaccine is extremely small (if any). The major difference most of us will immediately see is that a nosode is not injected, but taken orally or applied topically. It works its way through the body in a more natural way…through the skin mostly. It's kind of like magic really, as the "energy" pattern, not the "substance" does the job in a homeopathic remedy.

Nosodes can be used in two ways: 1) to protect against disease (called homeoprophylaxis), or 2) as a remedy for illness. Most research or studies seem to discuss homeoprophylaxis methods. Nosodes produce an immune response that is similar to the actual exposure to the disease. The body recognizes the imprint from the disease through the cellular structure. The most successful uses of nosodes happen when no pharmaceutical immunizations are given prior.

With an injected immunization, a modified or live virus is injected into your dog, which sensitizes the immune system to that particular virus, thus potentially protecting the dog from the fatal infection. The idea is that as your dog is exposed to the disease, his or her body will quickly respond and produce antibodies to overcome any infection. The idea seems okay on the surface, and much like the concept of the nosode, actually. But the immune system is stimulated in an unnatural way, which can confuse it. For example, whatever is in the vaccination then might cause an unnatural allergy to itself... causing a fight against itself inside your dog's body. I think of it as being like a kind of war going on with no end in sight. At what point does it exhaust your dog? However, as with any medical procedure, we should ask, "Is it safe? Is it effective? Do the benefits outweigh the risks?" And with puppies, should vaccines be given when their mother's immunity is still present? I will discuss this in a bit.

A NOSODE'S PURPOSE IS TO "IMMUNIZE" THE BODY AGAINST A SPECIFIC DISEASE AT THE POINT THE BODY SHOWS SIGNS OF WEAKNESS.

There are some limitations to the use of nosodes. Most states require rabies vaccinations for dogs, and the rabies nosode, called Lyssin, will not satisfy that legal requirement. However, I have learned that all vaccines, including rabies, are legally and medically approved for use in healthy animals only! So if your dog is showing any signs of acute or chronic disease, he or she is exempt from that requirement and should not be vaccinated. What is considered acute or chronic? Does this mean that we have an out from the law? I know that my Shiitake died from her rabies shots and it's too late for her, but I don't know how I would have gotten her into Hawaii without them. But I wonder…can I claim that Bella has an autoimmune deficiency that would likely cause her to have an unfavorable reaction? What about Blue? He has an acute bad toe. Leilani has chronic runny eyes. How can this be monitored? Do they have to have cancer already? Who stands up for my dogs when the government is behind the laws created in the first place? I'm wondering about animal rights here and the idea that they are entitled to live lives free from chemical vaccines with the constitution God gave them! Do we have to make up stories or find educated veterinarians willing to put their license on the line for the sake of our dogs' health and well-being? Note: There is a form in the back of this book that you can use with your local government to see whether you can avoid required immunizations for your dogs. I talk in a bit more detail about this in the next chapter.

My vet told me that my Bella was not strong enough for any immunizations, and to wait until she was healthy again to administer them. That led me to discovering other alternatives while I waited. I think her health issues became a godsend so I could go on a mad search for options that led me to researching and learning all I have.

Today, the safety and efficacy of vaccines are being questioned, and pet owners (and others) are seeking alternatives to keep their pets healthy while preventing disease. There is an alarming increase in conditions such as cancer, allergy, kidney and liver dysfunction, and other health issues. Nosodes are friendly for all users because they work their way in through the skin or the mucus membranes and don't taste or smell bad. The immune response to nosodes is a more natural response to disease that doesn't weaken the immune system. Nosodes are working with a degree of efficacy so they warrant further data collection, study, and research.

Human Nosode Research

In the early 2000s, a homeopath from Australia (Dr. Isaac Golden, author of two books, *Vaccination and Homeoprophylaxis: A Review of Risks and Alternatives*, and *Homoeprophylaxis: A Ten Year Clinical Study*, did extensive clinical research on homeopathic childhood immunizations. His research is often cited because so few studies have been done, likely due to the lack of funding or common knowledge on the subject. He concluded that homeopathic immunizations were 90.4 percent effective and that children who received standard vaccines were fifteen times more likely to get asthma, seven times more likely to get eczema, and two times more likely to get allergies than those who were using homeopathic solutions.

Similar studies have been conducted in Cuba and Brazil using homeopathic immunizations during disease outbreaks. In 1997, a large-scale leptospirosis outbreak happened in Cuba. Homeoprophylaxis was used and given to over two million people in high-risk areas with great success. The incidence of leptospirosis fell and homeoprophylaxis was successful in controlling the epidemic. Earlier, in 1974, Brazil used homeopathic immunizations during an outbreak of meningococcal disease. Of the 18,640 children given homeopathic remedies, only four cases of meningococcal infection occurred—resulting in a 95 percent effectiveness rate for the homeopathically-immunized children.

These types of studies provide a good reference point upon which veterinary studies can base their understanding. Success stories are emerging that support the use of nosodes as a worthwhile alternative for veterinary immunizations as well. Yet many veterinarians still practice old school ways of thinking and give vaccines without fully understanding what they are injecting and the lifelong dangers they are inflicting on their patients. Others believe in their efficacy, and some are now open to new possibilities or a combination of natural or homeopathic options and orthodox pharmaceutical ways.

Of course, it goes without saying that any animal that is properly cared for and fed a nutritionally-balanced diet will have a heightened resistance to disease. With fewer toxins in their bodies and a diet that enhances and fortifies their immune systems, I believe our dogs can live longer and healthier lives than ever before.

When I set out to write this book, I was still a bit naive about the specific side-effects and dangers of vaccines. As I started to piece things together, my mind could no longer comprehend the benefit of them, but I generally don't like to form an opinion on any subject until I've done more research. So that's just what I did. I went into my research a bit skeptical about vaccinations since I just lost my Shiitake from her multiple rabies vacs, but I tried to hold an open mind as I plugged forward in my self-study. I suppose I approached this much like many who have wondered about the subject. I was unaware and uninvolved until I was forced to be by an unfortunate experience. Once I started to question things, it seemed as if all kinds of information came flooding into my awareness. Before I knew it, I had a much larger amount of applicable research for this book than I ever originally intended.

“There are three faithful friends – an old wife,
an old dog and ready money.”

— Ben Franklin.

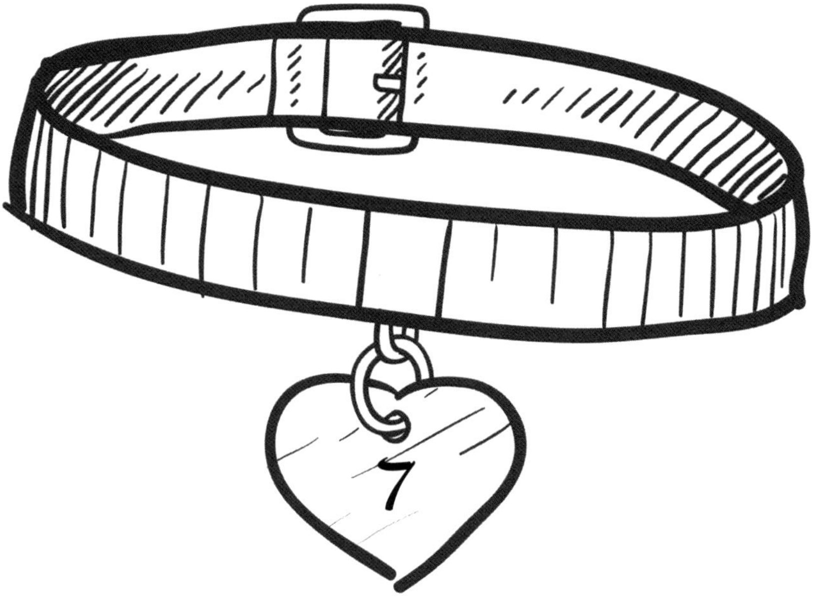

Vaccinations

"To err is human, to forgive, canine."

— Author Unknown

In 2018, the animal vaccine market is predicted to be worth $8.6 billion.[9] In 1908, the first county health departments were formed. Shortly thereafter (1914), the first human rabies vaccine was licensed in the U.S. In 1962, President John F. Kennedy signed the Vaccination Assistance Act into law. It allowed the CDC to support mass immunization campaigns and to initiate maintenance programs.

---

9 According to (www.vaccinenation.org)

It's hard to pinpoint when exactly the animal vaccines all began. I found some cases dating back to the late 1800s, or when The United States Department of Agriculture and the drug companies joined forces and put the recommendations for annual vaccination into action. But, there has been little argument over it since then, likely due to the financially-sound residual income it produces for the veterinary and drug industry as well as, in some cases, local government municipalities that make some vaccines law in our communities. Not to mention that we have been programmed to believe in their efficacy (just as we have been programmed to believe dogs should eat kibble, despite the fact that it may not contain meat or any other beneficial ingredients). In fact, the USDA puts the annual vaccination recommendations right on the product label, enforcing the several-decade-old belief that your dog needs to be vaccinated every year. There is no motivation for any of this to change because no one is providing any substantial evidence or sound studies indicating that vaccinations cause animals any harm.

With vaccines, the earning potential is large. It would cost a lot of money to go up against Big Pharma, and big profits would keep many from listening even if someone did. Who would be the one to go up against them? Many veterinarians make a living giving them. Vaccines are a large percentage of the average veterinary practice's income and create a kind of economic dependence.

Let's just say that a single rabies vaccine costs the vet about sixty cents per unit because a large veterinary clinic has purchased them in bulk. You are charged between $15 and $40, plus a standard $35 office visit. Did you figure out that percentage of markup? The markup is astronomical! According to one estimate[10] I found, "eliminating the one-year rabies vaccination and the accompanying office visit for dogs alone would decrease the average small vet's income from $87,000 to $25,000, and this doesn't include cats or other vaccinations. According to James Schwartz, author of *Trust Me, I'm Not a Veterinarian*, "63 percent of canine, and 70 percent of feline, vet office visits are just for vaccinations."

10 "Pet Vaccinations—Dr. Becker's Bites." Retrieved from http://www.drbeckers-bites.com/pet-vaccinations

If profits aren't enough, there's big money in making your dogs sick! With adverse reactions and other medical issues caused by the vaccines, vets aren't the only ones cashing in.

> *"There is little scientific documentation that backs up label claims for annual administration of most vaccines."*
>
> *— Journal of the American Veterinary Medical Association (1995)*

So vaccines make big money for those involved, but do they work? And what's in them anyway? When I did some research, what I began to find was shocking. To begin with, there are many heavy metals in vaccines! What? Vaccines are known to contain mercury, aluminum, and formaldehyde (to name a few). My first question was, "Why are these used and what side effects do they have?" Isn't mercury known to be very dangerous? And wouldn't I basically "pickle" myself or my dog if I put formaldehyde inside either of our bodies? Aren't researchers now finding links between aluminum and dementia and a host of other problems? Everywhere I looked I found that the overall side effects vary, but some common issues with vaccines can affect the brain, nervous system, intestinal tract, kidney, liver, lymph glands, and bone marrow. They have been known to cause debilitating nerve disorders, dementia, seizures, and hyperactivity, as well. When do these issues show up and how will I know if I vaccinate whether there is an issue? From what I could tell, it's not always obvious that vaccines are directly related to these issues because sometimes they take time to show up. The toxicity may not be apparent for many years; it could be subtle, or it could build with boosters. It seemed as if no one has done the research, but people are simply noticing changes in their dogs' health or behavior after the vaccine. I think the situation works much the same in our human children. As a parent or pet parent, we just know something isn't right, but we can't, with our limited knowledge, prove the relation to inoculation…we just know it.

But if vaccines contain all these bad things, what do they have in them to help my dog? I understood that the aluminum and mercury and formaldehyde had something to do with preserving the virus.

And that is fine in a chemistry lab until those things are also injected into my healthy dog. I started doing some reading and found that many vaccines for dogs are grown in labs and on hamsters and monkeys in particular…oh, and sometimes dead puppies. Monkey kidneys, chick embryos, dog brains and kidneys, and cat brains and kidneys are all commonly used as well. When we think of doing something healthy for our dog, we often don't realize that the virus needs to grow on some other being's tissue before it is injected into our innocent pups. And here's the catch. Sometimes those other beings are not healthy and contain a virus that can permanently alter the genes of the patient receiving the vaccine. Once I learned that, I really questioned the efficacy of the biological matter being injected through these vaccines. And what about the strain? Is it a strain from the area where we actually live? And the number of vaccines given? And the age in which they are given? And is there really a threat these days of the virus creating a practical need for concern? I was gathering so many more questions than answers with the research I was doing. Let's begin to walk through this a little at a time. It's a huge subject and there are many directions in which we could go. We believe we have to follow a schedule of immunizations immediately after a new puppy joins our family, so let's start there.

IMMUNIZATION SCHEDULE

Have you ever asked your vet, or yourself for that matter, what you are immunizing for and whether it's necessary in this day and age? And is there a healthier way to vaccinate? Maybe by limiting the vaccinations that aren't necessary? I took a look deeper into what some of the more conservative vets were suggesting to see whether I could understand the thinking behind the continuing efforts of veterinary vaccines despite their dangers.

Let's take a closer look at a typical immunization schedule, keeping in mind that studies are now showing that the mother's antibodies are present 12-26 weeks of age. In other words, it is not likely immunizations are needed or will work, but it is likely you are simply injecting poison that would degrade the immune system any time prior.

Vaccines are generally classified as either core vaccines or non-core vaccines. Examples of core or required vaccines are canine adenovirus, canine distemper, canine hepatitis, and parvovirus. Examples of non-core vaccines are bordatella, canine coronavirus, canine parainfluenza, giardia vaccine, Lyme disease, and rattlesnake vaccine.

TYPICAL IMMUNIZATION SCHEDULE

	6-8 wks.	10-12 wks.	14-16 wks.	Annually
Adenovirus	x	x	x	x
Bordetella	x	x	x	x
Coronavirus	x	x	x	x
Distemper	x	x	x	x
Leptospirosis		x	x	x
Lyme Disease		x	x	x
Parainfluenza	x	x	x	x
Parvovirus	x	x	x	x
Rabies			16 wks.	12-36 mths

If a combination vaccine (often called a 5-way or 7-way vaccine) is offered, it is a sure sign your vet doesn't understand vaccines and their dangers. I might just run out of that vet's office as soon as it was suggested and find a new vet. I say it is dangerous because, if there is a problem, what part of the vaccine caused it?

CAV-2 vaccine (Adenovirus) has been shown to create issues in puppies for ten days after vaccination.[11] FYI: There have been zero cases of Canine Infectious Hepatitis in North America in at least twelve years. If your breeder tries to do vaccines before you get your pup, this one might be done. You might suggest they are not the breeder for you if they insist upon it.

11 Phillips et al. "Effects of Vaccines on the Canine Immune System." Canadian Journal of Veterinary Research. *1989. Apr; 53(2): 154–160.*

DR. JEAN DODD'S IMMUNIZATION SCHEDULE

	9 wks.	12 wks.	16-20 wks.	Annually
Adenovirus				
~~Bordetella~~				
~~Coronavirus~~				
Distemper	x	x	x	x
~~Leptospirosis~~				
~~Lyme Disease~~				
~~Parainfluenza~~				
Parvovirus	x	x	x	x
~~Rabies~~				24+ wks

Dr. W. Jean Dodds, suggests that recommendations for annual vaccines are just that—recommendations—and they are not based on any scientific evidence.

Dr. Jean Dodds suggests that each of the above vaccines gives 7.5 to 15 years of immunity, if not lifelong. She is considered by many to be conservative in her approach to vaccines.

New vaccine models are showing that excessive and frequent vaccination of our dogs can be risky. One reference I found stated that all twenty-seven veterinary schools in North America have changed their protocols for vaccinating dogs and cats, yet many vets in practice are either reluctant to listen or too busy to know the protocols have changed. Needlessly vaccinating dogs compromises their immune systems and makes them more subject to disease and chronic health problems.

Purdue Veterinary School did a study of 1.5 million dogs (published in the 2005 *AVMA Journal*, and widely cited) that said a significant increase in adverse reactions occurs when multiple vaccines are given in one visit. It is believed that immune disorders, thyroid problems, allergies, and skin conditions are the top problems linked to vaccines.

"Vaccinations are not always effective, and they may cause long-lasting health disturbances."

— Robert Pitcairn, D.V.M., PhD

My personal research has shown me that we are immunizing too young, when the mother's antibodies are still in place, therefore, making the immunization null and void, but still presenting dangers to our sweet baby puppies.

IF YOU HAVE TO GIVE VACCINES

Dr. Charles Loops, D.V.M., is a veterinary homeopath who does not recommend routine vaccination for dogs (except for rabies vaccination for healthy dogs...for legal purposes). He suggests the following recommendations if you decide that you must vaccinate your pet:

- **Do Not Vaccinate under Three Months of Age:** It is stressful on the underdeveloped immune system.
- **If You Do Vaccinate:** Give one distemper/parvo vaccine spaced two to four weeks from each other. Give rabies after six months. Do not give Lyme, Coronavirus, and Bortatella.
- **Boosters Are Not Required:** Lifetime protection after one vaccine is likely.
- **Homeopathic Nosodes:** Use when at risk before three months of age.
- **Do Not Vaccinate.**

Following is a list I have compiled based on suggestions I have read from a variety of homeopaths over the years:

- **Never Vaccinate a Sick Dog:** Never vaccinate an animal with health problems, at the time of surgery, or during times of high stress.
- **Avoid Combo Vaccines:** Vaccinate for one disease at a time—

avoid combination vaccines. For dogs, give parvo separately from distemper.

- **Do Not Vaccinate:** Do not vaccinate for leptospirosis, hepatitis, or parainfluenza.
- **Rabies Vaccine Goes Alone:** Never give the rabies vaccine at the same time as any other vaccine.
- **If You Have to Give Rabies:** Rabies vaccinations are sometimes dictated by state laws. Lyssin, the homeopathic nosode, should be given within a few hours after the vaccination. The rabies vaccination is effective for many years more than when state laws require booster vaccinations.
- **Avoid Live Virus Vaccines:** Avoid modified live virus vaccines. Get killed virus vaccines, especially for rabies and canine parvovirus. (Note: The canine distemper/hepatitis vaccine is not available in a killed virus form.)
- **Do Not Vaccinate Yearly:** Vaccinate middle-aged or older dogs every two to three years, instead of yearly.
- **After Vaccination:** Give dose of homeopathic thuja 30c remedy immediately after vaccination. One week later, give a dose of homeopathic sulfur 6x daily for a week. Thuja and silica can be used before and after vaccination to protect your pup from possible vaccine damage.
- **Booster Vaccinations:** Are unnecessary and can cause setbacks if your pup is being treated for other chronic problems. These vaccinations are effective for many years if not possibly for life. Nosodes can be given if you are concerned your pup is at risk.
- **Do Not Vaccinate at All.**
- **Choose a Healthy Lifestyle:** Eat a diet of fresh foods, exercise, and avoid antibiotics and other allopathic medicine unless you need to use them for a life-threatening situation. Work toward enhancing your health. Ask yourself whether what you are doing is enhancing the life force of your pup.

WHO'S ACCOUNTABLE?

Although drug companies are responsible for vaccine safety, they are not held accountable for the vaccines' effects. Many studies are beginning to show that people and dogs still contract disease, regardless of getting their inoculations. Additionally, I repeatedly see reports claiming that vaccines cause more and more autoimmune disorders in an increasingly large number of dogs. In fact, many young puppies still hold maternal antibodies that can block the vaccine from working. Some maternal antibodies can even last as long as twenty-six weeks, according to some reports I have read. I've even had some vets tell me that the first vaccine "primes" the immune system and the second one creates the immunity. That just sounds absurd to me! But it only takes one vaccination at the right time to protect your puppy, and this fact has apparently been known for over thirty years. So why are we not being educated?

One large vaccine manufacturer tested the parvo response to its vaccine with titer testing. It vaccinated puppies at six, nine, and twelve weeks of age and then measured their response to the vaccine by measuring their titers to parvovirus. At six weeks, only 52 percent of the puppies had developed an immune response. At nine weeks, 88 percent of the puppies showed a response to the vaccine. At twelve weeks, 100 percent of the puppies were protected. So should we just wait longer to vaccinate?

The practice of vaccinating puppies at 6-8 weeks of age is a high risk! The chance that the maternal antibodies are blocking the vaccine are quite high...and by taking your puppy repeatedly to the vet's office, there is a higher risk of him or her being exposed to parvo and other strange viruses and disease. The fact is that the worst place a puppy can be is a place other sick dogs frequent.

There are two schools of thought here: 1) It would be a lot safer for your puppy if you were to socialize him in lightly trafficked places and keep him away from the vet's office or dog park until he is old enough (twelve weeks or more) that you know the vaccine is likely to work. 2) Expose your pup with short visits to places where the virus exists so he can develop his own immunity to the local strain versus some strange injections from wherever the strain came from. After all, isn't this really what the vaccine is doing anyhow? That way, he might get immunity to a local strain versus what you might find in a dangerous, and injected, strain.

And speaking of strains, nobody is checking to see whether the strain of virus infecting the dogs is the same as that from the vaccine. If no one is tracing the strain of the infectious disease, how can anyone say with any degree of accuracy what is in the vaccine and whether it will work? Shouldn't we make our vaccine manufacturers and veterinary clinics responsible for, at minimum, knowing this information?

VACCINE FAILURE

A study conducted by Canine Health Concern in 1997, involving 2,700 dogs, showed that 68.2 percent of dogs in the survey with parvovirus contracted it within three months of being vaccinated. Similarly, 55.6 percent of dogs with distemper contracted it within three months of vaccination; 63.6 percent contracted hepatitis within three months of vaccination; 50 percent contracted parainfluenza within three months of vaccination; and every single dog with leptospirosis contracted it within that three-month timeframe. *So vaccines represent—at best—only a 50/50 chance of protection.* In a parvo vaccine trial conducted by Dr. Ronald D. Schultz, head of pathobiology at Wisconsin University, three out of six parvo vaccine brands totally failed to give protection, two gave only partial protection, and only one was shown to be effective, but likely only for a short period of time.

SO VACCINES REPRESENT—AT BEST—ONLY A 50/50 CHANCE OF PROTECTION.

So not only can maternal antibodies block the vaccine's effectiveness for as many as twenty-six weeks of age, but it can also be unsuccessful for the following:

- If the puppy is sick or stressed at the time of vaccination (removed from his family for example)

- If the immune system is suppressed by steroids or antibiotics
- If the immune system is compromised by improper nutrition
- If the immune system is compromised by deworming meds.

And scarier yet...are our dogs seriously fighting their own DNA? A team at Purdue University found that vaccinated dogs were developing autoantibodies to their own collagen. (About one quarter of all the protein in the body is collagen.)

> *"Our ongoing studies of dogs show that following routine vaccination, there is a significant rise in the level of antibodies dogs produce against their own tissues."*
>
> *— Dr. Larry Glickman, of Purdue University*

A study published by Purdue University in 2005 found correlations between vaccine reactions in dogs and variables such as age, size, and number of vaccines given. The study found that smaller dogs were more prone to reactions to vaccines than larger dogs (dosages are not changed for size so I'm guessing this is why); risk of reactions increase by 27 percent for each additional vaccine given per office visit in dogs under twenty-two pounds, and by 12 percent in dogs over twenty-two pounds. Risk increased for dogs up to two years old, then declined with age. Risk increased for pregnant dogs and dogs in heat. More reactions were found when dogs were on poor diets. Shouldn't there be some kind of protection in place for our dogs? Who is speaking up on their behalf? If we aren't educating ourselves, how can we expect this to change?

In her book *Vaccination Examining the Record*, Judith A. DeCava states "a person not vaccinated has one risk, catching the disease, where a vaccinated person has two risks; catching the disease and damage from the vaccine."

I was told by multiple vets that my pups should have had parvo, distemper, and lepto shots when they were young, so I did some research to determine whether or not those shots would be useful.

Lepto and parvo were said to be real concerns here in Hawaii. I decided that maybe it was best just not to take my pups to areas of possible outbreak; if I avoided them, I wondered whether I/they would be safe. But would I be causing more social harm long term?

Various people reminded me that vaccines had eradicated large-scale epidemics and that vaccinations are intended to keep such epidemics from happening again. I lost a friend over this argument. I did some research and found that many vaccines were introduced as the disease was dying out. Somewhere, I read that once 67 percent of a population has been exposed, the disease dies out. I wondered whether that was true. But I also read that some researchers believe *vaccines actually keep certain diseases in the ecosystem.* If they do die out and we keep creating them in a lab and injecting them into our dogs, then I guess they never do die. In fact, I imagine we are introducing possible new strains.

"I think that vaccines...are the leading killers of dogs and cats in America today."

— Martin Goldstein, DVM

As a pet owner, you have two choices—let your vet decide your dog's health and allow him or her to be vaccinated, or do your research on safety and efficacy. There are many vaccine ingredients you should be familiar with, such as aluminum, Thimerosal, contaminants ("xenotropic" means harmless in the original host species but will cause problems in different species), and animal proteins.

I've found that no one is doing any research to claim either that vaccines are safe or dangerous, but I also found that more people are reporting issues with their pets after having them vaccinated. In the UK, there is Vaccine Damage Compensation for humans. The parents whose children were made epileptic by vaccines have been paid up to 30,000 pounds. I'm sure the parents will make quick use of that money and spend their lives managing the side effects in their children. It's time to create a method of accountability, but because it may take time for side effects to show themselves, it's hard to make a link between vaccinations and possible side effects. I took some time to research each vaccine to determine what, if anything, was so pressing to put my pups through unimaginable possible side effects. I wanted to go into my research with an open mind, but the more research I did, the harder it was to remain neutral. In fact, I honestly just got really pissed off and wound up in tears! I wondered whether other people knew these things or they simply just hadn't taken the time to teach themselves and placed unbelievable levels of faith in their vets' hands. I wondered whether the vets even knew what was going on. Had they just been turning a cheek in order to pay off school debts, office equipment, and staff salaries, or were they fully aware and felt a sense of entitlement to live a grand life at the expense of our dogs...and our wallets and broken hearts? I was finding more information showing the reasons not to do vaccines than to do them. I began to wonder whether I was just missing something, but the more research I did, the more confused I became about why we are being brainwashed to believe in vaccines' efficacy.

"It's very disappointing to me to still have distemper, parvo, and adno [adenovirus] given every year when we know it provides a life of immunity."

— Dr. Ronald Schultz

THE CORE VACCINES

Let's take some time to talk about what the core vaccines have been used for, the viruses they are made to defend, and available natural treatment options because, believe it or not, there are other alternatives to vaccines. I want you to pay special attention to the herbs and homeopathic treatments because I believe if we did a bit of reverse engineering, we might be able to use a few of these herbs in daily feedings and avoid ever having to use them in emergency situations to make our babies well again. You see, it all really begins with a sound, healthy, natural, and organic lifestyle and diet...all giving strength to the individual's life force.

LEPTOSPIROSIS

In the rare case of exposure to leptospirosis, the potential exists for lethal consequences from renal failure. Not only is the disease scarce across most of the country (yet found on occasion here in Hawaii), but it is 100 percent treatable.

WHERE LEPTO EXISTS:

Lepto is a bacteria that generally exists where there is standing water and where other animals (generally farm animals like cattle, but also rodents, such as rats and raccoons) have been contaminated…they urinate in areas that leach into the standing water…and your dog either has a an open sore and enters that water and/or drinks it.

WHAT LEPTO IS:

An infection primarily affecting the liver (hepatitis) and kidneys. Within just a few days to a few weeks after exposure to the bacteria, you may see symptoms, including diarrhea, fever (103-104°), vomiting, muscle pain, loss of appetite, blood in the urine, green bile in stools, lethargy, and depression. Symptoms are similar to those of meningitis.

VACCINE DANGERS:

The same danger exists from getting the disease as exists with each and every vaccination…and the likelihood and severity of reaction increases exponentially with every shot given (which in the case of leptospirosis, may be twice a year). In fact, some dogs vaccinated with leptospirosis die of renal failure within forty-eight hours with the same type of pathology that the actual disease could create. And some dogs may never come into contact with it other than via a vaccine. Meningitis is a side effect of the vaccination, which is a life-threatening condition characterized by inflammation of the brain and spinal cord's protective layers.

The vaccine can actually be ineffective due to the inconsistency of the bacteria strains. Lepto vaccines have four serotypes: L. Canicola, L. Gripophytosa, L. Icterohemorrhagiae, and L.Pomona. Hundreds of different serotypes exist, and there is no guarantee you are getting protection against the one in your area. You must ask your veterinarian which type is causing the illness in your area; otherwise, the vaccines will be worthless. (I'm guessing most veterinarians will be clueless about the strain and clueless about what they are injecting.) Here on Maui, vets recommend vaccines as often as every six months because they say there is no cure. I'll bet we could put money on the fact that none of the vaccinations have local strains in them. In fact, most vets say they have never seen a case of lepto in the entire time they've been practicing.

Here is another alarming fact about the lepto vaccine: the vaccine is associated with adverse events that should really catch your attention. The most concerning issue is that of human contamination (a public health issue). Vaccination causes the pathology (bacteria or disease) of the natural infection itself, but not just in your dog—in you! It can be easily passed on to humans if your dog has been vaccinated! *What?*

I didn't want to think that if my pups had the vaccination, I was not only putting them at risk, but I would be putting my whole family and myself at risk! Can you imagine? Your whole family could be at risk of renal failure or meningitis because you did what you thought was right and had your pup immunized! I don't know about you, but the CDC didn't contact me to let me know I was putting people (and my dog) at risk if I gave my dogs the vaccine that several vets fearfully suggested. Do these vets even know they are at risk or putting humans at risk? Are we ever forewarned about these kinds of side effects? Have you signed a waiver at your vet's office stating you are aware that you or your unknowing family members may get lepto? Are we even given a map or statistics of outbreaks in our area before we inoculate? I tried to find more information about outbreaks with maps of specific locations, but I couldn't. Perhaps you can let me know if you find something. (I personally don't think you will find anything because this kind of research is either just not being done or maybe it's impossible to know.)

Oh, and did you know that after the immunization, there is actually only a two-week to maybe six-month window for your dog actually to be protected by the bacteria most likely to cause harm! *What?* I'm going to risk all the above for just six months of possible protection, and then risk it all again six months later?

NATURAL TREATMENT:

With all this danger, why vaccinate for something that is treatable? In 2009, Cuba successfully treated 2.4 million people with a leptospira nosode after hurricane season. Remember, homeopathy treats a condition if it is present; not if you think you might get it. This can be a scary thought versus a supposed inoculation to clear it from your being entirely. We have been trained to believe we need to deal with the possible side effects of vaccines in exchange for the peace of mind of never seeing a virus in our lifetimes. But, in the case of lepto, it does not really work that way. There really is no true inoculation, and the side effects are not worth it for the short period it might actually keep the bacteria or disease at bay.

When I started looking into homeopathic treatment, I found that the treatment varies depending upon the actual and particular individual symptoms your dog is suffering with. It's important to change the way we look at managing sickness when we are approaching things from a homeopathic perspective—it's a kind of re-training of our thinking process. We need to focus on the individual side effects rather than the disease as a whole. How is your dog behaving? What are the symptoms?

Side effects to exposure to lepto can be treated in various ways, but the following homeopathic remedies have been recommended in the various research I have studied:

Aconitum/Aconite: Always the go to at onset, in emergency situations, or to prevent shock.

Arsenicum: Best in emergency situations for the GI system and for dehydration.

Baptisia: For muscular soreness.

Berberis Vulgaris (also called Barberry): For pain in kidneys and liver with vomiting, stool or urine mucus, rectum pain, or tears, and to assist with bile reduction.

Crotalus Horridus: For liver support/pain and inflamed kidney, weak pulse.

Lepto Nosode: Can be found at: www.holisticanimalmedicines.com and contains some of the harder to find remedies in the nosode.

Mercurius Corrosivus: For bloody diarrhea, stool mucus, abdomen pains, burning urination, and bloody cough.

Phosphorus: For coughing associated with the respiratory system, for liver support, and to reduce vomiting.

Zincum Cyanatum: Known to treat meningitis, agitations, and hysteria. I have not been able to find this remedy for sale (other than in the lepto nosode above), but I have found references to the following as alternatives: veratrum, gelsemium, spalding, bryonia, apis, helleborus, zincum metallicum, sulphur, tuberculinum, bacillinum, and calcaea.

The actual dosing of these remedies will also be variable based on your particular situation, but the onset of any presenting situation of change in your dog's constitution warrants an immediate and a more aggressive response. Aconitum/aconite should always be the go to for most situations that come on quickly. Then I like to follow up with the appropriate remedy for the particular situation immediately following. For more acute situations, you can use 200c more frequently and repeatedly at first… maybe go with a dose every fifteen minutes or until you see a change.

From everything I have researched, there appears to be very little that can go wrong, and it's very unlikely you can overdose your dog with homeopathic remedies in such a situation. Therefore, in a crisis, I might opt to go the more versus less approach myself. If lepto or its side effects comes on quickly, treat it immediately with higher dosages. I do recommend speaking to a homeopathic practitioner for the best results. Homeopathy would be my preferred method of treatment, but I will also share what I've learned about the more traditional routes of treatment in case pursuing a homeopathic remedy feels too overwhelming and you decide to work locally with your vet. You can also use the above methods in conjunction with the traditional veterinary practices. In fact, it is recommended, because the IV and drug method alone is not always successful. It is very important to boost your pup's immune system during and after such an event. Holistic Animal Medicines recommends Cat's Claw as an "autoimmune modulator" post treatment.

DETOXING FROM THE LEPTO VACCINE:

If you have already given the vaccine to your dogs, but now you want to detox them from it, use the following:

Apis: For facial swelling or allergic reaction after vaccination

Belladonna: For seizures and meningitis.

Cadmium Oxide (also called Cadium Oxydatum): Usually used for metal poisoning detoxing, this remedy can be somewhat harder to find. (I found it at www.helios.co.uk/shop/cadmium-oxydatum.)

Nat Sulph: For meningitis symptoms.

Silica: For convulsions, nausea, diarrhea, swelling.

Sulphur: For swelling, skin irritation.

Thuja: For skin issues, vaccinosis side effects: convulsions, anxiety, inflammation, diarrhea, asthma, cough, paralysis, swelling, skin eczema. With silica, it is known to be antidote to vaccinosis.

TRADITIONAL TREATMENT:

I did some research and found that in a traditional veterinary clinic, lepto is often easily treated with antibiotics such as penicillin and doxycycline. (Though these antibiotics are not natural, they prove my point that lepto can be treated without having to give the vaccine.) Doxycycline is said to be the antibiotic of choice to rid the urinary tract of a leptospira infection. Doxycycline can be administered to dogs in renal failure and will clear the organism from the kidneys. This is said to make it effective in infections of both the blood and urine. Detoxing the body, normalizing hydration levels, and creating balance are important in removing the infection. Corticosteroids are also said to be prescribed in advanced stages.

PARVO

My vet and all the staff looked at me cross-eyed when I told them I didn't want to bring my dogs into their office because I didn't want them to catch parvo. They all tried to convince me just to give my dogs the shots so they could come in. I felt like I was a bad person, and I was treated as if I actually had the disease myself. Nevertheless, did you know that 100 percent of puppies are exposed to the parvovirus at the vet's office?

Despite countless public scare tactics and ominous veterinary warnings, parvo actually has a survival rate of about 85 percent. This means that 15 percent of puppies exposed to it—and who actually catch it—will die. The survival rate, however, is greatly influenced by the treatment options. From a homeopath's perspective, I've heard it said that parvo is one of the most common viruses that can be prevented.

WHERE PARVO EXISTS:

Parvo is highly contagious and spreads through exposure to feces from other infected dogs (for several weeks following infection). It can be carried on anything that comes in contact with it (your feet, dog crates, etc.). Puppies are at the highest risk of contracting the virus.

WHAT PARVO IS:

The virus either attacks a dog's gastrointestinal tract, circulatory system, or cardiac system—likely overwhelming the lymphatic system and causing white blood cell count to drop. Symptoms include a lot of vomiting, and the dehydration from that is usually what kills. The trick is to diagnose parvo quickly by knowing the symptoms (vomiting, lethargy, diarrhea) and keeping your dog hydrated. It is said that if you stop the diarrhea, you will cure parvo.

Vaccine Dangers: The vaccine is not without its side effects, and it is also *not* a cure. In fact, everything I read suggested that if your pup has *never* had the immunization, he stands a better chance of survival because his immune system is not compromised. I guess once your dog has had the vaccine, it is hard to know whether you are treating the vaccine or the infection itself. Not to mention, if your dog does get parvo, many veterinarians will simply hook the pup up to an IV and not do much more for treatment. Some will give drugs to help control the vomiting and others will give antibiotics to prevent secondary infections or an anti-inflammatory to control intestinal inflammation. There is no drug that can cure a dog with parvo. Treatment is mostly directed at controlling the symptoms for as many as three to five days.

What it comes down to is that the vaccine decision has some trade-offs. If you vaccinate your puppy for parvo, you are reducing the risk that he may be taken from you abruptly and viciously. But vaccination comes at a high price with possible side effects of chronic disease (cancer, hypothyroidism, allergies, Cushing's disease, Addison's disease, bowel disease, joint disease, heart disease, etc.). Is it worth possibly affecting the quality and length of your dog's life? I suppose this disease could be looked at a bit like our human chicken pox. I know I had the chicken pox very bad, but once you get it, you generally have immunity for life. The same can be said for parvo. When you teach the body how to heal, it knows how to do it forever.

Natural Treatment: Use Vitamin C (sodium ascorbate) daily in meals to protect your dog if you suspect contact with a live virus or you prefer preventative care. There are many herbs and homeopathic treatments that are very effective at treating parvo symptoms. Choices range from commercially-prepared products like Parvaid or Vibactra, to simple homeopathic remedies and nosodes by companies like Holistic Animal Medicines. These are not only inexpensive and easy to do at home, but puppies treated this way have a higher survival rate than puppies treated with orthodox methods. I've heard of many options for treating parvo, so here are a few:

- **Sodium Ascorbate (Vitamin C crystal powder):** Dissolve 2-3 teaspoons in 1 cup of warm water. Give five times the daily amount in water orally every fifteen minutes until recovered.

- **Slippery Elm Powder:** Add to sodium ascorbate/Vitamin C to make a very runny liquid mix—if pet is vomiting at all. Insert in side of mouth small amounts (5ml) every fifteen minutes for puppies. (20ml for adult dogs). This should stop infection spreading as well as stop diarrhea.
- **Syringe with Pedialyte**
- **Activated Charcoal:** This can be watered down and syringed into mouth.
- **Herb Pharm Intestinal Tract Defense:** Contains wormwood and black walnut. Use the self-contained eyedropper and administer into the mouth with a bit of water to make it more palatable.

There is no sense recreating a good thing, so I recommend using the following brands or remedies and the herbs they contain as an easier solution:

HAMPL Brand Acute Parvo and Parvo Herbs (www.holisticanimalmedicines.com) contain the following:

- Ars Alb 6C, 200C
- Nux Vomica 30C
- Ipecac 30C
- Parvo herbs 3X
- Parvo nosode 30C
- Scullcap
- Goldenseal
- Cats Claw
- Turmeric
- Olive Leaf

PARVAID (http://www.parvaid.net) contains:

- Peppermint
- Spearmint

- Chamomile
- Plantain
- Echinacea
- Oregon grape
- Rose hips
- Yarrow
- Garlic
- Goldenseal
- Hibiscus Flowers

Parvo-K by Pet Alive contains:

- Veratrum alb (for vomiting, dehydration, fever)
- Belladonna (for acute fever, pain, inflammation)
- Zingiber officinale (ginger) to soothe the digestive tract
- Agrimonia eupatoria (agrimony) relieves diarrhea and eases digestive system

VIBACTRA (https://ambertech.com) is commonly sold with PARVAID to boost the immune system and rid bacterial and parasitic infections of diseases like parvo. It contains the following:

- Olive leaf
- Mustard seed
- Black seed
- Pau d'arco
- Cloves
- Grapefruit seed extract
- Jatoba

Outside of the brand names, here are the typically recommended homeopathic remedies:

Aconitum/Aconite: Always the go to at onset, in emergency situations, or to prevent shock.

Arsenicum: Best in emergency situations for GI system and for dehydration and diarrhea.

Crotalus Horridus: For use with considerable blood loss.

DETOXING FROM THE PARVO VACCINE:

If you have already given the vaccine and want to detox from it, use the following:

Apis: For facial swelling or allergic reaction after vaccination

Belladonna: For seizures

Silica: For convulsions, nausea, diarrhea, swelling

Sulphur: For swelling, skin irritation

Thuja: For skin issues, vaccinosis side effects: convulsions, anxiety, inflammation, diarrhea, asthma, cough, paralysis, swelling, and skin eczema. With silica, it is known to be antidote to vaccinosis.

TRADITIONAL TREATMENT:

Hydration through IV fluid to balance electrolyte levels. Antibiotics, pain, and anti-nausea medicines are first approaches to treating parvo traditionally. Blood transfusions are also sometimes done if too much blood is lost. Maropitant is an anti-nausea drug (which is said to actually cause vomiting) and Convenia is an antibiotic often used. Not much is typically done to boost the immune system in a traditional veterinary approach.

DISTEMPER

Distemper has been said to be the "greatest single disease threat" to the dog population. Almost all dogs are exposed to it. The fear tactics used to persuade people to vaccinate for distemper are everywhere. There is no doubt distemper is a serious virus, but fortunately, it is easily treated and even can be prevented altogether with the proper holistic approach. Advances in treatment, especially holistic treatment, make it a very curable condition.

WHERE DISTEMPER EXISTS:

Exposure to the distemper virus is through the air (from exhaling or sneezing) or by contacting contaminated bowls, toys, etc. Because canine distemper also affects animals in the wild (e.g., foxes, raccoons, skunks, wolves, etc.), contact between these wild animals and domestic puppies and dogs has been said to facilitate the virus' spread. But other evidence suggests exposure to these environments can actually immunize your pups against the disease.

WHAT DISTEMPER IS:

Distemper affects and causes serious damage to the respiratory, gastrointestinal, and central nervous systems. Distemper develops in stages. In the beginning, there is generally a 6-9 day period where no signs of infection can be observed. After that, a fever develops and the dog becomes lethargic. The dog may become normal for a few days or a week, and then it will suddenly show typical symptoms, such as: appetite loss, coughing, diarrhea, fever (103-105°), lethargy, nasal discharge, shivering, vomiting, loss of appetite, and watery or pus-like discharge from the eyes. Within a short time, the condition deteriorates and the dog may develop one or more of the following symptoms: eye inflammation (conjunctivitis) with a thick discharge that sticks the lids together, heavy mucus or yellow discharge from the nose, and foul-smelling diarrhea.

Within the first two weeks of infection, the distemper symptoms tend to fluctuate. At this point, some dogs may be able to get over the disease. However, for others, the virus may attack the brain cells and affect the neurological system, resulting in seizures, encephalitis (severe inflammation of the brain or spinal cord), and other neurological problems. One strain of the virus has some dogs also experiencing a hardening of the nose leather and foot pads. Secondary infections can also become a problem.

VACCINE DANGERS:

Many more vets today than in years past believe that if puppies are vaccinated after 12-16 weeks, they will be protected for life, but we are still being sold on the annual shot at our vets' offices.

If you still choose to immunize, receiving a distemper vaccine once when your puppy is twenty-two weeks old is sufficient in most holistic veterinarians' view. A lot of misconception exists that many distemper shots are needed over the dog's lifetime and there is no cure. Vets are beginning to realize (with titers testing proving immunity) that only one shot given at the right time is enough for the rest of the dog's life. Some dogs may require a second distemper vaccine as puppies if maternal antibodies block the first one (because it was given too soon), but if a puppy is vaccinated at twenty-two weeks of age, he will most likely be protected, for life, with just one distemper vaccine.

Like many vaccines, the distemper vaccine has been known to create the disease it was intended to prevent. And the risk of what is called "Vaccine Induced Autoimmune Disease" is said to be greater than the risk of distemper. In my research, I even found cases indicating that the distemper vaccine has been known to cause parvo in some puppies. With any vaccination, the inoculation suppresses the immune system for several days and the puppy risks developing disease. In fact, I'm fairly certain that my Bella might not have had all the skin issues she has if her breeder hadn't unknowingly put her at risk by giving her the vaccine at eight weeks old—since it's been linked to persistent skin problems and allergies.

Of course, with every vaccine, there is always the risk of life-threatening anaphylaxis or an allergic reaction occurring. I read that killed virus vaccines cause more allergic reactions than live vaccines. A killed virus is generally a larger vaccine where more needs to be injected into the body. As well, more additives are included in them to stimulate the immune system. But a live vaccine can actually cause the virus to grow and live inside your puppy's body. Yuck!

If there is an allergic reaction, it will usually occur within twenty-four hours of the vac and require your dog to be put on oxygen, IV fluids, anti-histamines, anti-inflamatories, and other related drugs. So now your dog has the virus and is getting pumped full of all kinds of other things. How is this supporting the life force of your pup? And how do you handle this the next time your pup is "due" for his or her annual vaccines? And if you had multiple vaccines of various types given, how do you know which one caused the issue? And after all this, are you sure the strain injected matches the local strain causing the virus? Is all the risk worth it? Who wins…medicine or God?

NATURAL TREATMENT:

If left untreated, distemper can be fatal, although advances in treatment—especially holistic treatment—make it a very curable condition. I always have to remind myself that the principle of homeopathic treatment is to treat the symptoms as they appear and that there isn't always a one-pill, one-shot, or one-remedy cure. This approach is a different philosophy from modern medicine.

One of the best ways to make your dog immune to any disease is actually to expose your pup to it! I know that sounds scary, but there was one case I read where a doctor (Dr. Manziano in New Jersey) suggested that her clients take their pups to a park where distemper existed and, for short periods of time, let them be exposed to the ground, water, and other places that either raccoons or other dogs frequented. In the end, she ran titers tests on the pups of the clients who took her advice, and she found strong immunity in them. What I found most fascinating in her studies was that after eleven years of sending her clients to the raccoon park, the disease no longer existed. The raccoons had either left or found a way to cure their distemper. She then began sending them to the dog park where it still existed. I have begun to believe that humans are actually becoming responsible for keeping these viruses alive by injecting them into our dogs!

Homeopathic vets have managed to treat distemper much more successfully than the traditional vets by using the distemperinum nosode—having success in both immunizing dogs as well as with infected dogs. We'll talk a bit more about nosodes shortly. The most commonly used mainstream remedy for distemper that I have found in my research is called Vi-Pro Plus, and it's readily available. I have found the Distemperinum nosode to be harder to find, and it generally requires a homeopathic vet to supervise, but I have also found it for sale at www.homeopathiclaboratories.com (for professional use only) and www.remedia-homeopathy.com (unable to deliver to the USA). It is always good to keep something on hand in case of an emergency, but good luck finding this one without some help from a homeopathic professional.

Vi-Pro Plus by Natural Remedies contains:

- **Astragalus:** For immune boosting.
- **Bryonia:** For nausea, vomiting, sensitive stomach.
- **Echinacea purpurea:** For immune boosting.
- **Pulsatilla:** For mucus and watery stool.
- **Veratrum:** For gastric irritability, vomiting, diarrhea.

HOMEOPATHIC REMEDIES (remember, they relate to particular symptoms) that can be used for distemper are:

Aconitum/Aconite: Always the go to at onset or when loss of appetite, shivering, or other symptoms appear, for emergency situations, or to prevent shock. This remedy may be capable of cutting short the disease. Give every half hour and up to as many as six doses at onset.

Antimonium Tart: For mucus in the chest and rattling cough, but nothing is discharged.

Argent Nit: For loss of control mentally and physically, trembling, use for abundant discharges, swelling, and redness of the eyes. Also use for thick mucus in the throat and stomach bloat and gas.

Arsen Alb: For great anguish and restlessness, eye and nose discharges, eye inflammation and burning, vomiting, or inability to stand the sight or smell of food; diarrhea, dry flaky or rash-like skin, inflamed liver or spleen, painful abdomen, nausea, small dark stinky or mucus stool, difficulty breathing, dry hacking cough, chest constriction or pain, restless sleep, fever, and when limbs or extremities are weak, swollen, restless, or painful.

Aurum Met: Known as metallic gold. For deteriorations of the bodily fluids and alterations in the tissues. Issues resemble syphilis. Assists in healing many emotional issues, such as depression. Also helps with violent head pain, eye soreness and pain, infections, inflammation, and swelling.

Baptisia: For vertigo, dizziness, confusion, can only swallow liquids, continuous desire for water, odor in stool, dazed from fever, or fever in general.

Belladonna: To calm pulse and create ease if pup is excitable; good for fits of convulsions.

Bryonia: For mucous membranes, lips, dry mouth, dry cough, or if finding it hard to breathe from chest, or is lying on painful areas to relieve pressure and provide relief.

Causticum: Generally used for rheumatic, arthritic, and paralytic issues such as pain and restlessness, retention of urine, incontinence.

China/Cinchona: For control of diarrhea, debility from exhausting discharges, throbbing headache, pressure in eyes, abdomen pain and bloating, liver pain, distended belly, vomiting bile or blood, undigested stool, breathing labored and head low, extremities or limbs in pain, restless sleep, chills, fever.

Conium: Think of this remedy for all the aging dog symptoms, especially for weakness of the body and trembling of the mind. Use for symptoms of old age, such as paralysis. Can also be used for burning during stool or the urge to create a stool or urinate with no discharge. Use for issues with genitals.

Euphrasia (also known as Eyebright): For watery eyes, coughing up of mucus, eye swelling, nose discharge.

Ferrum Phos: For red or inflamed throat.

Gelsenium: For motor paralysis, dizziness or drowsiness, muscular weakness, influenza, eye inflammations.

Hyoscyamus: For severe nervous system agitation, such as mania, insanity, twitching of tendons, delirium, dazed as if drunk, vertigo.

Hydrastis (also known as Goldenseal): For the mucous membranes to treat thick, yellowish secretions and discharge from any part of the body. Note: It has been known to help as a remedy to smallpox.

Ipecacuanha: For frequent coughing, coughing up, or vomiting red blood.

Lycopodium: For urinary or digestive disturbance, and for faint or withered looking pups that may be malnourished.

Merc Corr.: For severe tearing, inflammation, or yellow discharge from eyes. For when pup is straining to urinate or defecate without the ability to do so. For bloody, slimy, mucous-covered, or stinky stools and funny-colored urine. For raw, burning, or swelling in throat or genitals. Also for coughing with blood and eye ulcerations.

Phosphorus: Use if pneumonia sets in.

Pulsatilla: For inflammation and mucous discharge.

Pyrogenium: For septic fevers, all discharges are horribly offensive.

Silicea: Good for scar tissue and other skin issues. I always think of it as being like the tweezers to pull out the thorn.

Stramonium: Focus is on the disturbances of the brain with issues such as delirium, vertigo; pup then does best in a dark room.

Strychninum: For all muscle twitching, spasms, jerking, trembling, and restlessness.

Sulphur: For red, inflamed, itchy skin or skin breakouts; issues of the rectum and unusual stools; cloudy urine.

Veratrum Alb.: For profuse and violent vomiting, collapsing or signs of collapse, abdominal pain.

ADDITIONAL NATURAL METHODS OF TREATMENT:

Astragalus: For the immune system.

Canned Pumpkin: For diarrhea.

Colloidal Silver: Syringe or drop into mouth and even into eyes to protect against disease. Give as much as four ounces daily for larger dogs and only a few tablespoons for smaller dogs.

Echinacea: For the immune system.

Epsom or Sea Salts: Soak on inflamed eyes. You can also use a drop of olive oil in each eye to facilitate healing.

Fasting: Withhold food if fevering. Your pup will use up all its energy to fight the virus and the fever. Fast for two days. After fasting, feed vegetable broth and water only until fever drops.

Oregano Oil: Use veggie cap to avoid strong taste in your pup's mouth, but great for infection.

Probiotics: For digestive health and diarrhea.

Vitamin C: For fighting infection. Dr. Pitcairn recommends buffered Vitamin C (calcium ascorbate) at 250 mg every two hours for puppies and small dogs, 500 mg every two hours for medium-sized dogs, and 1,000 mg every three hours for large dogs. After fever passes, change to every six hours and continue until fully recovered.

Water: Syringe lots of water into the mouth to keep hydrated.

If you are able to identify the disease early, treating your dog with one or more homeopathic remedies should significantly reduce the severity and duration of the illness.

DETOXING FROM THE DISTEMPER VACCINE: If you have already given the vaccine and want to detox your dog from it, use the following:

Apis: For facial swelling or allergic reaction after vaccination.

Belladonna: For seizures.

Silica: For convulsions, nausea, diarrhea, swelling.

Sulphur: For swelling and skin irritation.

Thuja: For skin issues and the following vaccinosis side effects: convulsions, anxiety, inflammation, diarrhea, asthma, cough, paralysis, swelling, and skin eczema. With silica, it is known to be an antidote to vaccinosis.

Other Alternatives: Other homeopathic remedies used will depend on the symptoms your pup is displaying. Remember, homeopathy treats the symptoms.

In 1929, veterinarian Dr. Horace B.F. Jervis published his research titled "Treatment of Canine Distemper with the Potentized Virus." This research reports his frustration with many years of failed attempts at treating canine distemper with conventional treatment. That frustration led him to turn away from conventional veterinarian science and to begin treating his patients using the principles of homeopathic medicine.

TRADITIONAL TREATMENT:

Conventional veterinary medicine has very little to offer in the way of dog distemper treatment. While a conventional vet may try things like antibiotics or other drugs, these remedies are unlikely to be effective other than to relieve some of the symptoms. While there is no known cure, conventional treatment usually involves antibiotics for secondary infections and intravenous fluids.

OVERVIEW OF NOSODES

"Based on my clinical experience, I think I can safely say that protection with nosodes is as reliable as with vaccinations and without the added advantage of few unwelcome side effects."

— Richard Pitcairn, D.V.M., Ph.D.

I've talked briefly about nosodes, but let me explain a bit more about them before we continue. The homeopathic nosode is a remedy prepared from the diseased tissue or a product of the disease itself. It can be used to treat the associated disease. Nosodes are most effective when given at time of exposure to a disease…both at onset and after exposure. They can also be given to protect against disease (homeoprophylaxis). The biggest benefit of nosodes is that they are safe and have no side-effects.

As reported in *Dogs Naturally*[12]:

> The nosode is generally thought to be the most effective and safe manner of prevention by qualified homeopathic vets. John Saxton MRCV presented research showing the distemper nosode's ability to reduce an outbreak by around 65 percent in only five days with a reduction from 11.67 percent infected to 4.36 percent. When the entire population of the kennels' results were analyzed, an even higher success rate was reported with a drop from 8.05 percent to 2.81 percent (*IJVH*, Vol.5, 1, 1991).

12 The full article is available at http://www.dogsnaturallymagazine.com/pet-vaccination-risks-and-benefits/

SCHEDULE OF IMMUNIZATION WITH NOSODES

The following is recommended by various homeopathic vets:

	Pre-Birth	3 weeks	3 days	1x per wk.	1x/mo.
Treatment	Pregnant females may be given nosodes to pass immunity to the unborn puppies.	Puppies can begin at three weeks old. (Suggested dosage for dogs of all ages is the same.)	One dose given daily by mouth for the first three days; then give 1x per week.	One dose once a week for six weeks; then give 1x per month.	One dose given once a month for one or two years.

Another great nosode to be aware of is the psorinum nosode. It is used for skin conditions when you have tried many things and nothing is working. It is actually made from the discharge of the scabies mites. Kinda yucky sounding I know. It can be used for glandular swelling, foul skin odors, for pups where no amount of washing makes the foul smell go away, and for various other skin issues. It can be complementary to the sulfur remedy and easily found on Amazon.

RABIES

Making rabies vaccination a law is what killed my Shiitake. Rather than just asking for a titer test, she was needlessly injected twice to meet the requirements for the quarantine for the Hawaiian Islands. I have no way of proving this other than the fact that shortly after she was vaccinated, she became ill with lymphoma, and eight months later, she died. Then it was too late! I'm forever grateful for the lessons she taught me to share with others, but I'd rather still have her here next to me any day! My anger over this situation has been the motivation to write this book, so I suppose it has served its purpose. I'm far better educated now for each dog that lives in my home from this day forward.

RABIES AS LAW:

It is important first to know that rabies laws are generally not made by experts in immunology or rabies vaccination—they are made by state legislators—very few of whom have medical training. State veterinary officials or public health officers who aren't likely vaccination or rabies virus experts assist many legislators. It's unlikely they know how to inject a vaccine, and they are probably lacking expertise in vaccinology or virology. It's hard to apply a blanket law over each individual animal because, just like people, they all have a different physical makeup, weight, age, and medical condition.

A law or proposed change to protect animals from rabies may sound like a great idea, but good intentions aside, it is still bad science. In an effort to protect the public and other animals against the threat of exposure, we may be doing more harm than good. And laws may be pushed through because of irrational fears about rabies...or for financial or political gain. Many localities and veterinarians require rabies vaccinations more often than medically or legally necessary. Why? Personal beliefs? Because it's hard to be a veterinarian and also actively stay abreast of the changing laws? Do veterinarians fear losing their steady income from the county or city licensing fees that make for all the nice profits? Or do veterinarians have no choice because of the laws being enforced by uninformed or uneducated legislature. I really feel bad for veterinarians today who are simply trying to treat animals in need, but who also have to watch their medical licenses and adhere to all the laws and rules of our challenging society. It takes a sharp person to manage the care of an animal, stay abreast of the laws, and keep up with medical advancements. It's really a lot to manage. It's up to us dog owners to assist our veterinary offices in keeping them abreast of the changing times and finding ways to work together for our dogs' best interest.

WHERE RABIES EXISTS:

Rabies is most often transmitted through the bite of a rabid animal. According to the CDC, the vast majority of rabies cases reported each year occur in wild animals like raccoons, skunks, bats, and foxes. More than 90 percent of all animal cases reported annually to the CDC now occur in wildlife; before 1960, the majority were in domestic animals.

WHAT RABIES IS:

Rabies is a virus transmitted through saliva or brain/nervous system tissue. You can only get it if you come into contact with these specific tissues or secretions. If you pet or hold a sick animal, you will not be exposed. Coming into contact with the animal's blood, urine, or feces will not expose you either. And when those items are exposed to sunlight and dry out, they become non-infectious anyway. An animal showing the signs of a rabies infection may drool, foam at the mouth, or suffer paralysis. Pets with rabies do not act like themselves. For example, a rapid dog may act shy when he or she is normally friendly. Wild animals with rabies will show no fear for humans. The virus can appear within as few as ten days after exposure, but usually, it takes two to eight weeks before signs are noticed. There is no accurate test to diagnose rabies in your dog.

Although human rabies deaths are rare, the estimated public health expenditures[13] associated with disease detection, diagnostic testing, prevention, and control in the U.S. have risen between $245 and $510 million annually. Only 2-3 human deaths per year are caused by rabies. From 2003-2014, the CDC reported only thirty-three cases on its website of humans who died from rabies, and many of those incidents happened out of the country, and only a few involved dogs; in fact, many occurred because of organ transplants. One might argue that a decline in cases is due to vaccination programs, but someone else might argue that the requirement for rabies vacs is out of date. But $510 million sure is big business, so who's gonna change it?

VACCINE DANGERS:

Within 24-72 hours after the vaccination, adverse reactions may occur. Homeopaths suggest that the vaccine can carry the energetic imprint of the original disease itself and cause strange behaviors and health risks in your dog, including the appearance of aggression or separation anxiety; obsessive behavior, such as self-mutilation and tail chewing; fear of people and water or shiny objects; eating of strange objects or stools; destructive behaviors; seizures, epilepsy; injection site fibrosarcomas; autoimmune diseases that affect the bones, skin, blood cells, joints, eyes, skin, liver, kidneys, bowel, and central nervous system; chronic digestive issues; and muscular atrophy or weakness.

According to all vaccine manufacturers' labels, only healthy dogs should be vaccinated. If your dog has a documented history of health problems, or serious reactions (to the rabies vaccine or another vaccine), and your dog's lifestyle makes him unlikely to contract rabies, you may be able to get a special exemption or postponement from your local licensing institution. Vaccinating an unhealthy animal may prove disastrous, or even deadly. But, as I found out, there is no getting a dog into a rabies-free country or state like Hawaii without following the rules. I did find that with rabies, though, many states are beginning to consider changing legislation to protect our dogs, including a few states now looking to make some changes in the rabies laws. Such changes will not eliminate the need for the rabies

13 According to the Centers for Disease Control and Prevention at cdc.gov.

vaccine, but it will allow more reasonable standards to be put in place. For example, a rabies titer blood test is a way to determine your dog's level of protection. If your dog is bit, you might also get a titer test done on the dog that bit your dog...if indeed it was a dog. Sometimes, a titer certificate is suitable for legal purposes, if needed.

RABIES VACCINE EXEMPTIONS:

In 2012, the American Veterinary Medical Association (AVMA) recommended that dogs with health problems receive exemptions. If your state doesn't allow exemptions, become an advocate to change the law. You can find the form at https://www.avma.org/KB/Policies/Documents/annual-rabies-vaccination-waiver-form.pdf.

Once you fill out the form, there are no real instructions on what you do with it from there. I suppose you can take it to your local government, but there is no guarantee it will do much good since many government officials may not know how to honor it. I have included a similar form in the appendix that you may copy and use as well.

You can also have a veterinarian or local animal control official give you an exemption, which varies from locale to locale. But if your vet doesn't believe in vaccine reactions or doesn't support the idea, getting an exemption may prove to be an issue. Unfortunately, many vets may feel their licenses are threatened if they do not follow their state's rules, so anything outside the norm may be challenging to get them to buy in to. Not many vets are going to risk all those years of training and their license for the few people conscious enough to stand up for their dog's rights or who are advocates to buck the system that has been in place all these years. Their clinic and income are also at stake, which means getting them involved in protecting our pets' healthcare is just plain not fair to them. It truly brings tears to my eyes and pain to my heart to know how far we still need to journey for the love and good health of our best friends. We are making headway on equal rights for humans; now what about our planetary animals?

The Rabies Challenge Fund (www.rabieschallengefund.org) exists to help with avoiding unnecessary rabies vaccinations for your dog. Dr. Ron Schultz, Dr. Jean Dodds, and Kris Christine are currently heading up the fund to determine the duration of immunity conveyed by rabies vaccines. This group's goal is to prove the original vaccine gives protection for five to seven years instead of the current one to three.

At present, every state in the United States (except Hawaii) requires an initial "one year" shot, followed by a three-year vaccine every three years thereafter. In 2011, California signed a bill to allow dogs with health problems an exemption from rabies vacs until their health improves enough to get the vaccine. Although the exemption keeps the dog confined and never able to leave your control or step off a six-foot leash, it is a step in the right direction, but we still have a long way to go. The law is called "Molly's Law." It can be found at: leginfo.ca.gov. There is also a website I found (www.dogs4dogs.com) where you can get updated information on laws in your state.

NATURAL TREATMENT:

Soap and water: Use first after possible exposure.

Cumin seeds: Counters toxic effects of a rabid animal bite.

Echinacea: To boost immune system.

Garlic: Natural antibiotic.

Lavender: Compress applied to wound.

Vitamin B: Produces antibodies to fight infection.

Vitamin C: Helps fight infection.

Walnut: Neutralizes the poison of a rabid animal bite.

Homeopathic Remedies:

Acetic Acid: For intense thirst.

Belladonna: For seizures. (Also use if developing a high fever, seizures, glassy eyes with dilated pupils, and/or development of aggressive or dominant behavior after vaccination.) There is a thirst for water but a fear of it or liquids.

Chamomilla: Used to treat the most common rabies virus. Patients are extremely sensitive and cannot tolerate sound, light, or touch.

Cuprum Met: For strained muscles, convulsions, violent spasms, nausea.

Curare: Said to be an antidote to rabies.

Hyscyamus: Over-excitability, restlessness, disruptive behavior.

Lachesis: For thirst, delirium, trembling, tremors, confusion, mania, insanity, head pain, offensive stool, genital pain.

Phosphorous: For sudden symptoms like fainting, sweats, pains, impaired thinking, dizziness, head pain, mouth and throat issues, great weakness after stool, issues of the heart, lungs, and chest.

Plumbum Met: For progressive muscular atrophy.

Ruta: For painful body parts, weakness, and despair.

Stramonium: For aggressive behavior.

Tanacetum Vulgare: For shortness of breath, abundant saliva, mental fatigue, nausea, and vertigo.

DETOXING FROM THE RABIES VIRUS:

If you have already given the vaccine and want to detox from it, use the following:

Apis: For facial swelling or allergic reaction after vaccination

Lyssin (also known as hydrophobin): Neutralizes vaccine side effects. Medicine prepared from rabid dog saliva. (Also use if there is a fear of water, fear of drinking water, or hypersensitivity of all senses.)

Silica: For convulsions, nausea, diarrhea, swelling

Sulphur: For swelling, skin irritation

Thuja: For skin issues, vaccinosis side effects: convulsions, anxiety, inflammation, diarrhea, asthma, cough, paralysis, swelling, skin eczema. With silica it is known to be antidote to vaccinosis.

TRADITIONAL TREATMENT:

All bite wounds should be washed with soap and water or a virucidal agent (agent for destroying viruses) such as povidine-iodine solution. A new rabies vaccination is given if your pup has already been vaccinated. If the disease progresses, it's very likely your pup may have to be euthanized. It is even suggested by the CDC that the head of the animal be severed and shipped to the CDC for testing. If your dog has not been vaccinated, it is suggested that he or she be euthanized immediately. If you are unwilling to have this done, then the pup must be kept in quarantine for up to six months. There is no treatment or cure for rabies with allopathic care, and you might as well say goodbye to your pup if you take him in for care. It can be dangerous to keep him at home if he becomes aggressive, so you may have no choice. Humans are given a series of antibodies if exposed to rabies, but for some reason, it is just easier to euthanize a dog. Something just isn't right here, and new methods of care are needed versus the old antiquated system we are all currently following in this country.

KENNEL COUGH

WHERE KENNEL COUGH EXISTS:

Kennel cough can be acquired in a variety of ways. Over forty viruses may cause it. The one we hear about most often results from when our dogs are boarded with other dogs in a care facility. It is inhaled and contagious. In fact, we can't even board our dogs when we go on vacation if we don't have our dogs immunized in most cases. This situation may create a need for in-home care. Dogs can acquire the bordetella bacteria that most often causes the awful choking and hacking noises in most episodes. Most dogs that acquire this bacteria already have a virus that makes them more vulnerable, such as distemper, herpes, the flu, or adenovirus, so be aware that there is already a need to boost the immune system prior to the kennel cough showing up...even more so thereafter.

WHAT KENNEL COUGH IS:

With kennel cough, the respiratory tract is compromised and weakened, and it is affected by inhaled infectious particles. The "honking" cough is a result of the inflamed larynx and trachea. Your pup may also have a runny nose, discharge from the eyes, and be sneezing.

VACCINE DANGERS:

As with all vaccines, the results will produce the appearance of similar symptoms to the actual disease itself. Other side-effects include swelling at the injection site, lack of appetite, lethargy, and possible fever. Dogs with allergic reactions can also see symptoms like diarrhea, vomiting, seizures, and increased heart rate. Of course, aluminum, formaldehyde, and other foreign objects may be contained in the vaccine. Any vaccine elevates the histamine levels, and that can cause a host of problems such as chronic inflammation that may eventually lead to cancer. By the way, I read something recently that stated that cancer always hides behind inflammation. It was an article related to turmeric paste…which is known to bring down the inflammation. Fascinating really.

Bordella vaccines by injection or nasal mist are given by many vets. The bordella vaccine usually also contains the parainfluenza virus, and it usually becomes a host, walking around spreading both viruses to other dogs. What? Isn't this kind of backwards? If you take your dog to a boarding facility with a dog that just had a shot to be there, you are actually exposing your dog to what it was supposed to be protected against! Unfortunately, this is why I always choose in-home care for my pups.

Therefore, this vaccine is ineffective and will not protect your pup from the variety of bacterial and viral agents that may cause the kennel cough. Even with vaccination, your pup can still acquire the infection.

NATURAL TREATMENT:

Most cases resolve on their own without medical intervention within about three weeks as long as no other underlying conditions exist. Note: In rare cases, your pup's health can decline into pneumonia.

Many natural remedies can be used for kennel cough, including:

Astragalus: For immune support.

Collar: Remove collar from neck.

Drosera and Ignatia: Remedies used for kennel cough.

Esberitox: Used to boost the immune system. This is a fast-acting echinacea to reduce infections. This remedy is available in a chewable tab or pill and easy to incorporate into your pup's daily meal. You can use this for any and all viruses in your home for you and your pup.

Essential Oils: Place essential oils of peppermint or eucalyptus in a humidifier near where your pup sleeps.

Garlic: Antibacterial and antiviral.

Olive Leaf: Antiseptic, antifungal, antiviral, antibacterial.

Oregano Oil: Antiseptic, antifungal, antiviral, antibacterial.

Raw Honey: To suppress a cough. I have used Manuka honey with a bit of lemon, licorice root, slippery elm, and echinacea via a syringe.

Vitamin C: An antiviral.

Vitamin E: Provides immune support.

USING NOSODES FOR KENNEL COUGH:

The kennel cough nosode has been shown to be very effective and has impressive results. A British homeopath named Christopher Day, DVM, did a fairly well-known clinical trial in 1985 measuring the use of the nosodes during a kennel cough outbreak. Out of a total of 214 dogs treated with the kennel cough nosode, the incidence of actual, full-blown disease was only 1.9 percent out of 214 dogs, and the majority of dogs who did contract it exhibited only minor symptoms.

The vaccinated dogs had a higher incidence of disease at 4.7 percent, whereas only 0.7 percent of the unvaccinated dogs showed symptoms. This study shows that nosodes can be effective in disease prevention, and when dogs do contract disease, the severity of symptoms can be reduced with their use. The study showed that nosodes can be effective in disease prevention. Also, when dogs contract disease, the symptoms' severity can be reduced with their use. Nosodes effectively stop an outbreak of a highly transmissible disease. In this case, nosodes were more effective in stopping disease than the vaccines. *Vaccination actually impaired the body's ability to respond to the nosode.*

In reference to his clinical trials on kennel cough, Dr. Christopher Day states:

> What appears to emerge from the study is: a) Nosodes can ef-

> fectively stop, in its tracks, an outbreak of a highly transmissible disease (viz kennel cough). b) That it does so, in this case, more effectively than the presently available vaccines. c) That vaccination impairs the ability of the animal to respond to the nosode.[14]

So much more needs to be learned about nosodes, but there is no doubt that they should be considered an integral part of homeopathic or veterinary care. They are safe because they work through the mucous membranes of the mouth and are easy to administer. The immune response to nosodes offers a more natural response to disease…and without introducing killed or modified viruses and harmful preservatives of vaccinations that can weaken the immune system.

Is it possible that nosodes could replace vaccines? They have been proven for homeoprophylaxis in human trials. Because of their safety record, health benefits, and even the lower cost, nosodes are gaining popularity among holistic veterinarians in the U.S., and pet owners are starting to hear about them and give them a trial. I suppose it's really a personal decision worth researching further.

DETOXING FROM THE KENNEL COUGH VACCINE:

Apis: For facial swelling or allergic reaction after vaccination.

Belladonna: For seizures.

Silica: For convulsions, nausea, diarrhea, and swelling.

Sulphur: For swelling and skin irritation.

Thuja: For skin issues and vaccinosis side effects: convulsions, anxiety, inflammation, diarrhea, asthma, cough, paralysis, swelling, skin eczema. With silica, it is known to be an antidote to vaccinosis.

TRADITIONAL TREATMENT:

Antibiotics are a typical course of action.

---

14 From "Pet Vaccinations and Risks." Dog Naturally Magazine. *http://www.dogsnaturallymagazine.com/pet-vaccination-risks-and-benefits/*

HEARTWORM

WHERE HEARTWORM EXISTS:

Many people are unaware that heartworm is passed by infected mosquitos. Where I live in Hawaii, we don't have many mosquitos, so we don't have much need for a heartworm preventative (unless you live in a rainy area). There aren't many places on the planet, however, where heartworm isn't an issue. Just to be safe, I occasionally give my pups' an herbal treatment and work to boost their immune systems. A natural preventative starts first with determining the risk. Through proper nutrition and immune support, your pup will maintain a resistance to the parasite. I find that just a bit of garlic in my dogs' daily meal keeps the immune system strong and the pests away! Before you go into an area where your pups might be exposed to mosquitos, you can boost their immune system with echinacea—just a few drops of liquid supplement in their food and they are all set. If you suspect a bite, you can administer a few drops of black walnut hull in their food as well. There is no need to give a monthly medicine and risk damage to the kidney and liver if you don't have to.

WHAT HEARTWORM IS:

It's not easy to get heartworms. It takes warm weather and standing water to draw hungry female mosquitos carrying the babies (microfilariae), a dog that is already infected with mature male and female heartworms at just the right stage, and half a year for the larvae to mature into adult heartworms...if the dog's immune system doesn't rid the worms from his system first. Heartworms lodge into the heart and lungs and can grow up to twelve inches long. They can live as long as five to seven years, and a dog can have as many as 250 of them. They do not pass to other dogs unless they are bitten by the same mosquito. Many times a respiratory issue presents itself if the manifestation remains untreated. You will notice labored breathing, a mild but persistent cough, loss of appetite, fainting, or even heart failure.

VACCINE DANGERS:

Heartworm prevention is a multi-billion dollar industry. There is always a conflict of interest when such high dollars are involved. In fact, heartworm meds actually do not prevent heartworm. They actually are poisons that kill the larvae from the previous 30-45 days. If your dog is having kidney or liver issues or is prone to them, a heartworm preventative may prove risky. Rather than I list all the possible side effects to the multitude of preventatives, I suggest simply picking up a box and reading them. There are countless issues. If the weather is consistently below 57° and you see no mosquitos, you can halt on the preventative, but many people continue it monthly.

NATURAL TREATMENT:

It is believed that healthy dogs don't get heartworm; therefore, everything starts with building a healthy immune system. Heartworm can easily be treated naturally, but that doesn't mean it's going away overnight. It may take up to six full months before the cycle of worms discontinues and then some time after that to restrengthen the damaged tissues and heart. Another preventative is to use a natural mosquito repellent when outdoors or if they are prevalent in your area. I use one from doTERRA myself, but many essential oils can be used if you do your research. Citronella is the most common. A small amount of garlic can be added to the food daily as well to deter many types of bugs. Don't use more than a tablespoon of fresh minced garlic per day, and use less if you have a smaller dog. You can buy it in a large jar already minced, which saves a lot of hassle. A variety of natural treatments are available for heartworm, including:

> **Black Seed Oil:** An antifungal, antioxidant, anti-inflammatory, with anti-cancer properties. It supports liver health, fights diabetes, prevents hair loss, is good for skin, and fights superbugs. It contains Thymol, which is commonly used to treat TB and vari-

ous other viruses. Note: It has a strong smell and flavor that your dog may not like. You can buy veggie caps at your local health food store and place a bit inside, close it up, and it will disguise the taste.

Black Walnut Hull and Wormwood Tincture: This is the most popular heartworm treatment. Note that some dogs are allergic to both, so it's best to start with small doses. Neither lasts very long, so you'll have to figure out ways to hide it in yummy food.

Diatomaceous Earth: Place in food daily for up to a month. Use food-grade.

Garlic: To repel parasites and boost immune system.

Grapefruit Seed Extract: Antibacterial, antifungal, anti-inflammatory, anti-microbial, and anti-parasitic. It has been shown to fight off countless bacterial and viral strains. It heals wounds and helps with skin diseases and fungal infections.

Hawthorn Berries: Promotes the health of the circulatory system, strengthens blood vessels, and regulates blood clots and blood pressure. Used for heart problems since the first century. Good during and after heartworm treatment. It contains quercetin to help with histamines.

Heartworm Nosode: Visit http://www.earthsongranch.com.

Oregano Oil: Treats yeast infections. Known for its antiviral, antibacterial, antifungal, and antiseptic properties. It's also an anti-parasitic and has shown the ability to neutralize worms. Treats issues of the skin and intestinal tract and assists in digestive disorders.

Paratox: A homeopathic and all natural wormer for cats, dogs, and horses. It's an anti-parasitic that you put in their water daily or syringe into their mouths. It contains five homeopathic remedies: Allium Cepa, Allium Sativum, Croton Tigliem, Interleukin, Lycopersicum, Tanacetum Vulgare. You can buy it online at http://www.earthsongranch.com along with many other great homeopathic products.

DETOXING FROM HEARTWORM VACCINE:

There are various other treatment methods I have heard about for post-vaccination care (for all vaccine types) that we have not previously talked about. Here is a comprehensive list of a few others to try in case of an adverse reaction or just as preventative medicine if a vaccine is forced upon either you or your dog:

Bovine Colostrum: To boost immune system.

Colloidal Silver: You can use in conjunction with probiotics to cleanse the colon and liver and detox the body. Several days of use prior to and following the vaccination are recommended. Large quantities of silver may produce flu-like symptoms or diarrhea, but once the body is able to flush the viral or bacterial substance out, it will return to normal function. A larger dose (an ounce or two depending on the size of the dog) is used immediately following the vaccination.

Detoxifying Bath: Sea or Epsom salts as well as Young Living's "Purification" essential oil can help.

Diatomaceous Earth, Bentonite Clay, or Zeolite: Give as a drink. 1 Tablespoon 1-3 times a day to bind toxins and draw them out.

Elderberry: It inhibits enzymes so viruses cannot penetrate and infect healthy cells. A product called "Elderberry Defense" contains elderberry, echinacea, royal jelly, and olive leaf.

Enzymes or Probiotics: Taken in larger than normal doses on an empty stomach several times a day for several days up to and after vaccinosis. Good bowel flora (taxed by vaccine) is required for proper elimination and to boost the immune system.

HAMPL Vaccinosis Detox: Contains homeopathics, nosodes, organ sarcodes, bach flower complex, sulphur, thuja, pulsatilla, cadmium, ethoxyquin nosode, sugar nosode detox, detox nosode of x-ray, ars alb, canine & feline immunization nosodes, nux vom, kali phos, flower essences crab apple, silica, lymph and skin sarcodes, heavy metal detox nosodes, lyssin nosode, thyroid nosode tonic and repair, heavy metal miasm nosode, vaccininum nosode, mercury chelate, copper chelate, lead chelate, aluminum chelate, chelidonium, shock formula, vaccininum nosode. (Visit https://www.holisticanimalmedicines.com/store/vaccine_detox_relief_from_past_toxins.html for more information.)

Hypericum and Ledum: Taken in water every two hours immediately after injection.

Liver Flush: Epsom salts, olive oil, dandelion root or greens juiced, grapefruit juice or essential oil. Be prepared for everything to come out and allow for easy access to outdoors! Fully-functioning kidneys are also needed to eliminate many of the toxins from vaccines.

Magnesium: To alleviate cellular stress. Increase iodine and selenium to neutralize mercury.

Magnesium Glycinate Powder or Ion Magnesium: Use as a relaxant.

Malandrinum: For ill effects of vaccination (use with thuja and silica). Effective in clearing cancerous deposits (use with copper).

Massage: To help release toxins caught in the lymph nodes.

Mercurius sol or mercurius viv: Used after for neurological effects from aluminum and mercury as well as bromide, MSG, phenoxyethoanol, and polysorbate 80…just to name a few.

Redmond Clay Conditioner: Make into a muddy paste and place on the injection site for one week.

Selenium: Taken several times a day for several days up to and following vaccinosis.

Silica: Pulls out toxins from the bloodstream and tissues. Helps release aluminum. For convulsions, stomach, nausea, rectum, diarrhea, general swelling of the extremities or limbs (a lump at the injection site).

Sulphur: For general swelling of the extremities or limbs (a lump at the injection site), skin, eczema: mezereum (thick, hard scabs), red, itchy eruptions. Can be used with Thuja 200c a month after last vaccines. Known in the medical literature to counter serious side effects of vaccination.

Sodium Bicarbonate (baking soda): Said to buffer poisons.

Super Nutrition: The best way to deal with vaccines is to give the body everything it needs nutritionally. “Eating lower in the food chain” is said to minimize chemical intake. Foods high in chlorophyll and magnesium have the ability to generate new blood cells as well as increase oxygen. Spirulina as well as juices of wheat, barley, alfalfa sprouts, and fresh juices of parsley, cilantro, and celery are awesome detoxifiers! EPA oil is a powerful immune suppressant too. Drink plenty of water or lemon water.

Thuja: For mental issues, anxiety, eye, inflammation, respiration issues such as asthma or cough, paralysis of lower limbs, convulsions, rectum, diarrhea, general swelling of the extremities or limbs (a lump at the injection site). Known in the medical literature to counter serious side effects of vaccination.

Vitamin C: Large amounts given one month prior to vaccination date and three months in meals thereafter. This is a potent detoxifier, especially with mercury poisoning. Start with 500 mg daily, and depending upon the size of the dog, you can go up to 10,000 mg daily. Dosing prior to shots is recommended as well.

Vitamin D: Large amounts given one month prior to vaccination date and three months in meals thereafter. Exposure to natural sunlight will help as well.

Water Hydration: To increase oxygen in blood and flush out and detox the body.

TRADITIONAL TREATMENT:

The drug typically used is called Immiticide. It is an injectable arsenic-based product. It will take two to three injections to kill the adult heartworms in the blood vessels of the heart. The dog must be kept calm and quiet as treatment begins in order to keep the worms that are breaking off from causing blockages in the vessels, resulting in death. Many vets will tell you there is no other way to treat heartworms than the arsenic-based chemical produced by one company that earns over three billion dollars per year making it. Many problems have been reported as a side effect to this chemical, including kidney and liver damage, hair loss, skin rash, thyroid problems, auto-immune disorders, and fertility issues.

"The secret is in getting your body so chemically unloaded and nutrient primed, that it heals itself."

— Dr. Sherry Rogers

VACCINES CONCLUSION

In the wild, animals instinctively seek out healing herbs to help them when they are ill or undernourished, but we have domesticated them and taken away so much of nature today. In fact, Asclepius, the ancient Greek god of medicine, respected dogs very highly for their ability to seek out and eat medicinal herbs in the wild. We are beginning to realize that nature often has the answers—but animals have always known this! The power that created us will allow us every opportunity to care for ourselves and others. Natural medicine can help your pet just as it can help you.

Thousands upon thousands of pets suffer from vaccine-related diseases each and every year, ranging from skin eruptions to cancer and sudden death. The effectiveness of vaccination is questionable, at best. Dr. Richard Pitcairn DVM, homeopath vet, concludes:

> Vaccines do not actually protect populations from disease in the way most people assume—though they do seem to modify the pattern in which the acute disease manifests.
>
> What I have observed is that if one can look at this question with an open mind, one will be surprised at the amount of evidence that is actually there. If you look at the larger perspective of disease incidence (of any type) in the weeks and months following vaccination, you will soon see confirmations of what I am presenting

> to you today. And once this is seen, the way is open for you to question the whole edifice.

Perhaps it is time we simply step back, stand in a place of faith, and trust in the power that created us to take care of us and all the creatures placed upon the earth...in their natural form. The problem here is that we have simply forgotten the ability to connect with earth; perhaps we have never even really truly known how to...in this lifetime, anyway. The solution is not to manipulate beings for the ultimate state of overnight good health, but to allow each of us beings simply to be. There is a more subtle and divine energy that can heal us and take care of us. I believe part of the problem is that we believe there is a problem—therefore, the mirror reciprocates one (or many). The other part of the issue here, simply put, is greed—at the expense of the innocent.

In summary, and without even doing any research, I can tell you that the number of dogs' lives ended by cancer far outweighs those claimed by lepto, parvo, distemper, or rabies. But I needed to do a bit of research to determine whether I was correct, just to ease my mind. I found a twenty-year study (1984-2004) from the University of Georgia that examined the cause of death in dogs. The researchers examined a whopping 74,566 dogs from the Veterinary Medical Database, which includes data from twenty-seven veterinary teaching hospitals. The results were an astonishing YES! Cancer was by far the most common cause of death in all but eleven breeds. More than one-third of dogs die from cancer. Trauma would be the next leading cause, followed by infection. I honestly knew I needed to look no further.

I could write an entire book on what is going on in the world of vaccinations. The subject is really starting to heat up; people are claiming that their civil rights are being violated, and there are conflicts in interest in policy with directors of government bodies and pharmaceutical companies flip-flopping jobs for higher paychecks and criminal activities that new policies are not made from, etc., etc. Once the pharmaceutical industry no longer drives policy, we may see drastic changes for our pets (and for us humans).

Diseases were beginning to decline prior to immunizations and vaccines, and proof is beginning to pop up about the dangers and side effects of vaccines—dispelling the myth that an unvaccinated person or dog poses a danger to the vaccinated. Vaccines' effectiveness is certainly in question. Would viruses even exist if they weren't still being made in test tubes? Recent evidence has come to light to show that unvaccinated dogs are now showing positive titers. For many years, holistic veterinarians believed that nosodes protected through an obscure energetic process, but now more scientific evidence has come to light to show that it is possible for antibodies to be produced in the body without the antigens from the vaccine.

I believe everything created on this planet was carefully thought out, is loved, and can exist in its natural form. Our pups are indeed perfect little miracles just exactly as they are, so perhaps it is time that we just let the source that created us take care of us.

Forgiveness comes in many forms. If you feel you have made a terrible mistake with regard to vaccinations, you must understand that you can live thinking you did...or live to improve a system of which you merely became a victim. When you awaken to the stage of full conscious awareness of the catastrophic state of our American healthcare system (human or animal), you awaken to a whole new state of awareness. It is unfair to yourself to be hard on yourself for making a mistake because God forgives and time heals. The only real mistake we can make is to know and not speak out for change.

Our animals cannot speak for themselves, but I believe that when we become aware and speak for them through positive action for change, we can lift the veil that separates us from the natural state in which God created us and that is enhanced by manmade fear. After all, isn't the vaccination process just a way of saying "I don't trust what God created and I'm fearful I (or my animal) will not be cared for by Him?" Live in balance, be aware, and eat healthy. Have faith and let God take care of the rest.

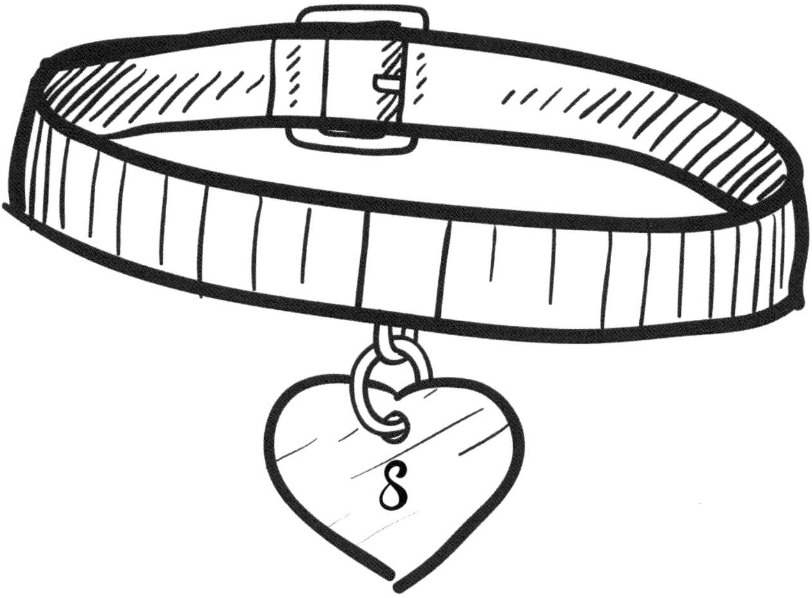

The Dangers of Spaying & Neutering

"The world is a dangerous place to live; not because of the people who are evil, but because of the people who don't do anything about it."

— Albert Einstein

Is it good medicine to remove perfectly good vital organs, and why should it be done? Is it in your pup's best interest? If your dog is always on a leash or in your control, how will she become pregnant? Is pregnancy the issue that causes Americans to fix their pups? Is it the pesky few days of the year that we have to deal with cleaning up the blood of our females? Or is it our males? Are they impregnating all the neighborhood female dogs? What is the reason we do it? Are we conscious? Have you taken the time to understand the risks? Is it worth it? Do you want the best for your pup? How long do you want to live with your pups? Will fixing them increase their lifespan? Are the risks worth it? Where do conscious veterinary medicine practices come into play here?

RESEARCH TODAY IS DISCOVERING THAT JUVENILE DESEXING, IN PARTICULAR, CAN CREATE A SEX HORMONE DEFICIENCY, WHICH ULTIMATELY TAXES A DOG'S ADRENAL GLANDS, CAUSING THEM TO WORK HARDER.

Let's take a minute to understand what is happening when we schedule that appointment. The traditional spaying or neutering is the removal of all sex hormone-secreting tissue. Sterilization is where the pup can no longer reproduce, but maintains sex hormone-secreting tissues. In North America, veterinarians are trained to teach their patients to desex their animals via the traditional methods of removing organs, and they nearly scold when pet owners fail to do so. In many European countries, there are far more intact dogs, which are simply managed or controlled by their owners during the heat cycle and they are desexed in a completely different manner when they are...their organs are left intact. The American system seems to suggest that it's irresponsible not to fix your pup because, as owners, we are unable to control our frisky pups from mass-producing millions of litters of puppies.

The reality of the female dog's cycle is that she only goes into heat once or twice a year for a few weeks. Let's say she is in heat twice for three weeks each time. That would be about forty-two days per year. Within those forty-two days, there are maybe four to eight days when she might become pregnant. So, in the whole scheme of things, the situation is truly manageable. I'm sorry, but men and women deal with their sexual urges far more days than dogs do, but we don't desex them, do we? Our pups don't have a voice or a choice, and we are taking valuable sex organs from them, a process that causes more complications than if we were simply responsible owners who managed a few days of inconvenience. Are we just programmed to have our beliefs based on an unconscious system? I'm asking you to do the research and know the risks.

Research today is discovering that juvenile desexing, in particular, can create a sex hormone deficiency, which ultimately taxes a dog's adrenal glands, causing them to work harder. Hypothyroidism has been on the rise in dogs, and it's believed to be related to desexing, as are a whole host of other problems. I'll talk about the hypothyroidism shortly.

HEALTH ISSUES LINKED TO SPAYING AND NEUTERING DOGS

A growing body of evidence suggests that desexing dogs, especially at an early age, can create health and behavior problems in them. Some of these problems are:

- Hip Dysplasia
- Shortened lifespan
- Higher rate of CCL (knee joint ligament) ruptures
- Increase in bone cancer for larger breed dogs
- Golden Retrievers are much more likely to develop hypothyroidism
- Increase in Cushing's disease
- Overtaxed adrenal glands
- Increased incidence of behavior problems, including noise phobias, fear behavior, aggression, and undesirable sexual behaviors
- Abnormal bone-growth development for dogs under one year of age

SIDE EFFECTS OF NEUTERING MALE DOGS

- Before one year of age, neutering can significantly increase the risk of bone cancer in medium to large dogs.
- Increased incidence of urethral sphincter incontinence
- Increases the risk of heart cancer
- Triples the risk of hypothyroidism
- Increases the risk of memory loss and dementia in older age
- Triples the risk of obesity
- Quadruples the risk of prostate cancer
- Doubles the risk of urinary tract cancers
- Increases the risk of orthopedic disorders
- Increases the risk of adverse reactions to vaccinations

SIDE EFFECTS OF SPAYING FEMALE DOGS

- Before one year of age, spaying can significantly increase the risk of bone cancer, common in larger dogs
- Increases the risk of spleen cancer
- Increases the risk of heart cancer[15]
- Four times as likely to develop heart tumors as intact females. Spayed females had a greater than five times risk versus their intact counterparts.
- Triples the risk of hypothyroidism
- Causes urinary incontinence in up to 20 percent of female dogs
- Increases urinary tract infections
- Increases the risk of recessed vulva, vaginal dermatitis,

15 *If you have any of the following dogs, the risk is higher: Salukis, French Bulldogs, Irish Water Spaniels, Flat Coated Retrievers, Golden Retrievers, Boxers, Afghan Hounds, English Setters, Scottish Terriers, Boston Terriers, Bulldogs, and German Shepherds. (Prymak, C. et al. "Epidemiologic, clinical, pathologic, and prognostic characteristics of splenic hemangiosarcoma and splenic hematoma in dogs: 217 cases."* J Am VetMed Assoc. *1988 Sep; 193(6):706-12.)*

and vaginitis (especially if done before puberty)

- Increases the small risk of urinary tract tumor
- Increases the risk of orthopedic disorders
- Increases the risk of adverse reactions to vaccinations
- Increases the risk of obesity
- Increased risk of cardiac tumors

Here are a few studies I found that indicate further the risk of spaying and neutering your dog:

A Study from the Journal of Veterinary Internal Medicine

Suggests there isn't much scientific evidence at all to support the idea that spaying of female dogs decreases or eliminates future risk of mammary tumors or breast cancer. The difference in death due to mammary tumors was not significant between spayed and non-spayed. The spayed group actually experienced a greater incidence of malignant tumor reoccurrence than the non-spayed group. Forty-two percent of dogs with a single tumor on one side had tumor regrowth on the opposite side. This study suggests that the removal of all mammary tissue is required at the time of tumor removal or spaying…increasing risks.

Michigan State University's College of Veterinary Medicine

There's a common belief that neutering a male dog prevents prostate cancer. However, this small study suggests that neutering—no matter the age—has no effect on the development of prostate cancer.

Gerald P. Murphy Cancer Foundation, 2009

This study established a link between the age at which female Rottweilers are spayed and how long they live. Females who kept their ovaries until at least six years of age were four times more likely to reach an exceptional age compared to those who were spayed at a younger age.

Texas Tech University Health Sciences Center

A study on cranial cruciate ligament injuries concluded that spayed and neutered dogs had a significantly higher incidence of rupture than their intact counterparts. While large-breed dogs had more CCL injuries, sterilized or desexed dogs of all breeds and sizes had an increased rupture rate.

Cornell University's College of Veterinary Medicine

In a study, results showed that both male and female dogs sterilized at an early age were more prone to hip dysplasia.

University of California, Davis

A study conducted involving several hundred Golden Retrievers. The study found that males neutered before the age of twelve months were twice as likely to suffer from hip dysplasia, and that three times more early-neutered males suffered from lymphosarcoma than intact males. Females spayed after twelve months suffered from hemangiosarcoma four times more than intact or early-neutered females. In either case, intact dogs came out better than those that had been desexed.

College of Veterinary Medicine at Texas A&M University

A cohort study of shelter dogs conducted concluded that infectious diseases were more common in dogs that were spayed and neutered before twenty-four weeks of age.

The American Kennel Club's Canine Health Foundation

This report pointed to higher incidence of adverse reactions to vaccines in spayed and neutered dogs.

COMPLICATIONS FROM THE SURGERY ITSELF

Of course, with all major surgeries, risk is involved. There can be a reaction to anesthesia, an infection, inflammation, a major hemorrhage, etc. Studies have found that the rate of complication with this surgery can be as high as 22 percent. But the death rate is less than 1 percent.

BENEFITS OF DESEXING

Some vets believe two medical conditions can be totally eliminated by desexing: 1) benign prostatic hypertrophy or BPH (enlarged prostate), and 2) pyometra (a disease of the uterus). However, the risk of pyometra or BPH in an animal's first year of life is incredibly low.

For the male, the only benefits found so far are:

- Eliminates the 1 percent or less chance of dying from testicular cancer.
- Reduces the risk of non-cancerous prostate disorders, reduces the risk of lesions around the anus (mostly in German Shepherds).
- May reduce the risk of diabetes. (The evidence here is inconclusive; perhaps it can be altered with diet more successfully.)

And for the female? If she is spayed prior to two-and-a-half years old, the benefits are:

- Greatly reduces the risk of mammary tumors (a common malignant tumor in some breeds of female dogs, such as Golden Retrievers, Boxers, Cocker Spaniels, English Springers, and Dachshunds). Although, the study mentioned above may debunk this.)
- Nearly eliminates the risk of pyometra (uterine infection); although this infection affects about 20 percent of intact female dogs, it only kills 1 percent, so I believe diet may be a factor here as well.
- If she is a German Shepherd, it will reduce her risk of anal lesions.
- A less than 1 percent reduced risk of uterine, cervical, or ovarian tumors occurring post-spay.

So unless your dog has one of the problems listed here, why are you fixing him or her? Convenience? Do you want to extend your dog's life? How important is that to you? I'm guessing it's important, so *please* start asking questions and consider the impact of your choice on your sweet kiddo.

HYPOTHYROIDISM

I became curious about the risk of hypothyroidism (underactive thyroid) with desexing our dogs. I found out that it is believed to be the most common endocrine system disorder in dogs and possibly the number one reason not to spay or neuter your dog because it seems to create a vicious circle that is hard to reverse.

According to the *Whole Dog Journal*, about 70 percent of the 140 breeds recognized by the American Kennel Club (AKC) recognize hypothyroidism as a major concern in their breeds. But many veterinarians believe it to be related to genetics or an autoimmune disorder. It is said to occur when the thyroid gland (found in your dog's neck) produces abnormally low levels of thyroid hormones. The gland produces two hormones: thyroxine (T4) and triiodithyronine (T3). Traditional medicine treats the disorder with a drug containing a synthetic thyroid hormone.

I have heard for many of the twenty-five-plus years I've had Shar Pei in my life that they are at high risk of developing thyroid disorders, though it's not something I ever had to manage with my dogs. So I dug a bit deeper to find out whether certain dogs are at a higher risk than others. In the most recent study I found, the ten breeds most susceptible include:

- English Setter
- Eurasier
- Spanish Water Dog
- Irish Red & White Setter
- Dalmatian
- Shetland Sheepdog
- Boxer
- Kuvasz
- Tibetan Terrier
- Welsh Springer Spaniel

Source: Orthopedic Foundation for Animals:Breeds having at least 50 evaluations January 1974 through December 2015 http://www.offa.org/stats_thy.html

Become an investigator; if your dog is already at high risk, that means you would likely put him or her at higher risk by spaying or neutering.

Some of the other results I found showed that both my Shar Pei and Bulldog made the top of the lists. But the list provided above was the most current information I could find. Here, my breeds were listed 91 and 93 of 112 dogs evaluated. Unfortunately, my partner was adamant about fixing our bulldog Leilani because he didn't want our male Shar Pei Blue to get her pregnant. So, unknowingly, she became higher risk, unfortunately prior to my research. My next question became what to do about it since it was already done. I started running in circles with all of it. At this point, I was led to researching the endocrine system. I found that getting a picture of the entire system in my head helped me see how few organs are really functioning as a part of the endocrine system and really how critical they are in the workings of the whole.

THE ENDOCRINE SYSTEM

Once I got a picture of the whole system in my head, I began to see how it would work if organs were removed and how the system might make up for their loss. I started to see the circular problems in my mind and in my research. When the sex organs are removed, it causes everything else to work harder to compensate for them not being there. It's like the body moves into a fight-or-flight mode.

The adrenal glands sit on the kidneys and both become taxed. Now I was more worried because I knew that the kidneys tend to fail in Shar Pei. I've always understood this to be because they get Shar Pei fever, which taxes the kidneys when the fever elevates. But I can't see how, now that the adrenals are working harder, it wouldn't also tax the kidneys. Shar Pei are also known to have thyroid problems, and the thyroid works harder when the adrenals work harder.

But then what happens many times is we don't always know it's a problem that could be possibly associated with the desexing, and we think the thyroid is failing or that our dogs have allergies when their skin has trouble and their hair falls out. So we give them allergy and thyroid meds and that can cause other issues, like Cushing's disease (also called hyperadrenocorticism). Cushing's happens when your dog makes too much cortisol. This is usually because there is a tumor in either the pituitary or adrenal glands, but it can also occur if your dog has taken steroids (for allergy treatment, for example) for too long.

Then cortisol levels increase and the adrenal glands have to work harder to keep up. Allergies, infections, physical trauma, excess exercise, emotional trauma, chemical toxins, anxiety or depression, prescription drugs, and lifestyle (lack of exercise or poor diet) can lead to even more adrenal fatigue. As I learned all this, my head was spinning! I started to cry and become overwhelmed the more I learned.

THE ENDOCRINE SYSTEM

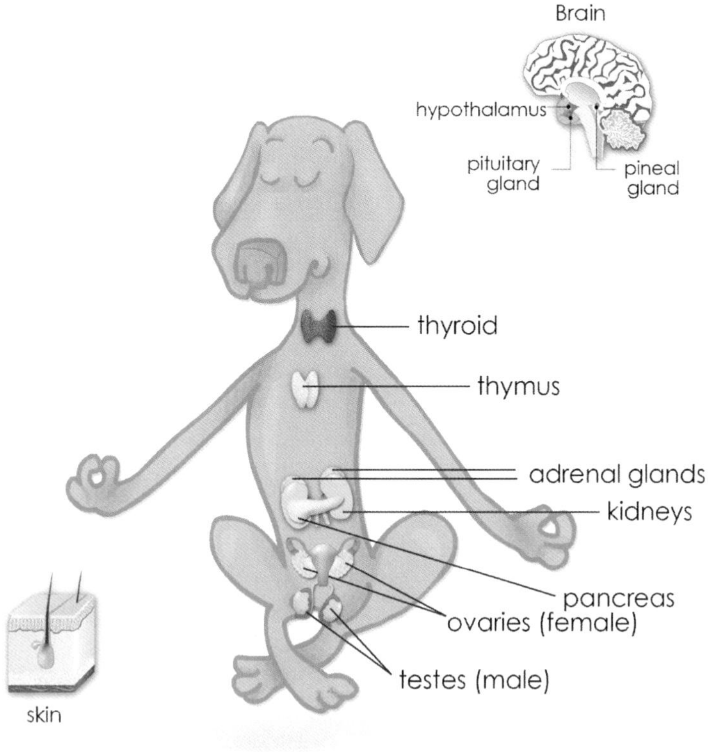

Again, my research pointed back to the importance of diet. Foods that calm the nerves can calm how the adrenal glands function…foods rich in calcium, magnesium, Vitamin A and C. Licorice root can stimulate the adrenals (if your pup doesn't have high blood pressure) and because the body can become fatigued, a good digestive enzyme with each meal can give extra digestive support.

Also, believe it or not, when your dog barks, it can stimulate the kidneys and adrenals through the vibration. In fact, in yoga this is referred to as the power of the "naad." Naad is the power of sound… healing sound to boost our health and increase our vitality. It is believed that in the human, mantra, rhythm, and breath used together can create a healing response in the immune system. So why wouldn't our dogs have this ability too? Could howling at the moon be explained as a healing ritual for our canine friends?

SUMMARY

It seems to me that when we remove the sex organs, the body begins playing a game of catch up to re-work the whole endocrine system. My mind is still stuck on the fact that if God wanted our animals to be born without their sex organs, wouldn't they be? I wonder whether, if we just honored our pups as they were created, managed the situation, and let our dogs be dogs, how our world would look different.

Again, the subject of conscious doctoring or pet parenting comes into play here. Have you done your research, or are you simply trusting that because everyone else is doing it, you should too? I ask you to take the time to think about the long-term health benefits of keeping your baby intact. I ask you to trust that God had a plan and there is a good reason to keep everything as it was created. Know the risks and choose wisely. Your baby is counting on you to do what is right. Unless there is a health concern or a reason to spay or neuter your pup, please consider leaving everything as God created it.

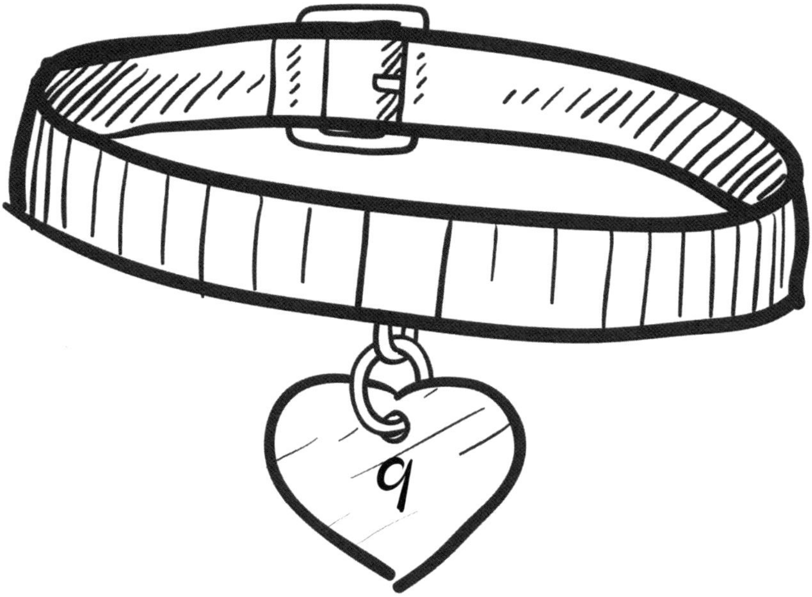

Essential Oils for Dogs

"God made the earth, the sky and the water,
the moon and the sun. He made man and bird and beast.
But He didn't make the dog. He already had one."
— Native American saying

Up to this point, we have discussed many fairly typical subjects you might expect to see in a book about healing your dog naturally. But I want to talk about the entire state of the dog—physically, emotionally, and spiritually. We will begin to drift into a few other subjects that may stretch your imagination a bit, but I believe that globally we are making a shift into becoming more consciously-aware beings, so today, the following chapters may not be as "woo-hoo" as they once may have been viewed. So let's start here with essential oils.

Because essential oils are able to pass through your skin and the air, they have great healing benefits. They can be applied topically, internally, or by being inhaled with a diffuser. Clove and frankincense can be diffused if you suspect a cold. The air can be cleaned with lemon. To improve energy, use peppermint. To relax or release a headache, use lavender.

Essential oils are extracted directly from the bark, flower, leaf, seed, or root of a plant or tree. They are distilled, yet highly concentrated. Imagine how many flowers of lavender it takes to get one pound of essential oil. You are getting the power of multiple flowers in just one drop. Essential oils can affect every cell of the body within twenty minutes of being used and are metabolized like other nutrients. Because a nutrient deficiency is really an oxygen deficiency, essential oils can transport nutrients to the starving human cells because they contain oxygen molecules. Disease begins when cells lack oxygen for proper nutrient assimilation. Therefore, essential oils stimulate the immune system. They are also high in antioxidants and create an unfriendly environment for free radicals...preventing fungus for example. They are anti-fungal, antibacterial, anti-cancerous, anti-infectious, antimicrobial, anti-tumoral, anti-parasitic, anti-viral, and antiseptic. They have been shown to detoxify the cells and blood in the body. They have also been shown to assist with Alzheimer's, Lou Gehrig's, and Parkinson's disease, as well as multiple sclerosis.

WHEN KING TUT'S TOMB WAS OPENED IN 1922, 350 LITERS OF ESSENTIAL OILS WERE FOUND INTACT IN ALABASTER JARS.

When King Tut's tomb was opened in 1922, 350 liters of essential oils were found intact in alabaster jars. They were a bit more solid in nature, and in 1926, they were analyzed and found to be primarily made of animal fat and a resin or balsam—making a more solid perfume that melted in the heat of the palm. Ancient

Egyptian papyrus, found in the temple of Edfu, contained formulations to make medicines and perfumes used by the alchemists and high priests and even for the embalming process. They were used by many kings and queens eons ago. In fact, the Bible references essential oils over 250 times. It was believed that the ointment of spikenard (a root) was used to anoint the feet of Jesus (John 12:3), and it was also found in King Tut's tomb. Spikenard was believed to carry mystical and romantic powers. Frankincense, myrrh, cinnamon, calamus, cassia, and olive were also commonly found in highly spiritual places. It is believed that essential oils were mankind's first medicines, and they were seen as quite magical in their ability to heal.

I only use three or four brands of essential oils because I trust in their quality and they are therapeutic grade. My preference is Young Living first, DoTerra second, and then a few I have found more readily at natural health food stores, such as Aura Casia and NOW Foods. You can muscle test to determine which brand is your best option. We'll talk a bit more about muscle testing in later chapters.

Essential oils are one of my favorite tools for invoking an environment of healing. In fact, when I go to bed at night, I love to fill multiple diffusers with calming oils or oils that assist with breathing to heal my whole family. As a family, we all benefit from them together. Eucalyptus can open the airways at night, and for a household with two Shar Pei and one English Bulldog, constricted airways and lots of snoring can be fairly typical. Diffusing essential oils can help to remove metallic particles and toxins from the air, increase atmospheric oxygen, increase ozone and negative ions (inhibiting bacterial growth), destroy odors and mold, and, of course, fill the air with a fresh aromatic scent.

Essential oils are non-toxic, and they support your dog's emotional and physical well-being. They can be dripped onto the spine directly for certain techniques (some oils need to be diluted or they will cause irritation). They can be used for allergies, sore muscles, healing skin conditions, to improve digestion, diffused into the air for calming and balance, used in cleaning, to invoke an altered state, to detox the body, or applied as a part of a technique for internal or topical healing. The most caution should be taken when they are used internally. I like Young Living for my kiddos because it has a newer line of oils called Vitality that are made as dietary supplements, so they are safer for internal use. Young Living also makes things easier by packaging certain blends just for animals. If you were to get started using essential oils for your pups, I would start with the Animal Connection Kit. It is great for emotional and physical well-being. Young Living also has an ointment and shampoo specifically for animals that provide great benefits as well. I promise that I'm not writing this chapter, though, to sell or promote these products, but I am a distributor if you'd like to use my information to sign up yourself. My ID is "VeganDog" or #1537886. My doTERRA ID is #882583. I just really believe in them because I have seen the results. For example, tea tree oil has healed many skin issues for the pups and me; peppermint has become a great breath freshener for all of us; a small dab of Thieves or oregano oil has healed many of our wounds; and here in Hawaii, we suffer from VOG, so eucalyptus or evergreen clears the air and makes it easier for us to breathe at night.

I tend to use my oils more in a diffuser than anything else…just because my pups are generally pretty healthy and don't need much topically. But the oils can also be used as a dietary supplement (with some caution) and topically (if diluted with a carrier oil). Because I have Shar Pei and an English Bulldog, essential oils are also great in our household for cleaning ears and other folds. But they are also my go to for cleaning the house. I do not use chemical products. Think about it…if you clean the floor, they walk on it, and then when they chew their feet, they ingest whatever you used to clean it or it leaches in through their skin. You can actually do some pretty amazing healing by simply washing your floors with the right products. How many times can you say that washing the floor was beneficial for your health? Because we live in Hawaii, we have year-round fleas, ticks (the non-Lyme's disease type), mosquitos (in the cooler, wetter areas), cockroaches, and centipedes. But because I wash the hardwood floors daily with Young Living Thieves, and the carpets monthly with citronella, I think many bugs are discouraged from coming in. These oils can also keep the bugs off the dogs. Before I give you a few great ideas with essential oils, let's talk about just a few of the best ones to have on hand for your pups.

TOP ESSENTIAL OILS TO HAVE ON HAND

Essential Oils	Properties & Uses
Bergamot	• Antifungal, soothing. • Excellent for ear infections caused by yeast or bacterial overgrowth.
Carrot Seed	• Anti-inflammatory, tonic—with moderate anti-bacterial effects. • Good for dry, flaky, sensitive skin that is prone to infection. • Can rejuvenate and stimulate tissue regeneration, thus effective for scar healing.
Cedarwood	• Antiseptic, tonifying, circulation-stimulating. • Good for skin and coat conditioning and dermatitis of all types. • Flea-repelling.
Chamomile, German	• Anti-inflammatory, non-toxic, gentle, and safe to use. • Good for skin irritations, allergic reactions, burns.
Chamomile, Roman	• Antispasmodic, analgesic, nerve-calming. • Good for soothing the central nervous system. • Effective for relief of muscle pains, cramps, and teething pain.
Clary Sage	• Nerve-calming. • Sedates the central nervous system.

Copaiba	• Supports healthy digestion. • Contains 50 percent beta-caryophyllene, which is used to support the body's natural response to irritation. (Beta-caryophyllene can also be found in the following oils: basil, oregano, black pepper, rosemary, cinnamon bark.)
Eucalyptus	• Antiviral, anti-inflammatory, an expectorant. • Good for relief of chest congestion. (Great for Bulldogs and short-nosed dogs in a diffuser at night or on a collar or cloth to help with breathing during exercise.) • Effective in repelling fleas.
Frankincense	• Said to be the most powerful essential oil in the world. • Known to shrink tumors and kill cancer cells, in some cases, better than chemotherapy. • Helps reduce inflammation and improve immune functioning.
Geranium	• Gentle and safe, antifungal. • Good for skin irritations, fungal ear infections. • Effective in repelling ticks.
Ginger	• Good for motion sickness; aids digestion and GI distress. • Effective for pain relief caused by arthritis, dysplasia, joints, strains, and sprains. • Anti-inflammatory • Known to heal leaky gut and strengthen immunity. • Reduces anxiety and slows aging. • Mix with peppermint and fennel for leaky gut, bowel disease, and other digestive issues.

Helichrysum	• Anti-inflammatory, analgesic, regenerative effects; extremely therapeutic. • Excellent for skin conditions and irritations (e.g., eczema). • Effective for healing of scars and bruises. • Effective for pain relief.
Lavender	• Very safe and gentle, antibacterial, anti-itch, nerve-calming. • Good for many common animal ailments, e.g., skin irritations; first aid for healing cuts, burns, stings, and other wounds. • Known to treat diabetes and oxidative stress. • Mix with Roman chamomile for rashes.
Lemon	• Helps release toxins and stimulates lymph drainage. • Rejuvenates energy. • Purifies skin and acts as a bug repellent. • May be the most powerful anti-microbial agent of all essential oils. • Improves neurological activity. • Freshens breath.
Marjoram, Sweet	• Strong antibacterial, calming, a muscle relaxant. • Good for bacterial skin infections, wound care, insect repelling.
Neroli	• Antihistaminic, powerful antibacterial properties, yet less likely to cause irritation than Tea Tree. • Good for ear infections and skin problems caused by allergies. • A “must-have” for dogs!

Peppermint	• Antispasmodic, stimulates circulation, insect-repelling. • Good for arthritis, dysplasia, sprains, and strains. • Works well with ginger to treat motion sickness. • Has been found to improve antibiotic resistance and healing from overuse of prescription antibiotics and other chemicals. • Relieves sore muscles when used topically. • Antimicrobial properties to freshen bad breath and soothe digestive issues.
Sweet Orange	• Calming, deodorizing, flea-repelling.
Tea Tree (Melaleuca)	• Ability to treat wounds with antiseptic properties. • Known to kill bacteria, viruses, yeast, and fungi. • Eliminates parasitic infections.
Valerian	• Nerve-calming. • Good for treating dog anxiety such as separation and noise anxiety.

Young Living Animal Scents Essential Oils & Thieves

Infect Away	• Supports proper healing. • 2-4 drops to your hands and pet into your pup's coat or belly. • 8-10 drops in a 1 oz. spray bottle with distilled water for immune boosting.
Mendwell	• Helps wound care. • 1-2 drops to the area to support healthy skin repair. Use a roller to apply a generous amount.
ParaGize	• For parasite elimination. Supports digestive system. 1-4 drops in water. • Can add to carrier oil and rub on belly. • 8-10 drops in a 1 oz. spray bottle with distilled water to support healthy digestion.
Puriclean	• For cleansing affected areas. • 1-2 drops to the area to support proper cleansing of skin and support a healthy coat. Use a roller to apply a generous amount. • 8-10 drops in a 1 oz. spray bottle with distilled water for quick skin cleansing. • Use a drop and pet from head to tail.
RepelAroma	• 2-4 drops on hands and pet into coat to freshen and promote healthy skin. • Insect repellant to keep bugs away. Dilute with water and place in spray bottle and apply. • Use a drop and pet from head to tail.
T-Away	• Diffuse for emotional freedom and joyful feelings. • Helps animals cope with emotional blocks. • Use a drop and pet animal from head to tail.
Thieves	• Clove, lemon, cinnamon, eucalyptus, rosemary. • Clove is ranked as the #1 herb in the world in anti-oxidant value. Known to kill candida. • Cinnamon balances blood sugar, protects again sickness and disease. • Rosemary protects the brain against dementia. Known to improve health of hair, skin, nails.

Top Ailments and Their Oils

Oils can be applied to the foot pads, a fabric or rope type collar, diffused in the air, or mixed with a carrier oil and applied topically for a wound. For breath, you can make your own toothpaste with some water and baking soda and a few drops of oil. My favorite way to treat nearly all issues is the least invasive, and that is to diffuse the oils at night and in my office by day while my dogs are hanging out at my feet. For the less invasive oils or those that don't have a bothersome effect on your pups' noses, you might be able to add one little drop in their water without them refusing to drink it. I actually like sometimes to hide a few oils in their food if I feel there is a need. A sardine will generally always hide the smell. Most often, though, I find diffusing is the least invasive…or bathing.

Ailment	Essential Oil
Allergies	Geranium, chamomile, lavender, rosewood, bergamont, cedar, citronella
Anxiety, separation anxiety, and car rides	Ylang ylang, chamomile, lavender, peppermint, ginger
Arthritis, Joints, Muscles	Clove, wintergreen, helichrysum, rosemary, peppermint
Asthma	Chamomile, peppermint, lavender, geranium, frankincense, rose, eucalyptus
Bad Breath	Spearmint, peppermint, clary sage, clove, lemon
Bowel Trouble	Peppermint, eucalyptus, thyme, chamomile

Ear Infections	Eucalyptus, lemon, rosemary, oregano
Fleas and Ticks	Lavender, peppermint, lemongrass, cedar, citronella, eucalyptus
Flatulence	Peppermint, lemongrass, cardamom, nutmeg, lemon
Grief	Rose, melissa, neroli, myrrh, marjoram, chamomile, bergamot
Immune System	Tea tree oil, eucalyptus, coriander, frankincense
Inflamation	Peppermint, lavender, rosemary, frankincense, myrrh, lemon, chamomile
Skin and Coat Issues	Lavender (#1 for burns), geranium, eucalyptus, helichrysum, chamomile, peppermint, orange, lemongrass
Ulcers	Lavender, lemon, frankincense, myrrh, yarrow, orange
Urinary Incontinence	Thyme, yarrow, sandalwood, patchouli, geranium, myrrh, helichrysum, eucalyptus, clary sage, bergamot
Weight Loss	Cardamom, spearmint

ESSENTIAL OILS & ALLERGIES

I began to wonder how I could use essential oils to assist with a few concerns I had going on with regard to Bella's allergies. I did a bit of research to see whether they would help block some of the inhalant type allergies, or even clean the air before it reached her system. I found out that the allergic reaction begins in the immune system and that an allergen is something that makes the immune system react to it like an invader. When the immune system over-reacts to something that is otherwise harmless, it produces the Immunoglobulin E antibodies we talked about earlier. These guys travel to the cells that release the histamine; in those cells is where the allergic reaction occurs. They then trigger symptoms, in Bella's case, on the skin. The body then responds and becomes inflamed. One of the most amazing benefits of essential oils is their ability to fight inflammation and boost the immune system. Some even work to help eliminate toxins. The best oils for allergies are:

- Peppermint
- Basil
- Eucalyptus
- Lavender (applied to sinus areas on face and neck)
- Lemon
- Tea Tree (topically)

For food allergies, you can use a drop of lemon or peppermint; for rashes, use tea tree or basil; and tea tree with lemon, water, and vinegar is a good air spray during allergy season.

EAR CLEANING WITH ESSENTIAL OILS

Basic Cleaner

- 1 cup apple cider vinegar (Braggs)
- 1 capful of rubbing alcohol
- 3-5 drops of lavender, neroli, bergamot, or chamomile

Mix ingredients and draw the liquid into the syringe. Put the syringe just slightly in the ear and slowly inject the liquid into the ear.

Rub in a circular fashion to get the liquid into the canal. Let your dog shake his or her head and release the gunk. Clean up with paper towel or slightly deeper (be careful) with cotton swabs.

Vinegar, also known as acetic acid, is a great cleaner that dissolves ear wax and kills parasites or possible bacteria. The vinegar for ear cleaning can be applied with an eyedropper or a syringe. If your dog has open sores, be careful because sometimes the vinegar may sting. I always test all products I make on myself prior to subjecting my pups to any discomfort. Herbal thuja can be added if you suspect a fungus.

Open Wound Ear Spray

- Witch hazel
- 1 Tbsp. oil (Young Living V-6 or coconut oil)
- 3 drops lemongrass oil
- 3 drops Thieves
- 4 drops copaiba
- 5 drops purification blend

If your pup has open wounds in his ear, the vinegar may sting. Witch hazel can be a good substitute. Add witch hazel to a 30 ml spray bottle with the above ingredients. Shake well and spray into ear once or twice a day. This spray is effective for yeast, bacteria, mites, and inflammation. Let your dog shake his head and release the gunk. Clean up with paper towel or slightly deeper (be careful) with cotton swabs.

For Tender Ears with Open Sores, Dampness, or Infection

- 2 drops of lavender
- ¼ cup of colloidal silver

Place drops in each ear and massage. Let your dog shake his or her head and release the gunk. Clean up with a paper towel or slightly deeper (be careful) with cotton swabs.

Note: Be extremely cautious if your dog has any open sores in the ear because the drops will sting and cotton swabs used too deeply may cause damage to the eardrum. I like to use liquid calendula mixed in either beeswax or coconut oil for healing open surface level sores as well, but be cautious not to block the canal because it would become a breeding ground for bacteria. Colloidal Silver or Witch Hazel are good replacements for the ACV if there are open sores and you still need to clean. Be aware that infected ears can be a sign of a more serious health issue. Sometimes adding garlic to the diet as well as colloidal silver can clear up the inside so the outside is healthier. And always address the overall gut health with a good probiotic. The gut can create all kinds of problems in the body that you never would have suspected were related.

ESSENTIAL OIL FLOOR WASH

Many times, you will see people recommending using a roller ball to apply essential oil to the feet pads, but why not also wash your floor at the same time and cause far less stress on your pup too! I like to wash with a bit of apple cider vinegar and whatever oil might suit the situation at hand. Then, while I'm washing, it's inevitable the pups will walk through it! In fact, I might even convince them to! I add essential oil to my carpet cleaner too! Here's the mixture I use:

- ½ cup Apple Cider Vinegar (Braggs)
- ½ bucket or sink of water
- 3-5 drops of Young Living T-Away for stress, Thieves for bacteria, or cedar wood or citronella for bugs

FLEAS IN CARPET

Mix vaporous (peppermint or eucalyptus) or citrus oils (citronella, orange, lemon, or grapefruit) with borax powder or food grade diatomaceous earth. Leave on for a few hours; then vacuum up. Note: Don't get it wet or you will have a real mess to clean up!

You can also mix these oils with a bit of food grade diatomaceous earth, and after you sprinkle that on the carpets, rub a bit on your hands and then on your pup for personal flea control.

SUMMARY OF ESSENTIAL OILS

Essential oils are far more than just yummy smells. They work with your pup emotionally, physically, and spiritually. It can be important to involve your dog in the process of choosing the right oil for him or her. If your dog is repulsed by the oil when it is presented, then it's not likely the one for him or her. If he licks it, paws at it, or tries to rub his entire body on it, then you may have a winner! You can also use muscle-testing or kinesiology to find the right one. Oils can be used for healing from various injuries and ailments, including car rides and anxiety, fleas and ticks, allergies, burns, ulcers, wound care, bad breath, and skin and coat issues to name a few.

There really aren't too many rules with essential oils, but remember that your dog has a far more sensitive nose than we do. Go lightly and respect that too much is never a good thing. If it's slightly too strong for you, imagine that times a thousand and that's how your dog experiences it. If you apply an oil to your dog, he cannot escape it. So be kind. A little oil goes a long way.

When it comes to addressing more emotional issues, essential oils are great, but what I find even better is the subtlety of the flower remedies. You and your dog will hardly smell these because they are far less invasive if your dog is sensitive.

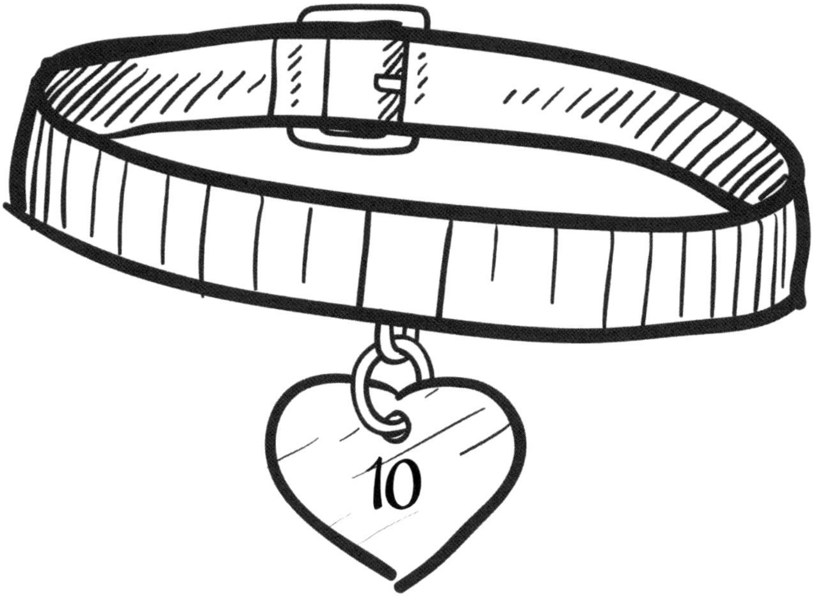

Flower Essence Remedies

"If a dog's prayers were answered,
Bones would rain from the sky."

— Turkish Proverb

If your pup is struggling with an emotional issue such as fear, anger, depression, or jealousy, then flower remedies can help. Companies like Feel Bach! have created a few remedies specifically for our pets.

Feel5ive for pets is a natural stress reliever. Home Alone is for stress when you leave your pet home alone. Thunder Storms will alleviate fear during thunderstorms, or fireworks, or when a gun goes off. Then of course, Rescue Remedy is excellent for trauma, anxiety, or to help your pet relax from any stressful situation like being in a shelter, riding in the car, going to a vet, or any rescue situation. And taken right from the Feel Bach! website:

> Our pets can suffer from the same situations that we humans do. Therefore, when we notice emotional distress in our pet, we should first examine whether we are exhibiting signs of that same distress. If we conclude that our pet is indeed exhibiting behavior that mirrors our own, or is manifesting a problem that we ourselves have, or is responding to something that has happened to us, then we should also be taking a Bach essence.
>
> Taking an essence along with our pet is a powerful motivator and a sign that we have decided to change a behavior pattern together with our pet. The result will be an easier and more rapid recovery.

I am so pleased to see that companies like Bach are making the connection between our pets and us. I have known for many years that my behaviors directly impact my pets. Dogs, in particular, are here to teach us about loyalty and stand as our angels, teaching us to treat ourselves (and them) the best we can. We truly are all connected.

LEILANI'S ANXIETY

My partner was struggling for some time with anxiety due to the loss of his father as well as some financial challenges. Our English Bulldog suddenly started becoming very fearful and started exhibiting some strange behaviors. She was sleeping in the bathroom much of the day and would run upstairs as soon as her meal was finished. In fact, sometimes she wouldn't even eat because of unknown fears. It got to the point where I was not sure I could stay in the relationship because I could see what it was doing to her, and I knew what it was doing to me. I realized the old saying though that "All things shall pass" and remained patient.

As her fears progressed, she also developed "head tremors." In some breeds, this head-shaking seizure-like head bobbing can be fairly common. When I did some research, I found out that the tremors were not treatable with common anti-seizure medication. In fact, there is little understood about the cause. I did find some reference to stress as a probable trigger. We certainly had stress. She had two episodes and I treated her with homeopathic belladona and aconite during the seizure. The first time it shortened the episode, but the second time it had no effect. I began looking into flower essences and homeopathy. I treated with Herb Pharm Anxiety Soother (contains kava, passion flower, bacopa, albizia bark, lavender flower, and essential oil). I just added a bit to her food, along with the flower essences and Anxiety Soother.

As my partner started working on himself and healing his pain, Leilani started spending less time in the bathroom and cowering less frequently when she wasn't. In a case like this, one might use Feel Bach! minimalus, Rescue Remedy, or aspen, but I also used another flower essence (Maui Flower Essence Technology's Plumeria) that we have here locally in Hawaii that is for "ease of being." I took it myself because of the stress the situation was causing me, and I also gave it to Leilani, through just a few drops in her mouth and in the water she drinks. I spent time with her talking to her and cutting as many energetic cords (we will talk about this later on) as I could, but because of her love for her daddy, she could not break free of "helping him" feel his pain. I would do some energy work and clearing for her, but within a short period, she would re-establish the link and be right back in the bathroom. Now that he has stepped up to do some personal healing, she no longer hides in the bathroom. Both are on the mend together and we have been head tremor free for almost a year now.

THE ENERGETIC CONNECTION TO OUR DOGS

Our dogs teach us great lessons about ourselves. I have a rule that I prefer not to allow food into the house unless it is something that is healthy enough to share with my kiddos. If I am suffering (or eating poorly), I am also aware that they are doing it with me. If I am dealing with emotional traumas and dramas, I am also aware that they are doing that with me as well. My dogs teach me daily to exist in a more healed state for their benefit and ultimately mine. It's very hard not to live with integrity, honesty, and healthily when you see firsthand how you are affecting those close to you.

Over the years, as I have taken my spiritual journey, I have become more keenly aware that the connection with our pets is far deeper than we realize. And I also know that during my divorce, for example, I put so much stress on my two dogs. I could not get my head out of my own troubles long enough to see that I was causing them pain and challenging their lives. Because they couldn't speak to me, they never outright told me how much they were struggling, and I was too caught up in all things me to see that I needed to turn around my emotional state, not just for me, but also for them. What a horrible feeling it is to know that the beings I loved the most were struggling due to my own lack of understanding! When I started to realize that this was happening, I began to live for my dogs. I was severely depressed at one point, but I did everything in my power to live for them, to smile for them, to think happier thoughts, to exercise, to leave the house more, etc. As I began to do more and more for them, we all began to enjoy life more. As Shiitake was beginning to pass over the rainbow bridge, I began to convince myself (for what I thought was her benefit) that I could be happier and live my life in her honor until I was strong enough to see that I was affecting far more than just her. I began to live for me and for everyone and everything around me. I used many flower essences to get through many challenging times. When I begin to sense my emotional state changing, I keep the ones I need within arm's reach for ease of use.

If you spend some time doing research, you will find that flower essences are far more than just a clear liquid with a funny, slightly alcoholic taste. They are little bottles that disconnect us from little inferior moments in our selves in order to make big changes in how we see the world. They make us see that we can turn little (or big) problems into catalysts for change for our futures and the world around us. I won't get into the details of each remedy since there are far more than I could explain here.

I have found many can also be combined with homeopathic medicine to make some even more powerful remedies that affect the entire constitution. Refer to the FeelBach! website for you own remedies. Here are a couple that might be great to try in the meantime:

Grief or Loss

Nat Mur, Ignatia 6X, with Feel Bach!'s Rescue Remedy, Gorse, Gelseminum, with Feel Bach!'s Star of Bethlehem.

Loud Noises

Phosphorus, Kali Phos, Arg Nit, Nit Ac, Aconite 6X, Sumbul 30C, and Feel Bach!'s Chestnut Bud.

Head Tremors

Aconite 30C, Belladona 30C, Herb Pharm Anxiety Soother (full dropper added to water), and Feel Bach!'s Rescue Remedy (substitute minimalus, or aspen), Maui Flower Essence Technology's Plumeria.

Summary

The flower essences are so subtle that you will wonder whether they are even working. You will have a certain state of mind at one moment, and within just a few minutes, if you have taken the right one, you will find that all of a sudden and out of nowhere, you are feeling more hopeful about life. I tend to find them great for people or dogs that just don't quite feel like they are living up to their highest potential or something unknown seems to be blocking them from their true bliss or joy. Remember, they are subtle, so be patient. They really do work!

"As wonderful as dogs can be,
they are famous for missing the point."

— Jean Ferris

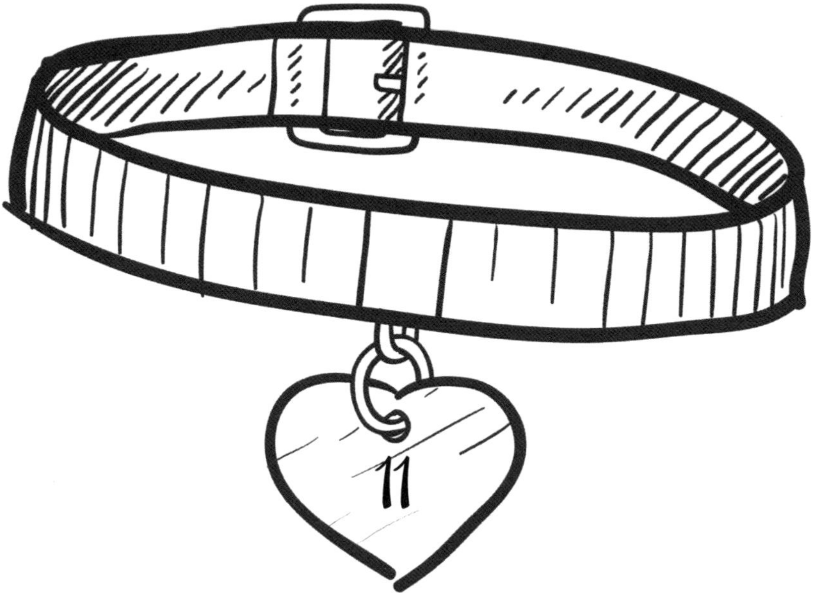

The Natural Energetic System

"If you want to find the secrets of the universe, think in terms of energy, frequency, and vibration."

— Nikola Tesla

We are all energetic systems. We each have a unique energy field whether we are human or animal. When it comes to identifying and maintaining these systems, the best method is with a "no tools required" way of thinking. God is very powerful if God created life. If God is that powerful, then why would God create anything less than perfect? We are perfect beings, but sometimes we have energetic (or emotional and physical) blocks that keep us from knowing this. We can learn all kinds of tools, tricks, methods, etc. that can sometimes become our very obstacles and bring more chaos to our lives. We need to understand that all these methods (yoga, Theta Healing, Reiki, Shamanism, Healing Touch Program™, etc.) are comparable to the training wheels on a bike. We need them to learn how to ride, but then we grow up and take them off and fly. I want to teach you the basics of how the energetic system works. My goal is that you seek out and find whatever training wheels work best for you until you learn how to connect to source/God to channel the energy that created you; then you will not only heal your dog and yourself, but exist in a more perfect state. Note: It is natural to feel a sense of connection to the tool or method that helped you find clarity, but do your best to let that go and simply connect deeper to your God source as you deepen your practice.

SO THE TRICK IN HEALING REALLY IS JUST THAT SOMETIMES—TRICKING THE PATTERNS OF THE MIND OR THE BODY INTO BELIEVING ALL IS WELL.

Earth is a very dense planet, and in the chaos of all things life here on Earth, we have so many distractions and obstacles. So the trick in healing really is just that sometimes—tricking the patterns of the mind or the body into believing all is well. Sometimes God just has a plan we cannot see (a plan we believe is not ours), and other times, we need to find a means to breaking up the blocks and reconnecting ourselves and our dogs to the power that created us… for healing and life's enjoyment. For example, earlier we spent a long time talking about food. Food can sometimes be the largest obstacle to our healing if something in the energetic process is "broken." Because the food process from farm to table (or dog bowl) can be filled with many unknowns, even horror stories, we must find ways to break down the obstacles that disconnect all of us from the power that created us. A lot of confusion can create blocks to healing or existing in that perfect state.

CONFUSION IN THE MODERN-DAY PACK

Many times, dogs' healing and health stems from the actions, behaviors, and mind-sets of their humans. Because dogs are pack members, they physically, energetically, and emotionally blend into that pack as a means for survival, and they begin to establish rules and pecking orders for the pack hierarchy. The confusion for all of us is that dogs have become so domesticated and we have become so insanely materialistic and disconnected from nature. Yet, I suppose, this is all a process in our planetary evolution....

We are pulled in so many directions that even our down time is full of distractions with personal devices upon which we check our social media sites, play games, and text our coworkers, families, and friends. We can't even take our dogs for a walk without our smartphone ready for the cute pic of them we need to take to post online (guilty). Because we are distracted, our dogs are confused. As humans, our world functions and flows with a certain reliance on fast responses, timely answers, and immediate feedback. Our dogs aren't always ready to comply with our needs. They are here to be the reminders of nature, love, companionship, and loyalty. All of the other things we believe to be so important are so superficial compared to the bond of the pack.

I like to think of the pack as a network of communication, messages, and signals circling around in a kind of energetic soup. Even if you only have one dog, there is still a pack and, guess what, you are in it! And to make matters even more challenging for your pup, every person you regularly communicate with (physically, emotionally, spiritually, and mentally) is in that pack. Stressors in the pack communication cause your dogs to be unwell in various ways. Maybe you've heard about how cellphone towers are linked with the decline in bees, due to their inability to get back to their hives? Honeybees are disappearing at a truly alarming rate all around the world. Up to 30 percent of the population is collapsing in North America.[16] It is believed that honeybees are disoriented because of cellphone signals, so they suffer from widespread miscommunication. This is similar to how we are now in-

---

16 http://www.naturalnews.com/032417_honeybees_population_collapse.html)

terrelating to our dogs. We are causing so much confusion for our pets! And the best way to fix it? Simplify your life! Get back to basics. Go natural. Remove chemicals. Remove the distractions. Less is more. Do you see any correlation here with your own life? Is it starting to make sense that dogs are great teachers? They mirror their environments. You can tell a lot about people when you meet their dogs!

PACK COMMUNICATION STRESSORS

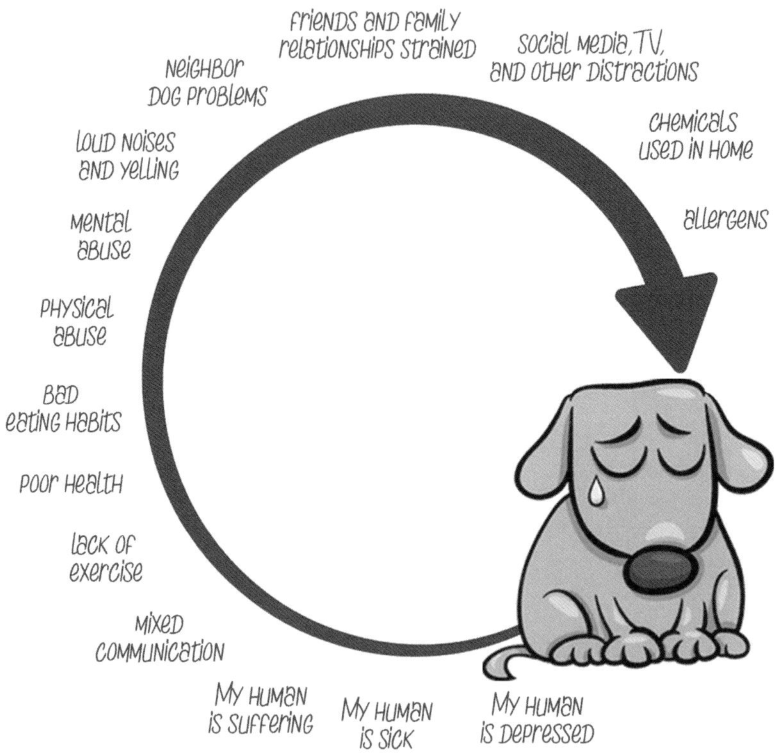

You see, the pack is so much more than a group of dogs. It's a group of dogs and people and their surroundings and how they interact with one another. When you start to harmonize with the pack, you begin to see when something is out of place. When a particular member starts leaving the pack, whether that is sleeping in the other room, developing different sleep patterns, arguing over food, running away, digging holes, hiding under the bed, staying out late, traveling more often, etc., then you start to see something is wrong. Watching the pack, you begin to see when health issues arise—whether those be emotional, physical, mental, or spiritual.

You are the pack leader, so you are responsible for shifting the energy of the pack. Our dogs will always remind us to put away the mechanisms of chaos and spend time in nature, help us choose the correct family and friends to spend time with and enjoy their company, and keep us in harmony with all the things that make life more balanced and complete if we work to create a happy pack. Happiness can heal.

THE HAPPY PACK

Intuition isn't something that some people have and some don't. We all have it. The difference really is that some people choose to slow down and use it while other people don't. Those who don't slow down are often bothered by things that simply don't go their way. And in the pack, the dogs wonder why you can't see it and don't act accordingly, so they "misbehave" to try to get your attention. So, with dogs, as with people, it's a matter of learning how to communicate. The problem with our human communication is that much of it is broken. How many times have you whined or stomped your foot and gotten what you wanted? Or texted a friend instead of just going over to his or her house? Searched the Internet for an answer rather than gone out and experienced life to find it? This works for us, but I bet if you whined or stomped your foot to get your dog's attention, your dog didn't do exactly what you wanted… unless, of course, you trained him to have a response.

Many people have asked me how I knew my Bella was allergic to certain foods. A variety of things taught me what to feed her, and it wasn't entirely easy to learn them. We still have moments of struggle with her hair loss or foot chewing. We learned what works and we keep doing it, but then there is an introduction of something new, or I simply forget to stick with the program…for example, I feel bad for not rewarding her with treats, but when I do, she has an allergic response. Consistency is the greatest tool for happiness.

Many things I do appear to be magical and intuitive to others, but they are second nature to me. I suppose that when you begin to open up and live more spiritually, it looks like magic to others who don't. I'd like to give you some great tools that you can use to help you better understand your pack—whether they be dogs or humans.

Every great transformation starts with understanding who you are. I began my spiritual awakening with the death of a dog—Tia Maria. When she died of kidney failure, my heartbreak motivated me to learn more about why she left, where she went, how to communicate with her, and most importantly, what caused the kidney failure. I travelled all over Central and South America after I got a baseline of training and understanding in various healing arts. The foundation for understanding any energy system usually begins with an understanding of the chakra system. So let's start there.

THE CHAKRA SYSTEM

The chakra system in a dog is pretty much the same as it is in a human. If you are unfamiliar with what the chakra system is, imagine your spine as a channel of energy. Then imagine that it has additional little energy systems spinning in a rainbow of colors in their own environment upon it. You might compare your spine to the sun in our solar system. Then each chakra is comparable to each planet. Each is its own environment independently, but a part of something more complete and quite a bit larger. Looking at chakras in this way really helps one understand the interconnectivity of all things. They are independent, yet they are not.

All living creatures have chakras. A few years ago, the concept of people, let alone dogs, having chakras was New Age thinking, and the subject was definitely not part of mainstream dog conversations. Alternative medicine is really not that alternative, though; it's just a more holistic approach to the health and healing of our dogs, and it's been around for a long time; we are just awakening to relearning it... mostly because big pharma is not proving to be a long-term solution, but merely masking the inherent problems.

Chakra is an ancient word that means "wheel" in Sanskrit. There are seven basic chakras that are represented by colors and symbols:

1. Root (red)
2. Sacral (orange)
3. Solar plexus (yellow)
4. Heart (green)
5. Throat (blue)
6. Third eye (indigo)
7. Crown (violet)

The three chakras found in the lower part of the body generally relate to our basic survival needs, while four upper chakras relate more to our mental or spiritual processes. No one chakra is more important than the next. They work together to create a balanced system. If one is out of balance, the entire system will tend to be thrown out of balance. If they are functioning correctly, they will be spinning in a clockwise motion; then, you will feel balanced and in alignment with self, source, and all life. Conversely, when one or more of our chakras is out of balance, we feel it throughout our entire system, and the energy there can be found spinning backwards (indicating a trauma or even a sign of a death…of an idea, concept, or even in the physical), side to side (a blockage), or up and down (too much energy getting through). When the chakras spin backwards, we can literally feel off-balance and like the world is against us…no matter how hard we try, whatever we are doing is just not working. If one or more chakras are under-active (not open enough), then the other chakras have to take up the slack and work extra hard to make up for the underactive or unbalanced chakra. (Does this remind you of the discussion we had earlier on the removal of the sex organs and their effect on the adrenal glands?) Over-active chakras pull energy from the other chakras and can cause a continued off-balanced state.

Remember how I talked about the influences in the pack's energy and communication? Well, chakras are no different. If our chakras are off, our dogs know it. They are much more sensitive than we are. They feel it emotionally, physically, and intuitively. We end up affecting our dogs' entire energy system. If this goes unchecked long enough, not only does it cause issues in our lives, but in the lives of our dogs. Imagine the energy running right out of your body and down the leash into your dog like an electric cord plugged into the wall. If you are nervous, unsure, have fear, etc. then your dogs will too! If you are calm, balanced, spiritually connected, and aware, guess what? Your dogs will be too! This is why I said earlier that I can tell a lot about a person by his or her dog. When you heal yourself, you will generally heal your dog. If you have ever watched animals in nature, you know they have in innate program to survive and thrive. If they are not surviving and thriving, it is mostly because they are feeding on our energy…in our modern-day domestic relationship.

It really takes more time to explain the chakra system than it does to balance it. I promise it's really easy once you get the hang of it! But before we start balancing our chakras, let's start getting more familiar with them through a chart to show you where the chakras are located on your dog and a bit about each one.

THE CHAKRA LOCATIONS

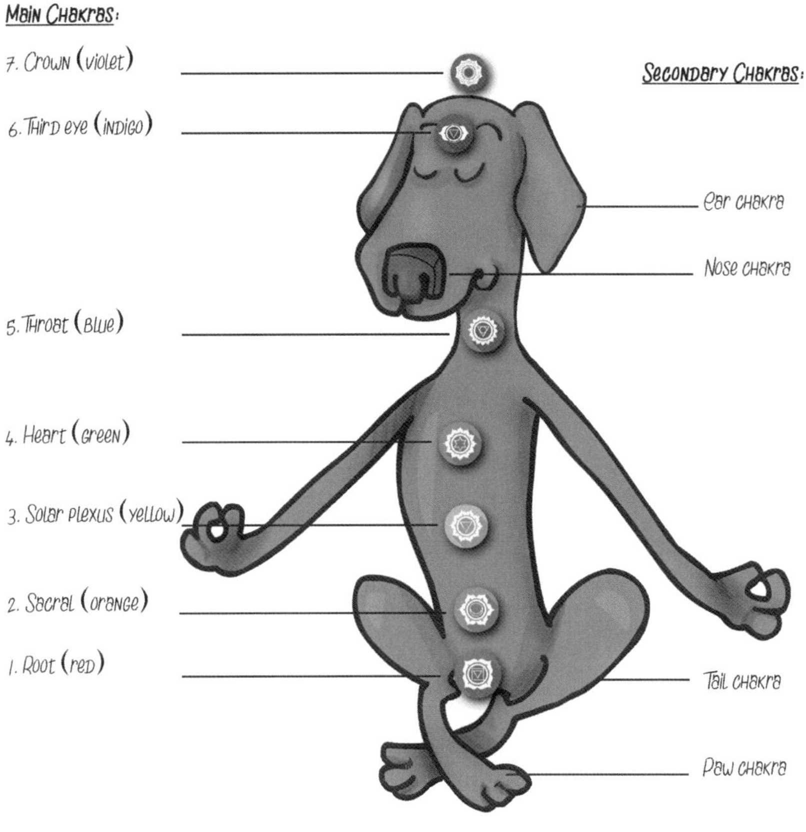

UNDERSTANDING INDIVIDUAL CHAKRAS

It is important to understand the chakras if you want to be better able to understand the behaviors of your dog, as well as for healing. When you dive deeper into each chakra, you may begin to understand particular patterns being displayed in your dog. I find that the most healing that needs to be done is with rescue animals where the bonds to humans have been broken and the dog is terrified or has been abused or neglected with little to no positive human contact. When a dog associates humans with being bad people, then a re-programming of the chakras can prove to be extremely useful, especially when the dog will not allow you to touch him or her. It's very easy to offer healing outside the cage or pen or even from home while the dog is in captivity. I can't tell you how many times I sit home and send energy and/or pray for animals in need. I talk to God and the animal and I pray. I cry a lot too. I have gone through many periods of severe depression over the mistreatment of animals on our planet, but I place my faith in the hands of the creator and work to balance the chakras to release whatever pain and trauma I can. Even if the dog's life is in jeopardy in a kill shelter, his pain can be eased prior to whatever is in store for him. Before I get myself (or you) too upset about the whole monstrous mess of homeless and neglected animals, let's start talking about doing some chakra clearing. Once you learn it, you will see that even if you have no money or feel helpless about any situation with animals, it is something you can do for free to help yourself and the animals of our world.

The chakra system runs up and down the spine. There are seven main chakras (the ear, nose, tail, and paw are secondary chakras) we will talk about here in great detail. The detail for each chakra is a listing of all the elements associated with each—essential oils, crystals, colors, symbols, etc. You see, there is more than one way to get a balanced chakra. If you notice that your dog constantly has a chakra that is out of balance, perhaps you can try hanging a coordinating crystal around his neck or close to the point representing the chakra. You can even place the crystal under the bed where he sleeps. If you feed your dog a rainbow of colors in his diet, then each of the chakras is getting some of the energy it needs. The chakras relate to particular functions in the body, so when something isn't working correctly, try balancing the chakra. When all else fails, look at your own! Your dog is feeding off of someone in your household. Become a detective and use the following as a guideline to help your dog release from any trauma, pain, or anxiety and heal. Once you have the hang of it, you can work to develop new tricks for monitoring or healing your dog's chakras.

THE SEVEN MAIN CHAKRAS:

1ST ROOT CHAKRA

- **Color:** Red
- **Totem Animal Association (Peruvian Tradition):** Snake
- **Function:** Stability, grounded, physical needs, survival instinct, security, tribal association
- **Body Functions:** Adrenals, fight/flight, bones/skeletal
- **Immune System:** Gonads, testes, ovaries
- **Glands (L5-S5 on the spine):** Adrenals, lumbar, coccygeal plexus
- **Crystal:** Red jasper, garnet, ruby, red coral
- **Essential Oils for Health and Wellness:** Ginger, cypress, cedar, vetiver, cinnamon, sandalwood, valor, Abundance, Grounding
- **Foods:** Beets, strawberries, cranberries, cayenne pepper, tomatoes
- **Herbs:** Noni, clover, goldenseal, ginseng, iron, echinacea, ginger root, cayenne pepper, yucca
- **Planet:** Sun and earth
- **Balanced Behavior:** Your dog should feel safe, secure, and grounded. There should be general trust of people, and your dog should have a confident demeanor. Territorial needs are appropriate.
- **Under-Active Behaviors:** Fearful or nervous.
- **Over-Active Behaviors:** May create a greedy dog, a dog that guards his toys, food bowl, or sleeping area. He may seem unsure and change may upset him.

Note: This chakra is extra important in rescue situations to help create a feeling of safety and security for animals in unfamiliar places and situations. Feel Bach! has a remedy called Rescue Remedy that is great for most animals with issues of insecurity and this first chakra. Many of the flower remedies will work best on this chakra.

2ND SACRAL CHAKRA

- **Color:** Orange
- **Totem Animal Association (Peruvian Tradition):** Jaguar
- **Crystal:** Citrine, carnelian, copper, tiger's eye, amber, citrine
- **Essential Oils for Health and Wellness:** Clary sage, rosewood, patchouli, melissa, bergamot, neroli, lemongrass, juniper, Peace & Calming, Harmony, Inner Child, Forgiveness
- **Food:** Peaches, mangos, melon, carrots, papaya
- **Herbs:** Licorice, Vitamins A, C, E
- **Planet:** Moon
- **Function:** Emotions, relationships, self-worth, sexuality, pleasure, procreation, primal instincts, creativity, physical power
- **Body Functions:** Sexual functions, elimination, water regulation
- **Immune System:** Spleen, bladder, pancreas, intestines, elimination
- **Glands (T9-L4 on the spine):** Lumbar plexus, sex organs, adrenals
- **Balanced Behavior:** Feelings are expressed appropriately, without being frantic or too intense. They are open to affection and loving.
- **Under-Active Behaviors:** Lacking in emotion or warmth.
- **Over-Active Behaviors:** Overly emotional, humpy, hyper dog. They may be needy, emotionally attached to people, and separation anxiety may be an issue. They may be overly protective of their home and people in it.

3RD SOLAR PLEXUS CHAKRA

- **Color:** Yellow
- **Totem Animal Association (Peruvian Tradition):** Hummingbird
- **Crystal:** Citrine, yellow topaz, yellow amber, or clear quartz
- **Food:** Lemons, melons, bananas, eggs, olive oil, yellow peppers
- **Herbs:** Gingko, milk thistle, yarrow, dandelion, parsley, nettle
- **Planet:** Mars, sun
- **Essential Oils for Health and Wellness:** Rosemary, geranium, fennel, juniper, copaiba, lemongrass, lemon, Harmony, E-R-Gee, Acceptance, Release, Sacred Mountain
- **Function:** Happiness, vitality, desire, personal power, will, energy, metabolism, social identity or dynamics within a pack of dogs or people
- **Body Functions:** Digestion, assimilation, muscles
- **Immune System:** Digestive system, stomach, adrenals, liver
- **Glands (T5-T9 on the spine):** Solar plexus, pancreas
- **Balanced Behavior:** Confidence, balanced joy, calmness
- **Under-Active Behaviors:** Passive, skittish and timid, depressed
- **Over-Active Behaviors:** Bossy, pushy, frustrated, tension, overly excitable, intimidating, domineering, and possibly aggressive.

4TH HEART CHAKRA

- **Color:** Green for healing or pink for love
- **Totem Animal Association (Peruvian Tradition):** Eagle
- **Crystal:** Malachite, rose quartz, jade, emerald, watermelon tourmaline, peridot, clear quartz
- **Essential Oils for Health and Wellness:** Rose, lemon, rosemary, fennel, cypress, tea tree, jasmine, ylang, Joy, Acceptance, Humility
- **Food:** Avocados, broccoli, cucumber, celery, kale, greens, squash
- **Herbs:** Echinacea, sage, alfalfa
- **Planet:** Venus
- **Function:** Love, understanding, water, calming, universal oneness, trust, hope, openness, compassion, forgiveness, balance, kindness, affection, expansion, circulatory system, heart, thymus
- **Body Functions:** Electromagnetic field generator, blood pressure, immune
- **Immune System:** Circulatory system, thymus
- **Glands (T1-5 on the spine):** Cardiac plexus, heart/thymus
- **Balanced Behavior:** Loving and friendly, a pleasure to live with
- **Under-Active Behaviors:** Fearful, cold, will keep you at a distance emotionally
- **Over-Active Behaviors:** Is it possible to be too loving? Too trusting? There might be a sense of being overly "clingy," which might be more related to security and 1st chakra issues.

5TH THROAT CHAKRA

- **Color:** Clear Blue
- **Crystal:** Turquoise, lapis lazuli, sodalite, blue agate, azurite, aquamarine, clear quartz
- **Food:** Blueberries, plums, fish, berries, potatoes
- **Herbs:** Chamomile, thyme
- **Planet:** Mercury and Neptune
- **Essential Oils for Health and Wellness:** Bergamot, tea tree, chamomile, eucalyptus, thyme, mint, hyssop, Believe, Valor, Envision, Hope
- **Function:** Self-expression, healing, creativity, communication, sound, vibration, listening, barking
- **Body Functions:** Metabolism and calcium regulation
- **Immune System:** Thyroid, nose, throat, lungs
- **Glands (C3-7 on the spine):** Pharyngeal Plexus, thyroid/parathyroid plexus
- **Balanced Behavior:** Calm, soothed, dog able to express self and make needs known
- **Under-Active Behaviors:** Timid, shy, even introverted dog
- **Over-Active Behaviors:** Barking needlessly, and manipulation

6TH THIRD EYE CHAKRA

- **Color:** Indigo
- **Crystal:** Tourmaline, sodalite, iolite, azurite, and clear quartz
- **Essential Oils for Health and Wellness:** Frankincense, myrrh, patchouli, Valerian, Vervain, cedarwood, lavender, Awaken, Dream Catcher, Transformation, White Angelica
- **Food:** Eggplant, berries
- **Herbs:** White willow, bilberry, kava, passion flower
- **Planet:** Jupiter
- **Function:** Insight, self-knowledge, intuition, knowing, clairvoyance, psychic senses, promotion of thought
- **Body Functions:** Hormonal/physiological regulation
- **Immune System:** Pineal, mid-brain, third eye, cooling, neutralizing, inner seeing
- **Glands (C1-2 on the spine):** Carotid plexus, pineal gland, pituitary gland
- **Balanced Behavior:** Lives easily in the world of dogs and people
- **Under-Active Behaviors:** Inability to think on own. Your dog may tend to rely on you too much and be easily confused.
- **Over-Active Behaviors:** Live in a world of fantasy and only want to play, play, play.

7TH CROWN CHAKRA

- **Color:** Violet or white
- **Crystal:** Amethyst, moonstone, sugilite, sodialite, fluorite, cle-ar quartz
- **Essential Oils for Health and Wellness:** Frankincense, myrrh, jasmine, ylang, lavender, Valerian, Vervain, Gathering, Inspiration, Three Wise Men
- **Food:** Light, airy, no color, and not very filling, soursop, garlic, bok choy, celery
- **Herbs:** Gotu kola, meadowsweet
- **Planet:** Uranus
- **Function:** Universal consciousness, understanding, air, promotes thought, all knowing, cosmic connection, The God source, enlightenment, gateway to other dimensions
- **Body Functions:** Circadian rhythms
- **Immune System:** Pituitary, left/right brain synchronicity, spiritual clearing, power of transcendence
- **Glands:** Carotid plexus, pineal gland
- **Balanced Behavior:** Allows your dog to be aware of the world and his or her place in it.
- **Under-Active Behaviors:** A dog who never quite fits in. The dog that no one will play with at the dog park.
- **Over-Active Behaviors:** A worried dog who works himself up over nothing.

OTHER SECONDARY CHAKRAS

Because dogs collect much information through their sensory systems, it is believed that they hold additional chakras, but we humans actually have these same sensory systems (except maybe the tail); we just don't always socially use them the same way. These could be called chakras in both humans and in our canines. When I've worked with particular clients, I have found energetic centers around the lymph glands and the hands and feet. I suppose I would also call these readable chakras, but they seem to be less developed in most humans. Dogs rely on them more. We will refer to these as secondary chakras because I have noticed they do have the ability to be balanced, even though they are not always recognized in many healing traditions. These chakras are:

Nose

An open, healthy nose chakra allows your dog to receive information via thousands of scent glands. A dry, extremely moist, or runny nose may be the indication of problems in your dog's energetic or physical body. Watch this chakra when using aromatherapy.

Ears

The ears allow your dog to pick up on a higher range of sounds than we do (for example, the dog whistle). Problems in the ears can cause your dog to be agitated, anxious, lose balance (vertigo), lose interest, or be depressed.

Paws

The paws allow your dog to connect to nature with a constant, connected flow of communication and harmony with the Earth's energy. If we walked without shoes, we would be able to feel this as well. When I learned how to heal with nature, I learned there is a constant rhythm with the Earth, and there is an ability to send and receive healing energies as well as give what is no longer needed into the earth for it to be mulched into the nutrients it thrives on.

Have you ever seen your dog kick his feet and dig at the earth after eliminating? Is it possible your dog is releasing a scent or energy, or trying to cover up an illness or disorder? Dogs never want to appear weak in the pack, and their elimination may be an indication of a problem that would be found out by other members of the pack.

Tail

The Tail Chakra in dogs acts as an extension of the root chakra in many ways by providing additional grounding and a feeling of security. I think of it as a kind of antenna to the chakra system as a whole. You can't see the spine and how all the chakras are inter-relating, but you can see the tail. Dogs share a lot of information via their tails. Docking a tail really throws the whole system off balance, so please give that some thought before you do it. You are actually cutting your dog's spine.

"If there are no dogs in Heaven,
then when I die I want to go where they went."

— Will Rogers

BALANCING YOUR DOG'S CHAKRAS

Balancing your dog's chakra system yourself is really pretty easy, but you may wish to have a Reiki Practitioner or a Shaman Healer do it for you. Although, doing it yourself bonds you deeper with your dog. There are multiple ways to balance your dog's energetic system or chakras. If you use any of the detailed information above as a starting place, you can do it easily. Whether you use essential oils, gemstones, food, herbs, or energetic manipulation, you can achieve much the same result, which will be to connect deeper with your dog. Working on your dog's energetic or physical system at this level is a great way to do that. You really can't do any wrong. Anything done with integrity and love is always done right in the world of energy. In fact, I have developed a kind of relationship with spirit where I believe all I need to do is say, "Balance the chakras" and it seems to work. You see, I just taught you all about chakras, but it doesn't even have to be that complicated. Ask and you shall receive, right? But knowing what you are asking for is sometimes the biggest hurdle. So let me explain just a bit more about energetically balancing the chakras so you understand what is happening. By understanding just a bit more, you can help your dog (or others you don't even know) to reduce stress, feel your love, ease his or her pain, and feel great comfort.

Since everything is energy, everything is pliable. You don't even have to be present to make great shifts happen in another place on the other side of the world. We are all made up of the same stuff.

Personally, I don't think you need to know what certain symbols mean (reiki) or have particular tools in order to perform a chakra balancing. All you need is to get out of your own way and ask the power that created you to come through you and into the person or dog you are looking to heal. The power that created us doesn't make things that complicated. But, sometimes, due to the busyness of the mind, we think healing is a complicated thing. I like to think of it as more of a study in life. When you study how things work versus trying to fix them, then you see their interactivity is more than surface level. It's kind of like the butterfly effect where one subtle thing affects the next. When you study the chakras, you begin to see that there is a certain flow that is optimal and one that is interrupted. The interruption can come in numerous forms. In the human, it is usually a cause of the mind. In the dog, it is usually picked up from the human. Dogs, like all animals, want to live and to thrive. Humans get bogged down with emotional traumas and dramas. When the dog attaches to the human's energy, that's when many issues start for the dog. Although, some issues can be independent of the dog. And some issues of the dog can be specifically for the heart opening of the human. I like to think of it as a co-created collaboration of the divine.

CUTTING CORDS

It is very important that in all relationships, we learn to cut the cords that bind us to a limited sense of self. Imagine that in the network of the pack there are little ropes or strings that attach to each member of the pack. These can be ideas or beliefs as well. In the world of spirit, everything is unlimited and infinite, but in the human earthly dense world we live in, we are subject to the limitations of our mind and body. These limitations cause us to lack in certain areas of our lives. I find it very important to learn how to cut all the cords that bind us daily. Have you ever attempted to do something, only to have your friend or lover tell you that you are silly for attempting it? Or have you ever thought you couldn't do something, but someone believed so much in your abilities that he or she pressured you in certain ways to achieve that thing that seemed nearly impossible? Or have you ever loved someone so much that you didn't want that person to get hurt so you tried to protect him or her from injury? Any and all things in our earthly, third-dimensional world are not consistent with the unlimited laws of the universe. Therefore, we must cut the cords that constantly bind us and cause us the limitations that keep us bound and unable to connect to the source that provides us a window into all things infinite. Sounds kinda far out, I know!

Remember the movie *Edward Scissorhands* with Johnny Depp? His hands were made of scissors. I want you to imagine either something like this for yourself or something maybe a bit less severe...holding a pair of golden ethereal scissors. These scissors are capable of cutting all cords that bind you or your dog in any area of life. Get an image of the being you want to heal in your head...a mental picture. See whether you can be shown the cords and who or what they relate to. If you can't, that's okay too, but some very visually-gifted people can actually sense or see these. I want you to imagine taking your energetic scissors and carefully cutting all around the energetic body of the being you wish to heal. I just do this in my head. Maybe you see imaginary little hairs coming out of the person's body and you are simply giving them a trim. Every day we live our lives, we develop patterns and belief systems, and deal with dramas and trauma, and they are all like those cellphone towers to the bees—they interrupt the pack. If we go to bed every night and just say a little prayer as we cut these...something like "God, please release all limitations from me and my dog(s)," it should help clear any imprints or limitations in yours and your dogs' lives. Do this daily and live with reverence of your actions and interactions.

Whether you are an intuitive person or not, working with the chakras and cutting cords will teach you that, as humans, there is a divine magic present in all life that we may just never fully understand. Let me share a story with you as we begin to understand the balancing of the chakras.

"Whoever said that diamonds are a girl's best friend never owned a dog."

— Author Unknown

MAI TAI AND THE DEATH OF THE CHAKRAS

My Shar Pei Mai Tai was preparing for his death at the end of a very full ten-plus years of life. I went off to work one morning knowing that I had a short day and he might pass before my return. I contemplated staying home that day but decided to honor him and allow him the choice to pass without me if he found it to be more peaceful for him. Death should be respected, and I was trying to honor whatever decision he needed to make. He was my protector, and it may have been easier for him not to have to show me any weakness. Since I had seen death shortly prior and was walking through life with much more faith, I gave permission for his spirit to pass while I was gone if that was his desire. I had one client to visit and knew I would drive home just after. I knew Mai Tai might not be alive when I got home. I drove home as quickly as I could that day. When I reached home and before I walked in, I prepared myself for what I might find and took a deep breath as I walked in the house. I found Mai Tai outside, trying to get in the house through the doggie door. He was such a strong protector that I had never seen him so limp and so weak. He was always so strong at my side. I wasn't sure whether he was still alive. I reached down with a tear in my eye, prepared to say goodbye. But, at that moment, I felt his breath. I knew he was close.

Because Mai Tai had always been my teacher, I decided to pull out a pendulum to monitor his chakras. (I will explain this more shortly.) I knew that if his chakras were disengaging, his physical and spiritual bodies were separating. I seemed to be intuitively aware of the process without having ever been in the presence of any other death prior. I held him in my one arm and on a dog bed on my lap. I tried to wipe the tears from my eyes as I watched the pendulum as I moved it up his spine. The chakras will all spin clockwise when they are healthy and strong. To my surprise, the first chakra was. I moved up to check each chakra and found the second was moving up and down and letting lots of energy in. The third, fourth, and fifth were doing the same. But the sixth was spinning just as healthily as the first. I instantly knew without a thought in my head that this was what death looked like. This was the "white light experience." I was being shown that the first chakra had Mai Tai still grounded in his physical body, but the other chakras were preparing for his release. And the sixth chakra was showing me that he was being held by spirit.

I had started training six months prior to this moment with Mai Tai… to learn the ways of shamanic healing, but I had never seen anything quite like this. I somehow knew to dive into an altered state (a shaman would call this a "journey") where I was interacting with his spirit body. The best way I can explain it was that it looked a lot like I'd imagine heaven to be. There was white light everywhere. I saw him—his light or spirit—but not his physical body. I intuitively saw him talking to what I could best understand as God. He was re-remembering home. He was being shown how to get back to the light. I flashed between this space in my consciousness to being in the physical form and holding his body. He looked to be struggling to go, so I started talking with God to take him home. And I still kick myself for this today, but I began screaming at God to take him. "Take him now!" It makes me upset to think I thought this was going to be a fast process and to know how unpleasant I was likely making the situation for him. Mai Tai saw my pain and discomfort, so I was making it hard for him.

All these years later, I know that death holds no judgment, but the processing does take a bit of time. I knew if I could take myself to the other side where I knew he was going, then I could convince him that I was okay with his passing. I don't really know how I knew this, but I did. Before I knew it, I was there. I could suddenly see his physical body. I called to him and he came running to me. I told him he was a good boy. I called again and again and continued to praise him as he ran faster and with a big smile on his face. He had more strength and presence in this heavenly place than I had seen in a while. I think what I was actually doing was giving him permission to pass. I saw him running into my arms, through me, and into the light. I immediately flashed back into my physical body to see whether he was still alive. Just as I did, I watched him take one last deep breath, wag his tail, and leave his body. I felt a tingle go through me. I was still holding the pendulum and watched as his first chakra released. But, much to my surprise, his third eye was still very actively engaged. I think he was still running and dancing with spirit. After quite some time, the activity in his third eye slowed and eventually stopped…and quite some time after, the breath left his body! There was no life left in his body. I sat in awe. I waited, and then I cried and cried. I wasn't sure whether I had just witnessed a miracle or this was something other people even knew about. But I knew that I needed to share it.

"Heaven goes by favor. If it went by merit,
you would stay out and your dog would go in."

— Mark Twain

How the Chakras Spin

Using a pendulum (you can buy one just about anywhere nowadays) will show you how the chakras' energy is spinning. You can actually create a pendulum with a string and something like a house key tied on to the end. You will need to hold the pendulum in your most dominant hand and hold it with your thumb and index finger. Hold it just above the chakras, starting with the first or root chakra. Simply ask the question, "Show me how this chakra is spinning." You will generally begin to see some movement. If you do not, then simply ask, "Show me yes" and "Show me no." Then your pendulum with usually swing away and toward you for yes and side to side or shoulder to shoulder for no. Once you get the hang of it, start holding the pendulum above each of your dog's chakras and see whether it follows any of these patterns below:

Clockwise: Generally everything is balanced in the energetic body. Sometimes, one chakra can spin faster than another, but for the time being, we will say things are balanced.

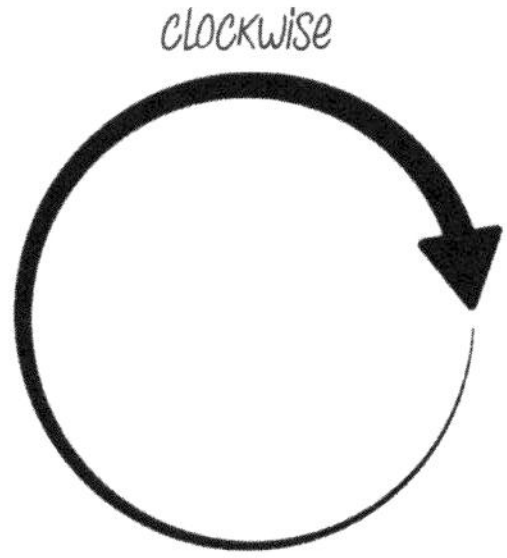

Counterclockwise: This is the sign of a great trauma or impending death. Please don't automatically assume someone is dying because 99 percent of the time, it is just a buried trauma.

Up and Down: Too much energy is coming in. Everything in the chakras above this one are not functioning appropriately. The chakras must be balanced and cleansed to correct this.

Side to Side: Energy is blocked. No energy is getting through. Everything above this chakra is generally not functioning appropriately. The chakras must be balanced and cleansed to correct this.

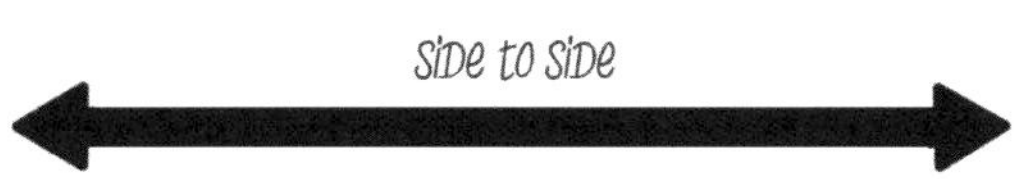

Once you get the hang of the pendulum, you will begin to be able to do the next stage—healing. And eventually, you will be able to use your intuition and not need a pendulum at all. You will either just see how the chakra is spinning or you will just know. You can also begin to establish relationships with totem animals or spirit guides or angels, and they will even do the work for you.

CLEANSING THE CHAKRAS AND USING A PENDULUM

You really don't have to be a reiki or energy master to balance the chakras. All you need to be able to do is to use a pendulum to see how they are spinning and to backwash them (spin them backwards) to release the heavy energy and send in white light for healing. Honestly, all healing can happen with white light. In order to use the pendulum, all you need to do is to get it to show you yes, then show you no. Once you have this down, it's as simple as asking, "Show me how the first chakra is spinning," "Show me how the second chakra is spinning," and so on. In order to clean the chakras out, simply spin them backwards; imagine pulling out whatever is causing the disruption and throwing it into the earth. Again, ask the pendulum, "Is the chakra clean?" Once it is illuminated with white light pulled down from the heavens a few times, you will get a "Yes." Then spin the chakra clockwise to close it. Voila! You are a chakra master! No classes needed. See, that was easy! Let's see how you do now on your first challenge. Here is a great test to practice on to see what your pup is allergic to, as we discussed earlier:

FOOD ALLERGY TEST

Ask the question: "Is <dog's name> allergic to <food type>?" Then just go down the list or add your own.

Food	Yes	No
Beef		
Corn		
Duck		
Lentil		
Wheat		
Soy		
Cow's Milk		
Lamb		
Venison		
Chicken		
Turkey		
Whitefish		
Hen's egg		
Barley		
Millet		
Rice		
Oatmeal		
Salmon		
Rabbit		
Quinoa		
Potato		
Peanut		
Pork		
Sweet Potato		

You just saved yourself about $300 by not having to go to your vet and wait weeks for results! Try this with anything you suspect to be an issue. You will really have fun learning all about your dog's likes and dislikes. Then, eventually, your intuition will kick in and you will see that you just know these things. Ask questions about where he likes to sleep, what are her favorite foods, does he like my husband, etc. But there is also another way to learn more about your dog… muscle testing.

MUSCLE TESTING

If you find that the pendulum isn't working for you in terms of the yes/no, there is another great way to test. I like to use my body when I'm in a store picking out vitamins and herbs (for myself or my pups). You can use the body to function much the same way as the pendulum. Ask your body to show you yes or no. Many times, the body will rock forward for yes and rock backwards for no. Hold a vitamin or herb in your hand and ask: "Is this going to help with xyz?" "Will this, or will it cause side effects?" Muscle testing is an easy way to learn to understand your pup's needs. If you are standing in the store in the vitamin aisle and wondering whether you should begin taking a certain product, all you need to do is ask yes or no questions. Hold the product in your hands. If you sway one direction with the product in your hand, then you have your answer. It works the same way for your pup. All you have to do is become your pup. Imagine you are your dog; then ask the same question. Energy is pliable and fun when you actually get to become your dog, right?

You can also hold the product on or near the part of the body you are wishing to treat. When it gets close to the body part that it will help, there is more strength in your body; when it isn't favorable, it will show weakness. The trick is to find the resistance. In a human, you might hold your arm out and resist the pressure of another person asking questions and pulling the arm down. This is called kinesiology, and it is a practice often used by chiropractors and acupuncturists, and it is now being adopted by many other healers as well. A dog is not likely to resist knowingly. If your dog pulls on a leash, you might be able to wave a few products near him and see whether he lets up on his tension. Otherwise, you must pretend you are your dog and muscle test on his behalf. The swaying body is one of the easiest ways to do that. You can also ask questions of your dog's subconscious. Examples might be: "Do you like that bed?" "Do you like that food?" "Is this food causing an allergy?" Is this the right homeopathic treatment? The right essential oil? The possibilities are endless. You don't even have to be a psychic. Easy! Another great tool to learn to communicate with your best buddy!

EXERCISE:

I want you to use the following pages to make copies and use for practice in balancing the chakras. Make notes on the left page of your findings and use the right hand page to check your dog's chakras. Because everything is energy and energy is pliable, I want you to pretend that the image to the right is actually your dog. This is a great tool to have because dogs don't always sit still. You can actually use this image as a model to heal your dog! Wow!

THE MAIN CHAKRAS:

7th CHAKRA NOTES: ______________________________

____

6th CHAKRA NOTES: ______________________________

____

5th CHAKRA NOTES: ______________________________

____

4th CHAKRA NOTES: ______________________________

____

3rd CHAKRA NOTES: ______________________________

____

2nd CHAKRA NOTES: ______________________________

____

1st CHAKRA NOTES: ______________________________

____

THE SECONDARY CHKRAS:

Nose: ______________________________

Ears: ______________________________

Paws: ______________________________

Tails: ______________________________

OTHER NOTES: ____________________

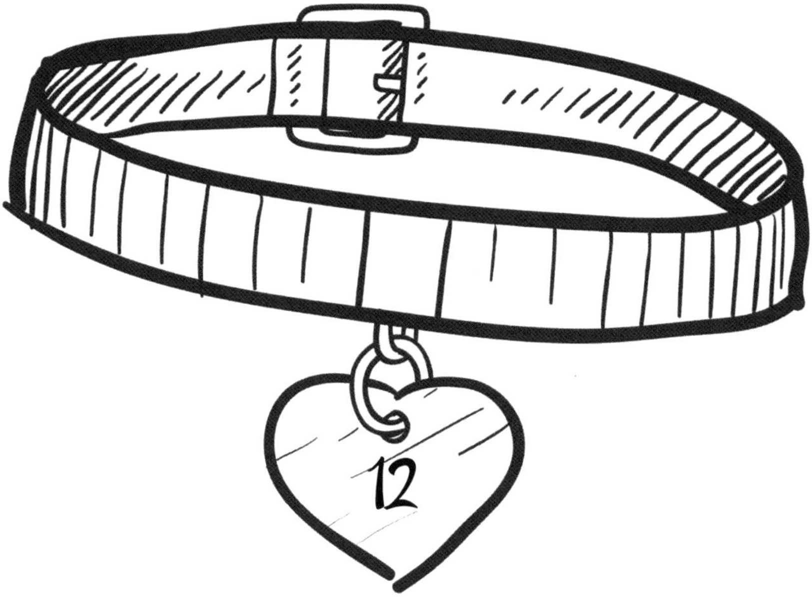

The Connection Between You & Your Dog

"If a dog will not come to you after having looked you in the face, you should go home and examine your conscience."

— Woodrow Wilson

As you spend time doing healing work with your dog, you begin to learn how to listen intuitively and hear your dog's needs. We are all connected to the same source that created us, and that source is no different for you or your dog. When you start to see the similarities of that for you and your dog, you begin to see that there is no separation. The language of energy is the same. How we communicate is not through our voice, but telepathically. How do you know when your dog is hungry? Has to go potty? There really isn't some mysterious woo-hoo thing going on there—you just know! There is an ebb and flow in your relationship, and the more intimate time you spend together, the more you get to know each other.

THE BIGGEST DISRUPTION TO YOUR CONNECTION WITH YOUR DOG IS THE CHAOS YOU BRING INTO YOUR OWN LIFE.

The biggest disruption to your connection with your dog is the chaos you bring into your own life. Be this diet, relationships, self-doubt, prescription medicines, TV watching, or video games, these are all disruptions. The more pure you can get all aspects of your life, the easier it is to connect. Clean up your lifestyle and simplify. For example, if you have a poor diet, it becomes a disruptor to your truest state. A life full of chaos, anxiety, poor relationships, worry, etc. creates distractions from the calm connected state of nature and the animals. Our modern materialistic lives create much static in our connection, not just to our best four-legged friends, but also to ourselves. As we learn to live more simplistically, we can clean many things out of the way that create so many blocks and obstacles in many places in our lives.

"When I am sad
There is not greater
Comfort than the
Silent devoted
Companionship
Of my dog."

— Author Unknown

I work from home, and I always play soft sweet music in my office. I diffuse pleasing essential oils and have created a comfortable environment for my dogs to be in at my feet. Not only does this create a safe place for them to retreat to, but it builds trust. There are many times here in Hawaii when the wind blows and things get knocked over or the blinds knock on the windows and my bulldog, in particular, sits at my feet. She isn't very fond of all the chaos as I explained in the flower essences chapter, but because she knows she has a safe place near me, that begins a trusting bond.

Once you develop a trusting bond with your dog, you can watch behaviors that also indicate trust and confirmed thoughts of love and safety. You see, animals count on us to keep them safe, and when we do, then they open up to us. Personally, I think that is pretty much the reason why they are here…well, also to break open our hearts. My Shar Pei Blue is very reactive when his safe environment is tested; in fact, so much so that when my partner comes barreling into the room with his wild energy, Blue barks and growls, letting him know that he has pierced the safe energy bubble with distractive energy and behavior. My partner is a motivational speaker, so by design, it is his job to pierce through what is still…well, until Blue makes him aware of the fact that he doesn't prefer it at home anyhow! I've asked him to take a deep breath and calm himself before entering, but he's too busy to remember. So for now, Blue will continue to let him know when he has violated *our* sacred space...because it bothers me as well.

MANY PEOPLE ARE UNAWARE THAT WHEN THEY ENTER A SPACE, THEY ARE NOT HARMONIZED WITH IT BEFORE THEY ENTER…OR EVEN THAT THEY COULD BE.

Many people are unaware that when they enter a space, they are not harmonized with it before they enter…or even that they could be. When you begin to see through your dog's eyes, that is when you begin to understand your dog's needs even more. Because animals have far fewer distractions than we do, they respond much quicker with all communication methods and healing modalities. Mostly, the distraction is surrounding the relationship with humans. When you begin by imagining a circle of trust around them, the first stage of communication is set. You can do this with soft music, essential oils, with healing, massage, or soft talk. You can also cover them in an energetic golden white light or bubble—just reach up in the air and imagine pulling down that bubble over you and them. When you do any healing, you should always do this beforehand to set the stage for safe, trusting healing to take place.

Animals communicate better with images, colors, and intuitive thoughts than they do with your voice, in my opinion. Have you ever been in nature and watched an animal run as soon as you used your voice? Next time, try sending feelings instead of abstract thoughts or try using visuals by drawing a picture in your mind for things you want him to do or know. Sometimes, you need to learn to get out of the analytical and logical mind to get into the telepathic. Once you are in the telepathic space, language is no barrier. When you begin to become your dog, you start to see through his eyes. Take a minute to see whether you can connect.

EXERCISE: CONNECTING AS YOUR DOG

The first step in all energy work is to create sacred space, so cover yourself and your pup with a ball of white light. Then ask for permission. Is your pup willing to work, or does he give you signals that now is not the right time? Hint: If he gets up and walks away, he isn't ready! Begin to imagine seeing through your dog's eyes. You will be smaller, shorter, under your desk, or at your feet. Start to feel your body. How does it feel to have four legs? How does your belly feel? Is it irritated, full, hungry? Do you feel any physical pain anywhere? Can you hear thoughts in your mind? Did you connect? If not, keep trying.

When you begin to understand how your body feels and know what is yours, then you begin to understand what is not yours. Doing a body-connecting exercise such a yoga can help you connect more deeply with and learn your own body, so as you become your dog, you will recognize what is you and what is him. If you had trouble with this exercise, begin first with understanding you. Is that pain yours? Make a note of what you feel in your body, and then begin to see yourself in your dog's body.

CONNECTING FOR HEALING

Healing animals isn't really much different from healing humans. The concept remains the same—find the obstacles that block the person or animal from connecting to the power that created us! Since I live in Hawaii, let me explain something I've learned since being here. The true nature of the aloha spirit is not entirely about forgiveness, as some may believe. Forgiveness indicates there is something wrong. There is never anything wrong, and asking for something from God simply means you are not truly connected. Truly being connected means that you walk with the power that created you each day and you trust and have faith with what is before you. The "aha moments" are not sporadic, but here now. The issues you are facing in your life (or your dog is facing in his or hers) are an illusion. Here are a few Hawaiian principles I discuss in my book *Stepping Into Your Becoming*. If you'd like to know them in more detail, you can read more about them there. But use the concept here as a guideline for healing your pup as well.

1. The world is what you think it is.
2. There are no limits.
3. Energy flows where energy goes.
4. Now is the moment of power.
5. To love is to be happy with.
6. All power comes from within.
7. Effectiveness is the measure of truth.

What does all this mean in a nutshell? Well, animals don't generally hold grudges, but they can remember pains that humans have caused them—whether physical, mental, or emotional. It can happen through separation from loved ones, mistreatment, or abuse. But, generally, they live in the moment, and they do generally forgive quickly. I always found it funny really that when I would run to the store, my dogs would hop in the car to go down the street, but other times, they would hop in the car and we'd take a long road trip. In neither case did they need to pack a bag or plan for the trip. By living in the present moment at each moment, they tend not to look too far back. Generally, when you can make them happy in each moment, they soon learn to forget past pains...if they ever even existed in the first place. They have always taught me that nothing in my past truly equals my present. In each present moment, I have a chance to start anew. I learned over a period of time on my spiritual journey into awakening that if I listened to my dogs, I would not live depressed in the past or full of anxiety for the future.

If you know anything about quantum physics, then you know that something may not even exist until thought is placed on it—thus, creating it. So if you don't want your dog to be sick, you must focus on his good health. The same goes for you. Do you always think something is wrong with you or your dog? Stop that thinking and focus on what's right! You can actually manifest the one thing you do not want by placing too much thought or energy there. Begin to see the gifts your dog gives you. In fact, honor whatever is there as a great teacher, even if you only see the bad right now. What is there is there to teach you. Then find joy in small things. Remind your dog of good health. What did your dog do as a small pup that brought you both joy? Focus on joy; do not feed the sorrow and pain. Joy and strength shared with love delivers more of the same. Get your vibration as high as you can get it, and then it will have a positive effect on your dog. If nothing else, it will at a minimum make things clearer about what is going on.

Keep in mind the idea of the homeopathic nosode versus a vaccination—when the body learns about an opposing force in one way, it is a problem (vaccination) causing an autoimmune problem, but when it learns about it in another way (a nosode), it learns how to create a solution or immunity. If someone gives you a solution, you are not as likely to remember how you got to the answer, but when you work it out on your own, you never forget how you got the answer. You and your dog must take all healing as a gift in your mutual ability to learn and grow. You are likely a mirror of each other in some way. In fact, as soon as you can figure out what is troubling you, you will likely heal your dog!

Dogs are not really here on earth to cause us problems; they are here to show us the reflection of ourselves, how to find joy, and to know true love. Drama always affects our dogs. And there is no such thing as a "bad dog." Dogs are simply acting out or showcasing a problem in your home or life. Generally, a dog's behavior of acting out in some way will teach us something about ourselves. When we correct the problem, we end up finding a solution for the whole household…and that usually means some kind of life change is required. When your dog complains, you must honor his or her wishes in some way. I promise it will improve your life in more meaningful ways than just giving your dog what he wants. Have you noticed that sometimes your dog will play without you? Try to get you to play? Does it annoy you? If so, it's even possible that your dog could be vibrating at a higher frequency than you and is trying to break your funk so you will loosen up and play too! It goes both ways. My bulldog Leilani is always trying to get her daddy to play, but he's so focused that it only makes him mad. She pulls bricks off the landscape and barks at them, and I just laugh. He takes them away! "Awe, c'mon, Dad…I was just trying to lighten things up and remind you of what it's like to have fun!" He's been struggling with the loss of his dad, and she's always trying to cheer us both up. It goes both ways. She is quite a healer. In fact, so much so that when she approaches me when I need a healing, I can see that her aura turns green, and I watch her jump on or touch spots where energy needs to shift. I actually believe that all dogs/animals are healers and are here to comfort us and remind us of the universe and the infinite connection from which we come.

When we take time to play in their world, dogs open up to us and show us their joys, their gifts, their ability to heal, their ability to shift the energy of a space. When we have bonding experiences like taking a trip, going for a walk, exercising, doing yoga, cooking and tasting in the kitchen, or just cuddling on the couch, we create a trust and a strong pack. The more time we spend with them, the more we can tell when there is a gift or, unfortunately, a problem.

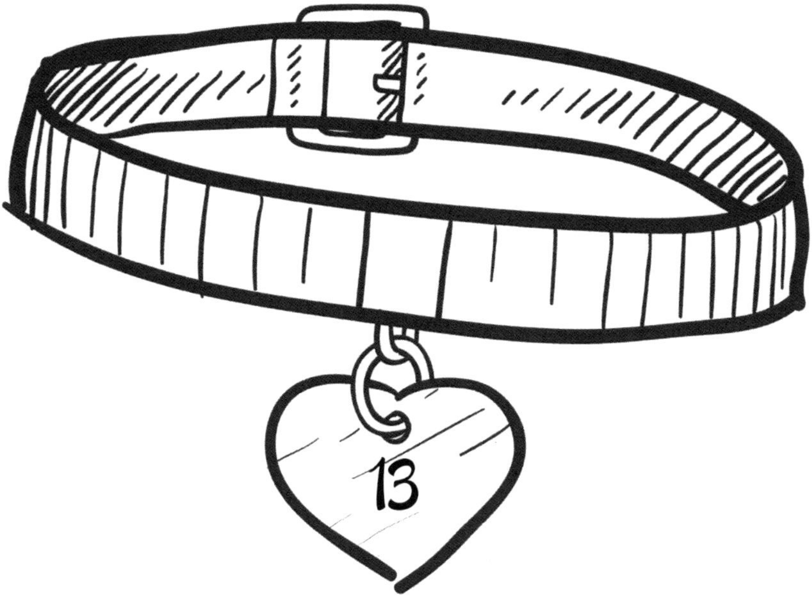

Signs of a Problem

"I've seen a look in dogs' eyes,
a quickly vanishing look of amazed contempt,
and I am convinced that basically dogs think humans are nuts."

— John Steinbeck

Knowing when to take your dog into the emergency clinic, for a regular or routine vet visit, or treating at home is a decision you need to know how to make on your own. Overall, you must do what feels right to you and your dog and trust your own judgment and intuition. I promise I'm not trying to give you a difficult answer here, but I think that to be the best pet parent, you have to be a great observer. The one thing you can offer your pet is the fact that you know his or her regular behaviors better than any veterinarian. You know when something is wrong. Trust in your gut. I know that every time my dogs run from me as I approach, there is a problem they are trying to hide from me—usually it involves a need for ear cleaning! It's part of owning Shar Pei, no matter how well you take care of them. I also have a dog who, when he is dirty and knows he needs a bath, hides under the bed. He actually loves baths, but he hates to succumb to me prior to getting one. You will learn your dog's signs, and you have a few new methods to try now too.

There is no one sure thing to tell you when the time is right for care outside of your own. But perhaps the following will assist you as it has me. And know that you might have a list of caregivers with many different approaches. In fact, I recommend that! It doesn't hurt to have a homeopath available by phone and a local vet for surgeries and one for regular care. Here on Maui, I have had to become my own homeopath because there aren't many vets knowledgeable in the subject. I just know when I go into a medical office I'm going to get an expensive medical list of products and solutions that I will most likely not agree with, but I'm smart enough to honor them in the presence of my vet. I just might not purchase everything from the girls at the counter on the way out. Know what you are going to be met with prior to your visit. Again, trust your gut.

HOMEOPATHY AND THE "VITALISM" APPROACH

According to the world of homeopathy or naturopathy, there is something in each of us called a "vital force" (or spirit) that you must stay in control of. Making decisions is easier when you know and understand your pup's vital force. This force includes all the things that make up his or her entire constitution like heredity, early environment, temperament, stressful life transitions, food intake, physical activity, exposure to toxins, etc. Being able to answer the question: "What is the state of my dog's vital force?" will many times give you the answers you need as to what to do next. When my Sushi was eighteen years old, I knew that the quality of her life was not the same as it once was, but toward the end, I had to ask whether she was enjoying her life anymore. Once the answer became no, then I knew it was time to assist her in her passing. I had never done that before, and honestly, I still struggle today with having made the decision to play god on her behalf. Every day I ask for forgiveness for that decision. She is well over it and flying high in spirit, but I'm the one who is stuck in the mind games. It's just never an easy place to be in.

The body's illness can be looked at in terms of the spiritual factors that might be contributing to it. Disease is simply a more advanced stage of the stress of failing to meet physical, emotional, or spiritual goals. So you might be wondering about how this looks in dogs? Are they so evolved that they know any differently? I actually think they are more evolved in this sense than we are. They have far fewer distractions than we humans do. Although, I will say it again, they are usually feeding on our energy and developing their own coping mechanisms… unfortunately, usually on how to deal with our issues.

So, you see, the issue of what to do when your dog is not feeling well most likely has a direct link to something going on in the household. When you can address that issue, you can address better what is going on with your dog. If you are in an emergency situation, then you might have simply missed the actions that led up to the incident. There was something going on well before the emergency, but due to the chaos in our human lives, we miss it. Unless, of course, your dog was hit by a car or poisoned. Albeit, if you dug a bit deeper, though, you might even find a deeper purposeful reason for this as well.

Some unique principles of healing in homeopathy will help provide a great foundation for you as it relates to not just your animal's vitality and needs, but also your own. Much of homeopathy rests on the philosophical foundation first established by Samuel Hahnemann in his book *The Organon of the Healing Art* published in the early nineteenth century. I find the following are great principles not just to practice healing by but also to live by. They are:

1. **The Law of Similars:** What caused it will heal it.

2. **The Single Remedy:** Prescribe one remedy at a time.

3. **Individualization of Treatment:** Treat each person individually.
4. **Suppression:** Addressing the cause of the problem is not an "out-of-sight/out-of-mind" approach.
5. **Order of Healing:** Allow your body to heal naturally.
6. **The Minimum Dose:** Prescribe the minimum dose required to achieve a therapeutic effect.

If these principles are followed even outside of homeopathy, they will help us heal. For example, let's say that there is a lot of stress in the household. If you don't address the original stressor in the home, but instead give your dog a medicine for his stress and anxiety, you have not addressed the cause of the problem—you are basically hiding it. Because you may not know the cause, you can begin with addressing the problem as it is expressed in your dog by, say, giving a pill for anxiety, but the stressor still exists. This would merely suppress the problem. If you can never find the original stressor, then perhaps a small dose of a remedy, such as belladonna, can give your dog the ability to adjust to it in a different way over time. If this doesn't work so well, then it's time to become a detective.

BECOMING A DETECTIVE

Where are we now? What caused the symptoms? What triggered the symptoms? If your dog is sick after you do one thing, what was that one thing and how do you improve the outcome? How do you stop doing that thing? Create a journal. How do you interact with veterinarians? Notice changes in body discharges or strange behaviors. Are the symptoms there more frequently? Let's try something else. If you keep doing the same thing and getting the same results, you need to try something totally different. What are your goals for your dog's health and what are the baselines you are working from? Are you moving toward a cure? Are you treating over and over again but losing ground, and now there is another problem? Have you gotten rid of the problem? Journaling might give you an "aha" solution. Here are a few things to look at when journaling:

JOURNALING QUESTIONS/ANSWERS:

Food

1. Did you change your dog's food? Was there a reaction?
2. Is the food organic? If not, should it be?
3. What is the food source? Is there a problem there?
4. Is there bad karma in the food source, such as tortured meats?
5. Are you feeding with a probiotic? What brand? Is it appropriate for dogs?

Vaccination/Medication/Chemicals

1. Did you just vaccinate, and was there a reaction?
2. Are you keeping a log of all events for a period after vaccination?
3. Are you removing toxins after vaccination?
4. Did you just give heartworm, flea, or tick meds?
5. Are you cleaning with a new product?

Healing Modalities

1. Make a note of the different ways you've tried to heal your dog.
2. Have you tried all of the following? Which one resonates with you and your dog?
    - Acupuncture
    - Animal Communicators/Intuitives

- Ayurvedic
- Bowen Therapy
- Chinese medicine
- Chiropractic
- Energy healing
- Essential oils
- Flower essences
- Healing Touch Program™
- Homeopathy
- Kinesiology/muscle testing
- Massage
- Reiki

Personal Interactions

1. Are you in a new house?
2. A new spouse? Child? Relationship? Job?
3. Did you move or start a new job?
4. Does your dog not like the veterinarian's office or someone in it?
5. Do you have a new animal in the house?
6. How does your dog interact with other dogs? Cats?
7. Are there changes in sleeping habits?

Watch for abnormalities and mentally or physically take note of when they happen. Watch the skin, the behavior, the digestive system (yep, you gotta dig in that poop sometimes!), body temperature, and the muscular/skeletal system.

Take some time playing detective and journaling. Sooner or later, the big aha will come, and it may be based on simply having good notes.

URGENT CARE NATURALLY

If you're stuck in a bit of a pickle and your vet's office is closed or you worry you won't quite make it there without a negative impact on your dog, then the following may help you in case of an emergency.

Vitamin C

For general health and for the prevention of disease, you can add calcium ascorbate crystals into meals or mix them with water and syringe (no needle) it into the mouth. Note: You can also use sodium ascorbate.

For emergencies, Vitamin C can treat cancer; distemper; poisonings; snake, spider, or tick bites; parvo; pneumonia; and can even be used for fading puppy syndrome. Mix 6-8 teaspoons of crystals or five times the daily dose in about a cup of warm water to dissolve; then give smaller portions orally every fifteen minutes for up to four hours or until back to normal. Vaccines severely deplete your pup of Vitamin C.

Slippery Elm

Slippery elm was used as a survival herb by the Native Americans during hard times; therefore, it is great to use in a syringe when your pup is not eating. It can be added to food for many stomach issues such as IBS, cancer, ulcers, inflammation, or gastritis. But if your dog is not eating and the issue is more acute, you can mix it with water and syringe (no needle) it into the mouth. Use three times a day when your pup is struggling with diarrhea.

Fever Reduction

At first sign of fever, give your dog a baby aspirin. Put alcohol on his feet to reduce fever. Do not give baths or use ice packs because they will cause shock. Use belladonna 30C and/or Aconite 30C.

When things don't go well in the case of an emergency, or the time has come for a transition, sometimes we can feel a sense of guilt that we have been poor caregivers or have done something wrong. Because dogs entrust us with their well-being, this can weigh quite heavily on our minds. Therefore, we'll turn now to that unpleasant topic all pet owners eventually have to deal with: death and transitioning.

*"All the darkness in the world
cannot extinguish the light of a single candle."*

— Saint Francis of Assisi

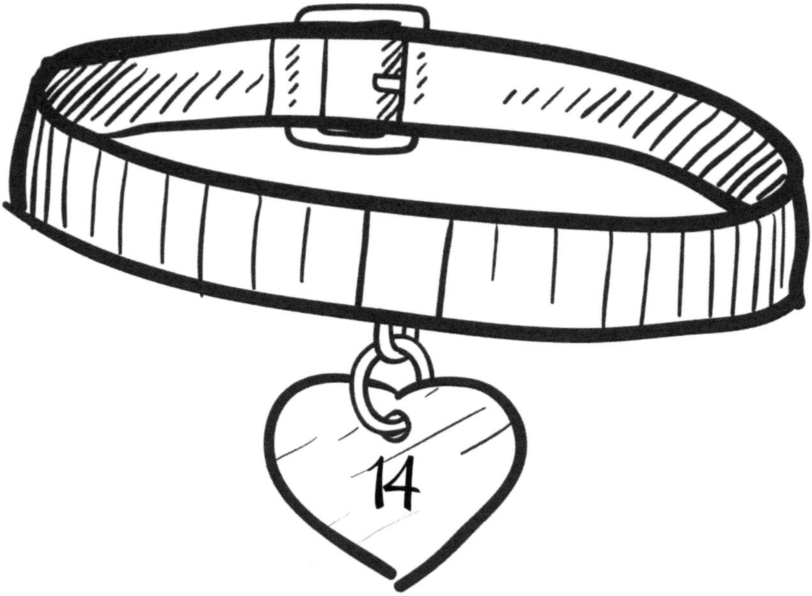

Death & Transitioning Over the Rainbow Bridge

"Dogs' lives are too short. Their only fault, really."

— Agnes Sligh Turnbull

It has been stated in the shamanic communities that one becomes a shaman in a variety of ways. One way is initiation through the death of a loved one. Another way is being hit by lightning. I'm not sure yet which one is worse. Loss is loss no matter whether that loss is a human or a pup. Often, there is no one there for us when we lose someone… especially when they are four-legged. There are churches and priests and ministers and other support systems in place for our humans, but not always so much for our pups. I know that many of us dog people get very attached to our four-legged kiddos…more so than our two-legged much of the time. And, for some of us, we don't have the two-legged kiddos and our pups become a replacement or a choice we make instead. I know the pain of loss firsthand. My loss was very deep and very real. In fact, not only did it send me into a deep depression, but it sent me all around the world seeking answers and fighting for my life. I gave up nearly all contact with my family and friends for many years as I tried to find peace and answers. I was embarrassed that so much pain was in my heart over "just a dog" (as others would say).

We often forget that our pups are not lifelong members of our family. Well, not the length of our lives anyhow. For them, we are their whole world and they choose us for such a brief time in their soul's existence. Do you realize that, with all the other people on this planet, they chose you? Your union was planned and purposeful!

ANIMALS PASS OVER TO BECOME OUR ANGELS AND GUIDE US ON OUR EARTH JOURNEY. BECAUSE THEIR LIVES ARE SHORTER, THEY CAN COME BACK TO US MULTIPLE TIMES IN OUR MUCH LONGER LIVES.

My babies spent more close loving time with me than I allowed any other human so their departure was very real. I struggled with the fact that so many simply saw them as pets...saying things like "just go get another!" They were not replaceable possessions! They were my loves, my best friends, my confidants, my shadows, my entertainers, my pillows to cry on, and no matter what I did, as long as I was with them, I was happy. When they left, my heart was pulled out. I truly believed that God hated me when I lost so many of my babies over such a short period. I was sad and angry at the same time.

Because we are our dogs' guardians, many times we can be left wondering whether we did everything right. Am I to blame for what happened? How could I have not seen this coming? Was I a bad person? How did I...? Then, not only are we dealing with loss, but we are dealing with the guilt of some idea that we caused their death. Take a moment and forgive yourself now. If you are asking this question, the answer is "*Yes*, you did everything right!" I used to think it was horrific when a parent lost a child before their own life ended, but then I realized that each soul is on a journey, a mission of their own. Answer these quick questions to understand God's love better:

How can God take _<dog's name>_ away from me?

Who gave _<dog's name>_ to me?

Who can tell God what to do? When you begin to understand that you were granted temporary stewardship over the care of your baby here on Earth, and the fact that this place is not our soul's true home, you begin to see the true gift that your kiddo was/is.

Whatever caused the passing of your baby over the rainbow bridge was a divinely-inspired action in a much larger plan. You were chosen as a guardian when this little soul chose to incarnate and you were chosen to be there as they depart. Of all the matches that could be made, you were pre-ordained to spend whatever time you have together. Their little soul chose you. Be thankful for that time.

I personally believe that animals pass over to become our angels and guide us on our earth journey. I also believe that because their lives are shorter, they can come back to us multiple times (as other animals) in our much longer lives. Wherever that sweet spirit goes, you will always be one. We are all a part of the whole, and lovers are always reunited. Love has no boundaries over space and time.

A Loan from God

God promised at the birth of time,
A special friend to give,
His time on earth is short, He said,

So love him while he lives.
It may be for eight or ten years,
Or only two or three,
But will you, till I call him back,
Take care of him for Me?
A wagging tail and cold wet nose,
And silken velvet ears,
A heart as big as all outdoors,
To love you through the years.
His puppy ways will gladden you,
And antics bring a smile,
As guardian or friend he will,
Be loyal all the while.

He'll bring his charms to grace your life,
And though his stay be brief,
When he's gone the memories,
Are solace for your grief.

I cannot promise he will stay,
Since all from earth return,
But lessons only a dog can teach,
I want you each to learn.

I've looked the whole world over,
In search of guardians true,
And from the folk that crowd life's land,
I have chosen you.

Whatever love you give to him,
Returns in triple measure,
Follow his lead and gain a life,
Brim full of simple pleasures.

Enjoy each day as it comes,
Allow your heart to guide,
Be loyal and steadfast in love,
As the dog there by your side.

Now will you give him all your love,
Nor think the labor vain,
Nor hate me when I come to call,
To take him back again?

I fancy each of us would say,
Dear Lord, thy will be done,
For all the joys this dog shall bring,
The risk of grief we'll run.

We'll shelter him with tenderness,
We'll love him while we may,
And for the happiness we've known,
Forever grateful stay.

But should the angels call for him,
Much sooner than we've planned,
We'll brave the bitter grief that comes,
And try to understand.

If by our love we've managed,
God's wishes to achieve,
In memory of him that we have loved,
And to help us while we grieve;

When our faithful bundle departs,
This earthly world of strife,
We'll get yet another pup,
And love him all his life.

— Author Unknown

I was once told by someone somewhere on my spiritual path that when someone we love passes before us, then we are seeking a level of mastery here on earth that requires this contract to play out...where our trusted advisor is on the other side to guide us into our mastery. Although understanding this hasn't brought back all those I have lost, it has given me far greater purpose for my life. I figure that I'm not really here alone and that my life must be very important for someone I love and trust to leave before me in order to assure that I am successful here. I've struggled with so much depression in this lifetime because all those I have loved have come and gone. You can feel so very alone when it feels everyone you love leaves. But I hold this little thought in the back of my mind that I am clearly very important and this life is clearly very purposeful because I am still here and they are not. I once thought it was unfair that I wasn't passing over with them because it was torture to exist here without them. I now see that there is a true divine plan that has set this all in motion. I now dedicate little things to each loss I've had as I go through my day. I talk to them as my secret confidants, and when I do something I think they would be proud of, I often feel their sense of pride as if we did it together...such as this book.

It is no different for you. Your life is purposeful and you have a very special being or beings over the rainbow bridge who are always there to look out for you. They do send signs when we ask. Ask for one now…what was your favorite thing to do together? A smell, a color, a treat, a car you always rode in together, etc. You are not alone and your life is very purposeful. Take a deep breath, close your eyes, and meditate on that for just a moment.

Remember animals are here to help and love us. When it is time for them to go, don't hold them back; release them with love and know they will return in another form. Soulmates are always reunited... even if now, it's just in our dreams.

"No louder shrieks to pitying heaven are cast,
When husbands or lap-dogs breathe their last."

— Alexander Pope, English poet

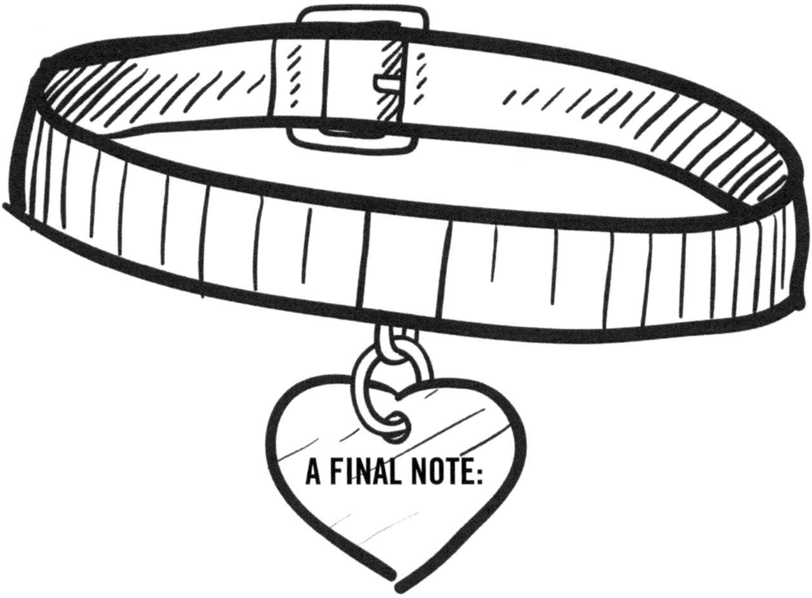

A FINAL NOTE:

A Big Mission

"He is your friend, your partner, your defender, your dog. You are his life, his love, his leader. He will be yours, faithful and true, to the last beat of his heart. You owe it to him to be worthy of such devotion."

— Author Unknown

There are many ways to go about healing your dog naturally, but it is my hope that your takeaway from this book is not all that is going wrong in our world, but that you learn how to take a proactive approach on not just healthier options for your dog, but also for yourself. Though I do not have an advanced degree in veterinary science, I do have two-and-a-half decades of personal experience that have taught me a kinder way to be and a gentler way to raise my pups. When we look at the entire span of our lives versus the brief moments in which our pups visit, isn't it only fair that they live with the least amount of suffering and the greatest amount of joy?

It may be believed by some that our pets naturally become ill and require regular veterinary care and a redirection from their natural state. But many holistic practitioners are saying that they become ill because of toxicities in the body from inferior pet foods, environmental toxins, vaccines, antibiotics, wormers, steroids, and the like. On top of this, nutritional deficiencies cause stress, and that leads to adrenal gland difficulties, which, in turn, cause allergies, arthritis, breathing difficulties, skin problems, cancer, ear problems, diabetes, seizures, and other disorders. The liver and the other organs become taxed. On top of all this there are other energetic and environmental issues. Our dogs, heck our animals…and people, are suffering! Our environment is suffering! STOP! I say, "Just stop all of it!" I cry nearly daily for our earth. Our planet is weeping and the only thing we can do is just stop all of it and go back to basics, loving each other, and trusting in the source that created us to watch over us.

During one of my meditations, I was shown that a group of us angels came down from what might be called heaven, or the source light. We came down with one mission: to save the planet. We didn't want to come because we knew it was a big job. As we descended, we cried for the planet. It had been many years since our last visit, and Earth was not as beautiful as we once remembered it. The animals were deformed, the trees not as green or full. We cried. We knew our job was going to be a big one, but we still came. I was not the only one. There were many of us. We must unite as was intended and speak out, ask questions, confront the faulty unconscious system, and wake up our friends and neighbors. Our planet depends on it!

To recap at a higher level, in this book, we talked about knowing when it is time to make a change in your and your dog's life; we talked about diet, nutrition, and meal planning. We talked about integrating homeopathy into your pup's life, about vaccinations and natural alternatives, the natural energetic system, and the connection between you and your dog, about death and the transition process, as well as how to use certain essential oils and flower remedies for healing, and finally, we talked about what to do when there are signs of a problem.

The problem is unfortunately greater than each one of us, but together, we can share the concepts in this book, and I also urge you to do some research and learn more; then share, share, share! I'm constantly sticking my nose deep into places that seem to cry out for help. I have often asked, "When is somebody going to do something about this?" I finally decided it was time to write this book. I'm no expert, but I'm a dog momma, I'm concerned, and I have a voice. I love our earth and our animals far too much to sit back and watch the innocent suffer.

As you move forward with your sweet four-legged beauties, I want you to know that you are not alone in your concern about what is going on. I'm right there with you. You may find that it becomes more challenging to work with your veterinarian with all these unique and different concepts, but holistic vet care might mean just finding a veterinarian willing to work with your different methods of treatment. You can have a homeopathic vet by phone and a traditional vet near home for emergencies. My hope is that you actually have such healthy babies that you require neither. I mean no offense to our lovely veterinarians, but honestly, I hope not to see you at the vet's office very often since that means I have a beautiful healthy kiddo by my side and so do you. I know that many vets are doing a great job and they care, and I hope that more and more learn the approaches of the homeopathic practitioner and the energy healer. Our pack is not just made up of dogs!

Many people feel guilty about vaccinating after they learn about vaccines. The truth is that you were doing the best you could. There is no right decision. There are morally right decisions. You do the best you can at any moment, and you educate yourself the best you can, and you forgive yourself and move on the best you can. Make yourself aware, educated, and become an advocate for your dog. Your health, your pup's health, and the state of our world are reliant upon you to help change it.

I may have forgotten something in these pages, or you may not agree with me. I'm so totally fine with that because my primary concern is our four-legged angels. This book was never about me. If you have a better approach or disagree with anything I've stated here, I challenge you to speak out and write your own book. I want to learn. We all want to know more. Please, write! And if you'd like to further our dialog, I honor your opinion and where you are on your path. I don't believe we are here to compete, but here to collaborate and heal a planet in dire need of change.

In love and light!

Yours truly,

Nicole K. Gabriel

"I may not be perfect but,
my dog loves me."

— Author Unknown

"Questers of the truth, that's who dogs are; seekers after the invisible scent of another being's authentic core."

— Jeffrey Moussaieff Masson

Resources

VACCINES:

- http://www.pandemicresponseproject.com
- https://homeopathicassociates.com/tag/reversing-vaccine-damage
- *Dogs Naturally Magazine,* www.dogsnaturallymagazine.com
- http://www.petwelfarealliance.org/stop-the-legislation.html
- http://www.blogtalkradio.com/homeopathyworldcommunity/2014/06/04/vaccinations-your-rights-choices-alternatives-homeopathy

HOMEOPATHY

- http://www.blogtalkradio.com/homeopathyworldcommunity
- http://theavh.org (Academy of Veterinary Homeopathy)
- www.holisticanimalmedicines.com
- www.nativeremedies.com
- http://www.earthsongranch.com

HERBS:

Herb Pharm Brand found at:

www.herb-pharm.com
www.pureformulas.com
www.iherb.com
www.amazon.com

NOSODES:

www.holisticanimalmedicines.com

ESSENTIAL OILS:

- www.youngliving.com
- www.doterra.com

FLOWER ESSENCES:

- Feel Bach! pet website questionnaire to get your pet's individual Bach compound (http://feelbach.com/qtp.asp)

ALLERGY OR OTHER TESTING:

- https://labordatenbank.com/cake/hemopet/samples/hemopet_form

  HOME HAIR TEST KIT

  A highly accurate hair test for deficiencies and toxins.

  Request a HAIR (fur) mineral analysis test at suggested labs below.

  (Snip fur from under the armpits, groin, and back of neck.)

  Analytical Research Laboratories, Inc.
  2225 West Alice Avenue Phoenix, AZ 85021 USA
  1-800-528-4067 Toll-Free Phone Number

ANIMAL RIGHTS:

- http://www.petwelfarealliance.org

ARTICLES:

- "Vaccines and Skin Problems" by Catherine O'Driscoll, *Dogs Naturally*
- "Food Allergies: A Man Made Problem?" Dana Scott, *Dogs Naturally*

BOOKS:

Feel Bach!:

- Graham, Helen and Gregory Vlamis. *Bach Flower Remedies for Animals.*
- Jones, T.W. Hyne. *Dictionary of the Bach Flowers.*

Homeopathy/Herbs:

- Basko, Ihor John. *Fresh Food & Ancient Wisdom.*
- Chambreau, Christina. *Healthy Animal's Journal.*
- De Bairacle Levy, Juliette. *The Complete Herbal Handbook for the Dog and Cat.*
- Goldstein, Dr. Marty. *Nature of Animal Health.*
- Hahnemann, Samuel. *The Organon of the Medical Art.*
- Hamilton, Don. *Homeopathic Care for Cats and Dogs.*
- Pitcairn, Richard. *Natural Health for Dogs and Cats.*
- Riviera, Michelle. *Vegan Dog Book.*
- Taylor, Beth and Shaw-Becker, Karen. *Real Food for Dogs and Cats.*
- Wauters, Ambika. *The Homeopathy Bible.*

Chinese Medicine:

- Schwartz, Cheryl. *Four Paws, Five Directions.*

Vaccines:

- O'Driscoll, Catherine. *What Vets Don't Tell You about Vaccines.*

SUPPLEMENTS:

Prebiotics:

- Prebiotic Plus from Animals' Apawthecary

Probiotics:

- GutSense (http://dr-dobias-natural-healing-usa.myshopify.com/products/gutsense)

ACUPUNCTURE:

- International Veterinary Acupuncture Society (https://www.ivas.org)

CHINESE MEDICINE:

- Chi Institute of Traditional Chinese Veterinary Medicine (http://www.tcvm.com)

CHIROPRACTIC:

- American Veterinary Chiropractic Association (http://www.animalchiropractic.org)

"The difference between a child and a dog is two extra legs."

— Author Unknown

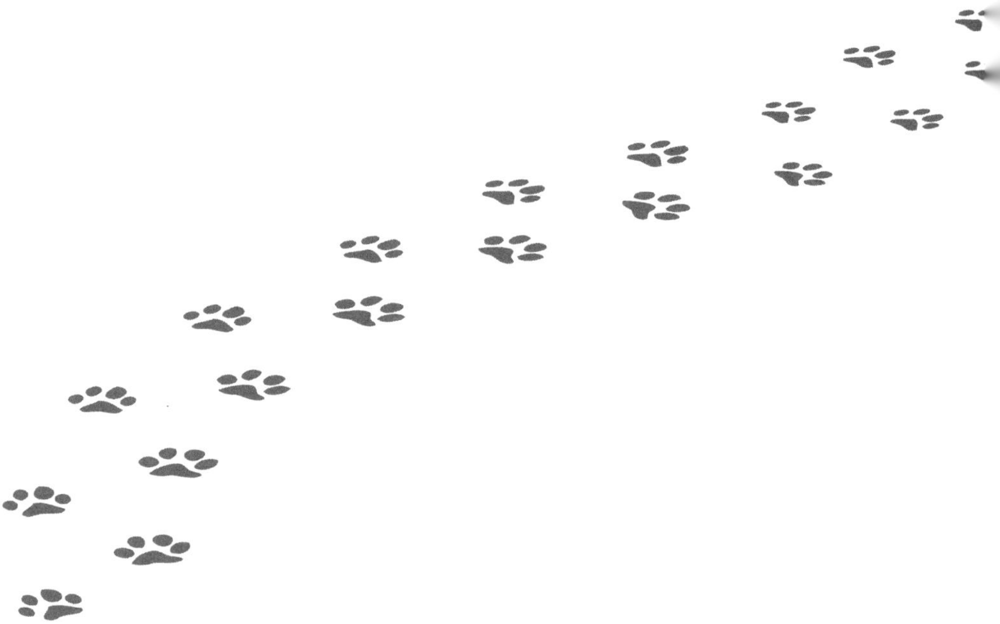

CERTIFICATE OF NON-VACCINATION

VETERINARY CLINIC

NAME OF CLINIC: ______________________

ADDRESS: ______________________

CITY: ______________________

STATE: ______________________

ZIP: ______________________

PHONE: ______________________

OWNER OF ANIMAL

NAME: ______________________

ADDRESS: ______________________

CITY: ______________________

STATE: ______________________

ZIP: ______________________

PHONE: ______________________

This is to certify that...

in my professional opinion this pet should not be vaccinated for rabies as s/he is not at risk for contracting rabies and/or has been adequately vaccinated in the past to protect against rabies and vaccination would be detrimental to his or her health.

PATIENT INFORMATION:

NAME: ______________________

SPECIES: ______________________

GENDER: ______________________

COLOR AND MARKINGS: ______________

HEIGHT: ______________________

WEIGHT: ______________________

AGE: ______________________

MICROCHIP NUMBER: ______________

DATE EXEMPTION ENDS: ______________

< insert picture of animal >

VETERINARIAN'S SIGNATURE: ______________________________ LICENSE #: ____________

States that accept this form: Alabama, California, Colorado, Connecticut, Florida, Illinois, Maine, Massachusetts, Maryland, New Hampshire, New Jersey, Nevada, New York, Oregon, Pennsylvania, Vermont, Virginia, Wisconsin.Go to http://www.dogs4dogs.com/rabies-laws for additional information on your state.

Index

*"All his life he tried to be a good person.
Many times, however, he failed.
For after all, he was only human.
He wasn't a dog."*

— Charles M. Schulz

About the Author

NICOLE GABRIEL, MBA, is an author, professional speaker, graphic designer, life coach, and animal health and well-being coach. She is also a vegan nutrition coach. She has been a student and teacher of Peruvian Shamanism and Kundalini yoga (RYT500) for many years. She is a raw vegan food enthusiast, seeker of truth, animal rights advocate, supporter of women in technology, and the owner of Vegan Dog Treats and Angel Dog Productions. As a former auto executive from Detroit, she holds an MBA in Technology Management. She is certified in Transpersonal Psychology at the Master's Level, has a B.A. in Communications, and holds a degree in Graphic Design and Commercial Art.

For more than twenty years, Nicole has studied business, personal growth and development, spirituality, health, nutrition, and wellness. She spent nearly a decade traveling the world in search of herself after a series of life-changing events—spending time in Central and South America working with shamanic healers, and more locally, studying the yogic philosophies of, in particular, Kundalini yoga.

Prior to retiring from a six-figure income in corporate America at age thirty-two, Nicole spent a decade in web-related technology management, marketing, and advertising as a "Big 3" automotive executive in Detroit. She followed that experience by successfully building and growing a $1.2 million per year chiropractic/spa franchise in three locations throughout Michigan.

Today, she lives on Maui, Hawaii, with her fiancé, Patrick, and their English Bulldog and Chinese Shar Pei. Among other things, she runs her businesses, Vegan Dog Treats (a healthy dog snack alternative) and Angel Dog Productions (designing websites, book covers, speaker presentations, and logos for aspiring new business owners and authors).

"Petting, scratching, and cuddling a dog could be as soothing to the mind and heart as deep meditation and almost as good for the soul as prayer."

— Dean Koontz, False Memory

About Healthy Dog & You Counseling

WORKSHOPS

If you'd like to spend time learning how to balance chakras, read energy, communicate with your dog, learn about specific healthy food, tips, and preparation, then stay tuned on the Healing Your Dog Naturally Facebook page, listed below, for additional information. If you'd like to arrange a workshop in your area, please let Nicole know.

FACEBOOK SUPPORT

The funny thing about having dogs is that they are almost like the hidden members of your family. They are not welcome in many stores, certainly not in restaurants, and at work, we have to put in eight-hour-long days and leave our babies at home. So when it comes to our dogs' health concerns, sometimes there is no one to talk to. For some reason, our world functions and flows like we are supposed to pretend they don't exist. When we go to the vet, we are rushed in and rushed out, and there isn't much community there to support us either. Many times a vet's office is run like a business. You come in for your service and you leave paying your bill. Nicole has often struggled with this herself. If you just need someone to talk to, she'd like to invite you to the following Facebook page:

www.facebook.com/groups/HealingYourDogNaturally

"Every dog must have his day."

— Jonathan Swift

About Angel Dog Productions

Nicole Gabriel has spent twenty-plus years in the arts, doing advertising, marketing, and website development, among other things. She began her other business (Vegan Dog Treats) with the help of her canine companion Shiitake. The brand needed a label, so Nicole started there. The logo was born with a cartoon image of Shiitake on the bag, website, and business cards. She also began doing the creative work for many client's book covers. After a short period, people started asking who did the creative work. Soon, Angel Dog Productions was born. Angel Dog Productions (ADP) designs book covers, interior book layout, websites, logos, and images that are used for personal or corporate branding.

Much of the focus for Nicole's clients is to get them set up with a "look" to launch their book, speaking, and marketing campaigns. Nicole also creates speaker presentations. ADP's goal in creating websites is to make the content simple and easy to manage for the owner. Nicole loves what she does and loves helping people, so please look her up. She'd love to hear from you! Call or text for a no-obligation, complimentary 30-60 minute consultation.

www.AngelDogProductions.com

*"If slaughterhouses had glass walls,
the whole world would be vegetarian."*

— Linda McCartney

About Vegan Dog Treats

After nearly a decade of watching her dogs struggle with daily and terminal health issues, Nicole Gabriel successfully created a new way to feed pets that is not only good for them, but a humane approach that leaves a smaller global footprint on the planet and doesn't require the taking of a life.

Dogs are classified as omnivores and are scavengers by nature. All the ingredients in Vegan Dog Treats are organic, natural, all vegan, dehydrated, and not cooked in most cases. The ingredients are kept primarily intact when they are not heated, which means they keep their nutrients. If you're going to feed your dog a snack, why not make it a healthy alternative that doesn't require killing one to serve another? It just makes sense!

www.Vegan-DogTreats.com

"The dog is a gentleman;
I hope to go to his heaven not man's."

— Mark Twain

About Shamanic Healing & Yoga Teaching

During her travels to Peru, Bolivia, and other locations in Central and South America, while working with shamanic healers, Nicole was told she would be a great healer and teacher, and through her life experiences, she would excel. In her yoga, she would be told that to master something was to teach it. So you could say she's still seeking mastery.

If you have always wanted to know how to heal yourself or another through shamanic healing techniques, Nicole teaches a series of classes that will start you on your way.

She is also available (as Nirankar Kaur) to teach Kundalini yoga. She is available as a guest teacher, lecturer, meditation guide, or "humanology philosopher" for your organization, studio, or center. Call or text for a no-obligation, complimentary 30-60 minute consultation.

www.NicoleKristinGabriel.com

"Dogs are not our whole life,
but they make our lives whole."

— Roger A. Caras

Life, Nutrition, & Wellness Coaching

Are you unhappy at work? Are you always tired and lacking energy? Have you put on a few pounds and your jeans no longer fit? Are you suffering from emotional or physical pain? Are you stressed and looking for both career and relationship solutions? Personal growth and development has been a keen subject of interest for Nicole Gabriel her whole life. While others her age were out doing silly teenager things, she was sitting at home reading books from self-help authors. From there, her interests flowed into diet and then spirituality.

Let Nicole show you how to move from tragedy, loss, death, or change into a better you! With certification in Transpersonal Psychology and several years of alternative therapy practice and research, Nicole will listen and help you through whatever stage of life you are experiencing. She can discuss diet for you and/or your pet. The light is just around the corner, so let's just find the switch! Your wellness is within reach. Call or text for a no-obligation, complimentary 30-60 minute consultation.

www.NicoleKristinGabriel.com

"Dogs do speak,
but only to those who know how to listen."

— Orhan Pamuk

Book Nicole to Speak at Your Next Event

When it comes to choosing a compassionate speaker for your next event, you'll find no one more capable of transforming your audience than Nicole. She will take your hand and lead you on a transformational journey. Her stories are inspiring, comical, tragic, and mysterious—yet, at the same time, by having just a little faith, you will be transported into a magical sacred space where the big "ahas" happen.

Whether your audience is 10 or 10,000, in North America or abroad, Nicole Gabriel will deliver a tailor-made message of inspiration for your meeting, conference, or classroom. Speaking topics include:

- Dog Health & Nutrition
- Learning from Animals
- Eating Food as Medicine
- Becoming Vegan
- Defining Self
- Letting Go and Having Faith
- Embracing Change
- Becoming a Leader from Within
- Transforming Your Life
- Peruvian Shamanism Theories & Practice
- Kundalini Yoga Theories & Practice

www.NicoleKristinGabriel.com

"I believe in integrity.
Dogs have it.
Humans are sometimes lacking it."

— Cesar Millan

If You Liked This Book, Get Nicole's Other Books!

Is something in your life shifting? Are you questioning its purpose and hoping that life's difficulties will end in peace, happiness and understanding?

When a chain of unexpected events occurred, beginning with the loss of her beloved Chinese Shar Pei, Tia, Nicole Gabriel felt her life was suddenly turned upside down. But as she overcame the hurdles of a career change, divorce, and the loss of many loved ones, she found her thoughts and perspective on life shifting into a new and amazing spiritual and psychic awareness. Now she shares her incredible journey for your benefit.

In Finding Your Inner Truth, Nicole takes you on a wild, mystical and soulful ride through the most traumatic and magical years of her life to share with you the confusion she felt, the questions she asked and the comforting answers she received. You will be surprised by what is in these pages—prepare yourself for explorations beyond our three-dimensional world, brushes with reincarnation, the foundational principles of shamanism, embracing yoga, engaging in alternative healing and following the loving guidance of her canine companions. But most of all, you'll be surprised by what you learn about yourself.

Prepare to know that following your heart will always get you where you need to be and lead you toward your inner truth. And when you find it, like Nicole, you'll realize that everything comes full circle, has a purpose and turns into love in the end. Let Nicole be your guide on this journey to finding your inner truth!

SEEK. TRUST. BELIEVE. LOVE

NicoleKristinGabriel.com

If You Liked This Book, Get Nicole's Other Books!

Has that little voice in your head ever said, "It's now time to step into your becoming?" Do you feel it's time to own and transition into your authentic powerful self? Are you ready to stop looking for something outside yourself and start becoming the person you wanted others to be for you?

Nicole Gabriel has been there and she's now ready to guide you on your rite of passage as you eliminate your mind chatter that holds you back and step into becoming your most divine self! Get ready to wash away all that isn't working in your life, learn how to have faith in that little voice, and step into your authentic self and your authentic power. Through personal and transformational stories, introspective questions, and guidance from various spiritual traditions, including shamanism and Hawaiian healing principles, Nicole takes readers' hands and leads them through the doorway separating the past from their glorious futures.

"Stepping Into Your Becoming" is what happens when you consciously choose what you will believe in, how you will live your life, and you become fully responsible for your own happiness. It's when you see yourself reflected in all things and then change yourself so the world you see will change and become what you desire. Finally, it's about finding your true freedom.

It's time to see the wounds of your past as healed experiences. It's time to step beyond your fears, to use your God-given gifts, and to own your power. Your greatness is awaiting you when you step into your becoming.

AWAKEN. TRANSFORM. REALIZE.

NicoleKristinGabriel.com